10,000 HOUSE NAMES

and their meanings

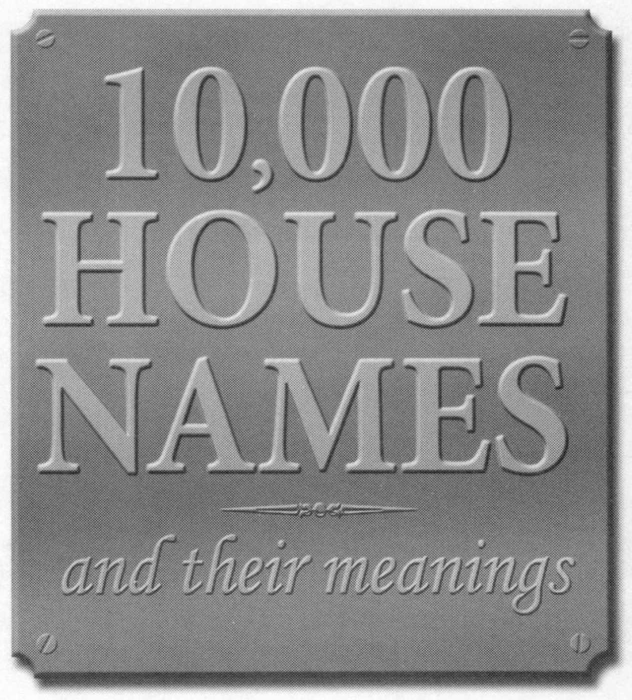

LORI COOPER

Thomas C. Lothian Pty Ltd
132 Albert Road, South Melbourne,
Victoria 3205
www.lothian.com.au

First published 2005

National Library of Australia
Cataloguing-in-Publication data:

Cooper, Lori
10,000 house names and their meanings.

ISBN 0 7344 0753 X.

1. House names. I. Title.

929.97

Cover design by Louise McGeachie
Front cover photograph © Comstock Images/Getty Images
back cover photographs author's own
Text design by David Constable
Printed in Australia by Griffin Press

CONTENTS

CHAPTER 1

THE EVOLUTION OF THE HOUSE NAME

Centuries ago, castles, stately manors, farms, houses and cottages were given a name of their own so they could easily be identified throughout a shire or county. There were no such things as street directories or street names for people to find each other. A stranger could ask any villager where *Ivy Cottage* was and be given directions.

As populations grew and cities emerged, it became apparent that a more exact system of locating people would be needed, so the street and numbering system was introduced. This method began in Paris in 1463, and was later introduced to Britain in 1765 and Australia in 1854.

Today, naming a house is back in vogue. Renovators and new homeowners are placing their personal mark on a house by giving it a name. It was a tradition our grandparents often indulged in, and a wander through your local neighbourhood will no doubt reveal name plaques such as *Hill View*, *The Cottage*, *Rosebank*, or something similar.

There is even a town in Tasmania, Australia called *Doo-Town*, where the locals display their wit with house names containing the ending 'doo'. Examples include *Love-me-doo*, *Much-ado*, *Xanadoo* and *Gunadoo*. This town has become a tourist attraction simply because of the quirkiness of its house names.

House names vary according to the taste and personality of their owners. Some homeowners may choose a name for their house to reflect a bygone era (*The Renaissance*); others, to give personality (*The Zany Zone*). Still others may choose a house name to reveal the heritage of the owner (*Maori House*) or choose a name that is fresh and individual (*The Yellow House*). House names can also give a wonderful energy (such as *Folly Farm*) or a certain aura (*Edenhope*). Names can also evoke feelings of power (*High Court Manor*) or strength (*The Pillars*).

Traditionally first named by the architect, builder or initial owner, a house name can mark its history, ownership, or the surrounding vista, or denote the wealth or power of its owner. Names such as *Windsor Castle*, *Admiralty House* and *The White House* suggest wealth, ownership and importance.

A name can promote the environment surrounding it (*Ocean View*) or the use of the land (*The Medicine Lodge*). Humour can also play a part in naming a home (*The Bank's* or *Dunroamin*).

It is important to choose a name that will be as fashionable tomorrow as it is today. To ensure the durability of your house name, consider adhering to traditional names.

Naming a house after a loved one is a good way to show respect, fondness and remembrance. A house may be passed down from one generation to the next and a much-loved grandparent may be honoured by naming the house after them (*Violet's Cottage*, *Theodore's Valley*, *Ruby Fields*).

A wished-for destination can inspire dreams of fancy for your house name—for example *Tuscany*, *Montana*, *Niagara* or *Paris*.

The beautiful countryside, flowers, rivers and mountains found in rural areas provide the imagery that makes choosing a name difficult but also inspirational. Beautiful views can inspire names such as *Bella Vista*, *Lovely Lea*, *Sea View*, *Golden Sands*, *Lake View*. Just look around at your environment for enlightenment: *Daisy Fields*, *The Woods*, *Wisteria Cottage*, *The Frog Marsh*, *The River Bend* or *Field Of Heather*.

Vegetation, scenery, animals, birds, reptiles, insects, flora and even fish can ignite the imagination to provide a perfect name for your property. Some creative names include: *Kangaroo Flats*, *Bear Bungalow*, *Lady Beetle Cottage*, *Koala Cottage*, *Pine Valley*, *Lazy Glen*, *Clover Fields*, *Cod Cottage*, *Rose Petal Manor*, *Seashell Isle*, *Green Forest*, *Stony Brook*, *Doe Haven*, *Magpie Nest*, *Cockatoo Cottage*, *Butterfly Haven*, *Feathered Friends* and *Sparrows Landing*.

Foreign languages have become more popular than ever for house names. Foreign words conjure up a special exotic feel for a house. They may show that the owner is well travelled or versed in language, for example: *La Maison Blanche* (French), *La Casa Blanca* (Spanish), both meaning the white house.

Reversing words for effect

Reversing the spelling of a favourite word can be a fascinating enigma to visitors who may try to work out the meaning of the name. *Emoh Ruo*, *Nevah*, *Tolemac*, *Nede*, *Emoclew*, *Evol*, *Reverof*, *Revolc* or (with apologies to Dylan Thomas) *Llareggub Hall* are a few examples of this naming method.

Real estate and the house name

In the real estate business, it is good to stand out from the crowd. From a real estate standpoint, a house name may give personality and evoke the feeling of a cherished, well-maintained property. A house known as *Eden's Garden* is more likely to draw interest than a house at number 42 Main Street. If you are considering selling your home, consider the appeal that a house with a name can offer.

Descriptive house names for the city

With most of the world's population residing in cities, it is obvious that not everyone can have beautiful views, rolling meadows, trickling brooks and homes named *Seaside Retreat* or *Sweeping Fields*. With a little imagination, inspiration can still be taken from the surrounding environment, for example: *High-rise Haven*, *City View*, *High Tower*, *Western View* or *South View*.

Family names

Surnames are a popular means for finding a suitable house or property name and also represent an attachment to the home that could last generations; for example: *Taylor House*, *Howard Hall*, *Montgomery Manor* and *Grantley Estate*.

By combining the names of children or family members, one can create a unique name for one's home. For example, combining *Shay* and *Lea* results in

Shaylea. *Glen* and *Gary* results in *Glengary* and *Sara* and *Anna* turns into *Saranna*. *Marwyland* is the result of mixing three family member names, *Margot*, *Wylie* and *Andrew*.

For something different, first names can also be reversed; for example: *Senga* (Agnes), *Eronelle* (Ellenore), *Samoht* (Thomas) or *Nawor* (Rowan).

Famous house and property names in works of fiction

Many houses with names have featured in movies. In one of the most famous, *Gone with the Wind*, the beautiful Georgian-style mansion that Scarlett O'Hara so loved is named *Tara*. *Mandalay* is the house in Daphne Du Maurier's *Rebecca*. The mansion property that featured in the novels by V.C. Andrews is called *Rolling Hills*. *Greenacres* featured in a television show of the same name. *Alnwick Castle* featured in *Harry Potter and the Philosopher's Stone*. *Greystoke* is the name of the mansion in *Greystoke: The Legend of Tarzan, Lord of the Apes*. *Xanadu* is the mansion in Samuel Taylor Coleridge's famous poem. *Bramasole* is the house featured in the movie *Under the Tuscan Sun* after Frances Mayes' book, while in the Australian television series *McLeod's Daughters*, the property is called *Drover's Run*. And who could forget *Melrose Place* or, if you're a little older, *Peyton Place* and *Harper Valley*?

Memorable places

There are many memorable places that could be easily converted into a name for a house. Some places may hold precious memories: where you were born, where you were married, where you went on your honeymoon and much more. *Paris*, *Tuscany*, *Palm Springs*, *El Dorado*, *Graceland*, *Hollywood*, *Santa Fe*, *Byron Bay* and *Kangaroo Valley* are just a few examples.

CHAPTER 2

HOW TO CREATE YOUR OWN HOUSE NAME

Prefixes usually are descriptive words added onto the front of another word to create a house name. For example, with the word ***Wood*** you can add the suffix *mead* to create ***Woodmead***, meaning wood meadow. Similarly, ***Meadow*** and *ville* become ***Meadowville***, meaning meadow village.

If you have already decided on an attractive word that describes your home such as ***Grove***, add a descriptive word or a prefix before it to make it more expressive: *Honeygrove* or *Bellegrove*. For the word ***Mountain***, add *Blue* to create *Blue **Mountain*** or *Lonely **Mountain***, *Misty **Mountain*** or *Cedar **Mountain***.

Suffixes are words that you can add onto the end of an existing word, for example: ***Sea*** and a word that will go pleasingly with it—***Sea*** *View*, ***Sea*** *Change*, *Seaville*, *Seatown* or *Seascape*.

Below is a list of suffixes most commonly used in house naming, to help inspire you to find the right name for your home.

Acres Land measurement; many fields or pastures.
Apartment Flat.

Bail/e A town.
Bank Edge of a waterway.
Bay Inlet.
Berry/Bury Where berries grow; castle; manor house; borough.
Billabong A waterhole.
Borough Municipal.
Bourn/Bourne Stream; boundary.
Brae/Bray Hill.
Brook/e A running stream.
Bungalow A cottage.
Burgh A town or county; borough.
Burn/Burne Stream.
Bury Borough; manor house or castle.
Bush Area with lots of vegetation.

Cabin Lodge.
Castle Large medieval or stately residence.
Chalet Small house.

Chateau Castle.
Circle An area circular in shape.
Clon A fertile meadow.
Close Private or enclosed area.
Cosey/Cosy A comfortable area.
Cottage/Cott Small country-style house.
Country Rural area away from the city; nation.
County An area of land with a boundary.
Court/Courtyard Area enclosed by a wall.
Cove A small recess in a shoreline.
Cover A secure area.
Crag/Craige A rock or rocky area.
Crest Summit.
Croft Small pasture area/farm.
Cubby A small play house for children.

Dale A valley.
Dell A small wooded valley.
Den/Denn A cave-like or sheltered area; a comfortable room.
Don Valley.
Down/Downe/Downes Rolling country hills; slope.

Eas Waterfall.
Estate A large property or manor house.

Fair/Fayre Light-coloured; good; fete.
Falls Waterfalls.
Farm Ranch.
Field/Fields Pasture or open ground area.
Flats Flat land or flat pasture area.
Ford/Forde Shallow river crossing.
Forest A wooded area; woods.
Fork A river or road that divides into two.

Gables Triangular section of a house near the roof.
Garth An enclosure.
Gate Access to the property; entrance way; door.
Glade Open area in a forest.
Glas/Glass Green.
Gle/Glen/Glenn Small valley.
Grange Country home.
Green A grass covered area.
Grounds A specific area.
Grove Small wood.
Gully Valley with water cutting through it.

Hall Large stately residence or a place where townspeople meet.
Ham Hamlet, small village or farm.
Hamlet Small village.
Haunt An area that is visited frequently.
Haven Refuge.

Heath A field of heather.
Hill A small mountain.
Hollow A valley.
Holm/e Hamlet, village or farm.
Home Where one resides; shelter.
House Where one resides; shelter.
Hurst A forest on a hill.
Hut A small, makeshift shelter.

Igloo An Inuit ice house.
Inis An island.
Inlet Passage between two islands or bay.
Inn A bar, tavern or pub.
Isle A small island.

Knock A hill.
Knol/l/Knole Small hill.

Lach/Loch Lake.
Lair A cave-like or sheltered area.
Land Pasture, acres.
Lea/Lee/Leigh/Ley Meadow.
Lodge Cabin.
Lower Under or below.

Magh Plain.
Maison House.
Manor The main house on a large estate.
Manse House occupied by a minister or landholder.
Mansion Estate or stately house.
Mead/Meade Meadow.
Meadow Grassland or pasture area.
Mere Lake or little.
Merth Merry castle.
Mews Attached residences or sets of stables.
Moor/Moore/Mor Wetlands or marsh.
Mor Short form of 'moor', marshland; big or great.
Mount/Mont Mountain or a large hill.
Mountain A very large hill.

Nest A home usually associated with birds.
Nook Small, secluded place.

Ohm Rhymes with home; in electronics, unit of resistance in which one volt produces a unit of one ampere (after German physicist Georg Simon Ohm).

Palace Residence of royalty; a very expensive house.
Park Area dedicated to fauna.
Peak The top of a mountain or hill.
Penthouse An apartment or flat atop a building.
Place A particular area or building one resides.

Pool/e A pond.

Ranch A farm.
Range A region.
Rath Circular fort.
Residence Where someone lives.
Retreat A safe and private place.
Ridge Long, narrow elevation of land.
Roost Nest; home.
Row/Rowe An area that is arranged in a line.

Shack A roughly built shelter.
Shanty A roughly built shelter.
Side/Siding/Syde Hillside.
Spa A beauty retreat for relaxation; pool of bubbling water.
Spring/s An area with a small lake or pond.
Sraid Street.
Station Large ranch.
Stead An area or the short form of 'homestead'.
Ston/Stone An area where there are lots of stones.

Teach House.
Terrace A row of attached residences.
Ton/Town A town.
Top Above or higher.
Tor Power.
Trees Two or more trees.

Upper Above or higher.

Vale/Valley A valley.
View A vista or the sights surrounding an area.
Villa A country house.
Village Small town.
Ville A village.
Vineyard Where grapes are grown and wine is made.
Vista View.

Way Leading from one area to another.
Wich Bay.
Wick Village.
Wish Desired.
Wood/s A forest area.
Worth Farm; or a village; valuable; enclosure.
Worthign/Worthing Enclosure.

CHAPTER 3

HOW TO DISPLAY YOUR HOUSE NAME

First impressions count. The style of your house name plaque is an important indication of your own personal style and may give the community and visitors a particular notion of your character. Clear and distinct lettering is a must for a house plaque or nameplate. You can use your computer to experiment with different fonts, styles, sizes and colour. Although not all manufacturers of nameplates or plaques will have the font style you desire, they may have one that is similar in style.

Fonts and lettering

Capital letters

Capital letters are commonly used as they allow for clear and easily understood words. Most house names done in this style can be viewed easily from the roadside.

ARIAL COTTAGE

GOTHIC HOUSE

are some examples.

Scripted letters

Scripted letters can give a beautiful, flowing appearance to a plaque; however, they may make reading difficult depending on your chosen name, so choose carefully.

The Laurels

Sherwood Forest

The Old Painted Lady

are examples of various script fonts.

Old English-style letters

Old English-style fonts have been popular over the centuries for shop signs and house name plaques. Such a font gives a traditional ambiance to a building. The kind of house that would suit this style would be an older building, perhaps with Victorian architecture. It would also suit old or traditionally renovated Victorian-style homes or apartments and bed and breakfasts or motels. Some examples of this are:

The Old Priory

The Old English Hall

The Old Post Office

The Old School House

American influenced fonts

The 'Wild West' of America inspired the type of font you would have seen on 'wanted' posters. These fonts immediately conjure up images of cowboys, saloons and ranches. This would be a good font selection for a farm or ranch. Some examples of this style of font:

The Ranch

THE STATION

THE FARM

Contemporary lettering

Modern lettering on signs may also be used as long as it suits the style of the house you are naming. Some examples of modern font styles are:

ELM COTTAGE

SEAVIEW

The Cottage

Different styles of nameplates or plaques

There are many different styles of plaques available in many mediums. Copper, wood, slate, sandstone, stone, brass, aluminium, ceramic, porcelain or plastic are all commonly used.

Copper is used for traditionally cast plaques that come in a variety of shapes and sizes. General maintenance such as polishing is needed to keep its sophisticated look.

Cast aluminium plaques come in a range of sizes and shapes. Raised letters, motifs or borders in white or gold lettering create a beautiful contrast to the usually dark background. Maintenance is generally low.

Ceramic and porcelain nameplates are frequently oval- or circle- shaped although other shapes are also available. Motifs and borders may be added or even hand-painted on to the plate and glazed. They are usually low maintenance, but are not shatterproof.

Stoneware plaques are usually made by hand and are kiln fired. They are traditionally available in the earthy colour of the clay used, but may be glazed with your choice of colour.

Sandstone plaques can be hand carved by a mason, and the stone itself, depending on its cut, size and beauty, may be expensive compared to other options. It may also discolour in weather conditions such as rain.

Wooden house signs were traditionally carved by hand, today they are often engraved by laser. In England, cherry wood, English oak and Sapele were traditionally used for their beautiful attributes. Several coats of lacquer are required to protect these sorts of signs from the weather.

Slate is a popular choice for house names in the United Kingdom as it is weatherproof, rot-proof and low maintenance.

Plastic signs may also be used for contemporary nameplates. A signwriter can design the name and choose from a variety of colours.

Metal pressed signs can give a rustic look and are usually laser engraved. They generally need some polishing to maintain their appearance.

Speak to your craftsman for more information on the maintenance of your house name plaque.

Illustrated designs

Motifs are repeated designs, such as a border design, that can be added to your nameplate to make it more decorative. Simple pictures such as a tree, cat, dog, flower, horse, star or heart are simple examples of decoration that will add a creative touch to your nameplate.

Where to place your house name plaque

Once you have decided upon a house name plaque, there follows the other decision of how to display it. There are a few options for displaying a plaque.

- On the wall beside the front door.
- In a place that can be seen from the road.
- On a wall at the front of your home.
- Beside the driveway on a wall or gate.
- On your letterbox. Some letterboxes even have a special place to stick a house name.
- On a large rock in your garden. You can either display a plaque or have the house name carved into it.
- Under a porch light for maximum illumination.
- On an old-fashioned-looking signpost. This will give a romantic feeling to a house.
- On a large front door.

Remember, if you are a tenant or if you own an apartment in a building, you will need to get permission before hanging the plaque.

CHAPTER 4

POPULAR HOUSE NAMES FROM AROUND THE WORLD

Below is an alphabetised list compiled from the most popular house names in the USA, UK and Australia. The ten most popular house names are: *The Cottage*, *Rose Cottage*, *The Bungalow*, *Woodlands*, *Hillcrest*, *Seaview*, *Treetops*, *Oaklands*, *Fairview* and *The Laurels*. The meanings and origins of these names are featured in various chapters of this book.

Aberdeen
Avalon

Babylon
Balmoral
Bay View
Beach Haven
Beachside
Beachside Cottage
Beachview
Blue Gum Estate
Bluegums
Brae Cottage
Braeside

Cherry Cottage
Cherrywood
Clear View
Clover Cottage
Cloverdale
Clover Hill
Crystal Creek

Dunmovin'
Dunroamin'

Edelweiss Cottage
Eden
Fairview
Ferntree Gully
Frangipani Cottage

Gone Fishing
Grandma's Cottage
Grandpa's Cottage
Grandview
Gran's Cottage
Green Gables
Greenacres

High View
Hill Crest
Hill View
Hillside
Hillside Manor
Holly Cottage
Holly Wood
Honey Suckle Cottage
How-Dee-Doo

Ivanhoe

Jasmine Cottage

Lake Cottage
Lakeside
Lake View
Laurel Cottage
Lilac Cottage

Meadowlea
Meadow Leigh
Meadow View

Nana's House

Oaklands
Ocean View

Ocean Views
Our House

Pinecroft
Pine View
Pinewoods
Primrose Cottage

River Cottage
River View
Riverwood
Riverwood Estate
Rose Cottage

Sea View
Seaside View
Sunnyside

Tara
The Barn
The Beach House
The Brook Cottage
The Bungalow
The Castle
The Coach House
The Cottage
The Country House
The Cubby House
The Estate House
The Gables
The Haven
The Hillside
The Hollies
The Laurels
The Loch
The Loch House
The Lodge
The Manor
The Manor House
The Meadows
The Mews
The Nook
The Old Church
The Old Post Office
The Old Priory
The Old School House
The Old Vicarage
The Orchard House
The Outback
The Painted Lady
The Retreat
The Rose Garden
The Stables
The Station
The Stud
The Valley House
The Villa
The Vines
The White House
The Willows
The Yellow House
Treetops
Treetops Estate
Tudor House
Twin Oaks

Waterside
Wattlebrae
Wattle Cottage
Wattlevale
Wayside
Welcome Willows
Weowna
White Cottage
Whispering Pines
Willow Cottage
Willows
Wisteria Cottage
Wisteria House
Witsend
Woodlands
Woodville

Yellow Cottage
Yew Tree Cottage

CHAPTER 5

A LITTLE BIT OF ENGLAND

The British have a superb way of expressing love for their homes by choosing a name that reflects their adoration. Nature, flowers and gardens inspire English house names, as do history and architecture. Often names are taken from areas people recollect from childhood, or from a place that holds fond memories. Churches, abbeys, schools, and other buildings are further sources of house names. The list of English house names, like English place names and personal names, also reflects the influence of other peoples who occupied Britain in earlier times, such as the Romans, the Vikings and the Norman French. With so many Australians, New Zealanders and Americans having English ancestry, English house names feature prominently in these countries. Their popularity can be expected to endure.

The use of old-fashioned spelling will add a special air to your home. Names such as '*Faerie Cottage*', '*Forest Gait*', '*The Meade*', '*Sunnymeade*' or '*Lavender Fayre*' are a few examples.

A

Abbey Gate
Entrance gate to the abbey.

Abbeymeade
Abbey in the meadow. *Mead is also a very sweet alcoholic drink made from honey, water, malt and yeast.*

Abundance Cottage
Small house of plenty.

Academy Cottage
Small house of learning.

Ackerley Cottage/Ackerly Cottage
Small house in the oak tree meadow.

Acorn Cottage
Small house by the oak tree.

Acorn Hills
Oak tree hill.

Acorn Oakes/Acorn Oaks
Oak trees.

Acreworth
A valuable land measurement.

Action Fields
Busy meadows.

Ado Cottage
Small house of bother.

Agray Cottage/Agrey Cottage
Small house in the open field; also a grey, small house.

Ainslea House/Ainslee House/ Ainsleigh House/Ainsley House/ Ainsly House
Home in the meadow clearing.

Alcott/Alcott Cottage
Old cottage.

Alderidge Cottage
Small house by the alder tree ridge.

Aldgate
Old gate.

Alfriston Manor
Estate house where the old adviser resides.

All Seasons
All the seasons (winter, spring, summer, autumn/fall) are experienced in this area.

Alton
Old town.

Alton Cottage
Small house in the old town.

Ambledownes/Ambledowns
To walk at a leisurely pace down the rolling countryside.

Ambleside
To walk at a leisurely pace down the side of the slope.

Amity Cottage
Small friendly house.

Amityville
Friendly village. *This usually friendly name is unfortunately associated with numerous horror movies based on a book of the same name by Jay Anson. The first movie was made in 1979.*

Annerlea Cottage/Annerlee Cottage/ Annerleigh Cottage/Annerley Cottage/ Annerly Cottage
Small house on the graceful meadow.

Apex House
House at the summit.

Appleby Manor
Estate house by the apple tree orchard.

Appletop
Apple trees growing at the summit of the hill.

Appleville
Apple village.

April Cottage
Small house built or bought in April. *This house may also be used as a holiday house in April.*

April Fields
Meadows that flower in April.

Arcadia Vale
The ideal valley.

Arctic Breeze
Cold wind from the north.

Ardent Cottage
Small and passionate house.

Arrow Court
Arrows in the courtyard; arrow-shaped courtyard.

Ascot/Ascott/Ascott Cotage
Small eastern house.

Ash Cottage
Small house by the ash trees.

Ashbourne
Ash tree stream or boundary.

Ashburton
Fortified town where the ash trees grow. *Lord Ashburton was president of the Royal Geographical Society at the time of the discovery of the WA river that was named in his honour. Towns in Australia and New Zealand are also named after him. As well as denoting a fortified farmstead, 'burton' also is the name of a type of tackle used in setting up rigging and a town in Staffordshire, famous for its ale of the same name, hence the expression 'gone for a burton', said of absconding soldiers, workers, etc.*

Ashdale
Ash tree valley.

Ashdon
Ash tree valley.

Ashford
Shallow river crossing by the ash trees.

Ashgrove
Ash trees in the small wood.

Ashton
Ash tree town.

Ashvale Manor
Estate house by the ash tree valley.

Aspenbrook/Aspenbrooke
The aspen tree stream.

Aston
Eastern town.

Atherton Cottage
Small house by the stream in the town. *The Atherton Tablelands is situated in Tropical Queensland and features World Heritage listed rainforests, abundant wildlife and rich agricultural land.*

Atlea/Atlee/Atleigh/Atley/Atly
At the meadow.

Atlea Cottage/Atlee Cottage/Atleigh Cottage/Atley Cottage/Atly Cottage
Small house in the meadow.

Aurora Cottage
Small house under the golden beauty of the dawn. *An aurora is caused by electrically charged particles from the sun accelerating along magnetic fields into the earth's upper*

atmosphere. As they collide with gas atoms they give off light. The cumulative effect of these collisions is a spectacular display of moving bands of light. The aurora of the Northern Hemispere is called 'aurora borealis' or 'northern lights'; that of the Southern Hemisphere is called 'aurora australis' or 'southern lights'.

Austin Villa
Little and majestic village.

Avon
River. *Stratford-upon-Avon was the place where William Shakespeare was born. He was also known as the 'Bard of Avon'.*

Avon Gables
Triangular section of roof that can be seen from the river. (See Avon)

Avondale
River in the valley. (See Avon)

Avonlea/Avonlee/Avonleigh/Avonley/Avonly
River meadow. *Avonlea was the town featured in the Anne of Green Gables series by Lucy Maud Montgomery.* (See Avon)

Avonmore
River marshland. (See Avon)

Avonmouth
Source of the river. (See Avon)

Avonside
Riverside; hill by the river. (See Avon)

Avonwood
River in the forest. (See Avon)

Ayr Forest
Airy woods.

B

Backland
The land at the back of the property.

Backton Creek Cottage
Small house by the creek in the back of the town.

Barndale
Barn in the valley.

Barnfield
Barn in the meadow.

Barnville
Village barn.

Barrington
Fenced town.

Barrington Estate
Large, stately house in the fenced town.

Bay Cottage
Small house by the inlet.

Bay View
Vista of the inlet.

Baybrook/Baybrooke
Small stream by the inlet.

Bayville
Village by the inlet.

Baywood
Forest by the inlet.

Beaconsfield
Signal fire in the meadow.

Beaconston
Light in the town.

Beau Desert
Beautiful desert.

Beau Ford/Beauford
Beautiful, shallow river crossing.

Bedford
Dry river crossing.

Beechworth
Beech tree farm.

Beanlea/Beanlee/Beanleigh/Beanley/Beanly/Beenlea/Beenlee/Beenleigh/Beenley/Beenly
Bean meadow.

Belgrave Cottage
Small house by the bell in the grove. (See Bell)

Belgrave House
Small house by the bell in the grove. (See Bell)

Belhaven
Beautiful sanctuary.

Belhaven Cottage
Small house in the beautiful sanctuary. (See Bell)

Bell
Hollow, bell shaped metal cup that makes a ringing sound when struck. *The bell was an important form of communication in the Middle Ages. It warned of fire, flood, invasion or other catastrophes. The person who resided closest to the bell had the job of ringing it when it was needed.*

Bell Cottage
Small house with a bell. (See Bell)

Belle Meade
Bell-shaped meadow; beautiful meadow. *Mead is also a very sweet alcoholic drink made from honey, water, malt and yeast.* (See Bell)

Belle Meadow
Beautiful pasture. (See Bell)

Bellhouse
Home with a bell; beautiful house. (See Bell)

Belton Hall
Town with a bell in the hall. (See Bell)

Beneficial House
Home of great benefit.

Berry House
The home with berries growing nearby.

Birches
Birch trees.

Blackacre
Burnt land; black land.

Blackford
Black, shallow river crossing.

Blackheath
Black coloured heather; burnt grass.

Blackmoor
Black marshland.

Blackwood/Blackwoods
Black forest; the burnt forest.

Blessed Cottage
Small and holy house.

Blessed Manor
Holy estate house.

Bloodwood
Red forest; red coloured wood; forest of battle.

Bloodwood Cottage
Small house by the red forest; small house made of red wood; small house in the forest of battle.

Blythwood
Cheerful and gentle forest.

Borderline
Boundary line; fence line.

Bottom Gardens
Property with gardens on the lower grounds.

Bouldercrest
Rocky hill summit.

Boundary House
Fenced house.

Boundary's Edge
Edge of the property marked by a fence.

Bow Cottage
Small house with an arch or bend.

Bow House
Home with an arch or a bend.

Bowen Estate
Large, stately house where the victorious one resides; the archer's friend.

Bradman Cottage
Small house where the broad man resides. *Sir Donald Bradman was the world's greatest cricket player and a holder of many cricket records.*

Brae Cottage
Small house on the hill.

Brae End
Hill at the end of the property.

Braemar
Hillside marshland.

Braeside
Hillside.

Braeside Manor
Hillside estate house.

Brentwood
Burnt, steep hill in the forest.

Briar Estate
Large, stately house by the wild rose forest.

Briarbank/Briar Bank
Wild rose riverbank.

Briarwood Cottage
Small house in the wild rose forest.

Bridge View/Bridgeview
Vista of the bridge.

Brightlands
Well-lit fields; sunshine fields.

Brighton House
Home in the bright town; home in the town with sunshine.

Britannia
From Britain. *'Rule Britannia' is an unofficial anthem, music written by Thomas Augustine Arne and the words by James Thompson in 1740. 'Britannia' was originally the name given to England by the Romans.*

Britannia Estate
Large, stately home whose owners are from Britain. (See Britannia)

Broad Estate
Wide and large stately house.

Broad Oak/Broad Oake
The large and wide oak tree.

Broad Oakes/Broad Oaks
Large, wide oak trees.

Broadacre
Wide land.

Broadbay
Wide inlet.

Broadhurst
One who resides in the wide forest on the hill.

Broadlea/Broadleah/Broadleigh/Broadlee/Broadley/Broadly
Wide meadow.

Broadmeadow/Broadmeadows
Wide pasture.

Broadwater
Wide waterway.

Brook Cottage/Brooke Cottage
Small house by the stream.

Brook House/Brooke House
Home by the small stream.

Brooklands/Brookelands
Fields with a stream flowing through them.

Brookside/Brookeside
Beside the small stream.

Brookside Cottage/Brookeside Cottage
Small house beside the little stream.

Broughton
Town on the hill.

Broughton House
Home in the hill town.

Browtop
Summit or edge of a hill.

Bumble Brook/Bumble Brooke/Bumbling Brook/Bumbling Brooke
Clumsy stream; winding stream.

Burn Cottage
Small house by the stream.

Burndale
Stream in the valley.

Burnleigh/Burnlea/Burnlee/Burnley
Stream in the meadow.

Burnside
Hillside stream.

Burwood
Prickly forest.

Bushgrove
Small, secluded bushland.

Bushgrove Cottage
Small house in the small, secluded bushland.

Byrock House
Home by the rock.

C

Canyon Valley
Valley in the gorge.

Canyon View
Vista of the gorge.

Cardwell
The strong and courageous one's stream.

Carlile/Carlill/Carlisle/Carlyle Hall
One who resides in the hall of the fortified castle.

Cascade Cottage
Small house by the waterfall.

Cascades/The Cascades
Waterfalls.

Castle Bay
Castle by the inlet.

Castle View
Vista from the fortified estate house.

Castlemere
Castle by the lake.

Castlemerth
Small and merry castle.

Castlemont/Castle Mont
Castle on the mountain.

Centennial Cottage
Small, one hundred year old house.

Channel View
Vista from the waterway.

Cheery Cottage
Small and happy home.

Cheery House
Happy home.

Chetwin
The cottage with a winding path.

Childerlea/Childerlee/Childerleigh/Childerley/Childerly
The children's meadow.

Church Cottage
Small house that was once a church; small house by the church; small house where the clergyman resides.

Churchwell
Well or spring by the church.

Cinder Hills
Burnt hills; ash hills.

Cinderfield
Burnt meadow; ash field.

Cinderford
Burnt area by the shallow river crossing; ashes by the shallow river crossing.

Cinderlea/Cinderleah/Cinderlee/Cinderleigh/Cinderley/Cinderly
Burnt meadow; ash field.

Claymore/Cleymore
Clay soil in the marshlands.

Clear Brook/Clear Brooke/Clearbrook/Clearbrooke
Clear small stream.

Clear View
Unobstructed vista.

Cliff House
Home by the cliff.

Cliffbrook House/Cliffbrooke House
Home by the small cliff stream.

Clifford House
House by the shallow river crossing below the cliff.

Cliffs Edge Cottage
Small house on the edge of the cliff.

Cliffside
Hillside edge.

Cliff Top House/Clifftop House
Home on the summit.

Clifton Cottage
Small house in the cliff town.

Clifton Grove
Small wood in the cliff town.

Cloverlea/Cloverlee/Cloverleigh/Cloverley/Cloverly
Clover meadow.

Cloverlea Cottage/Cloverlee Cottage/Cloverleigh Cottage/Cloverley Cottage/Cloverly Cottage
Small house in the clover meadow.

Cloverlea House/Cloverlee House/Cloverleigh House/Cloverley House/Cloverly House
Home in the clover meadow.

Cold Mountain
Icy mountain. Cold Mountain *(2003), is a movie starring Nicole Kidman and Jude Law. It is about an American Civil War soldier who makes a perilous journey back to his sweetheart.*

Cold Stream Cottage
Small house by the cold brook.

Cold Stream Manor
Estate house by the cold brook.

Coldstream Cottage
Small house by the cold brook. *Coldstream is also a town in Victoria, Australia, where singer Dame Nellie Melba lived in the later years of her life.*

Colonial Cottage
Small house in the colony.

Colonial House
Home in the colony.

Comfort Cottage
Small house of comfort.

Compass Cottage
Small house with views in all directions.

Copper Bell Cottage
Small house with a copper bell. *The bell was an important form of communication in the Middle Ages. It warned of fire, flood, invasion or other catastrophes. The person who resided closest to the bell had the job of ringing it when it was needed.*

Corner Farm
Farm at the corner of the property.

Cornerside
Corner of the hill.

Cornerways
Corner property by the cross roads.

Cornish Homestead
Farmhouse with Cornish owners.

Cosy Nook
Small and comfortable place.

Cottage Bell
Small house with a bell. *The bell was an important form of communication in the Middle Ages. It warned of fire, flood, invasion or other catastrophes. The person who resided closest to the bell had the job of ringing it when it was needed.*

Cottage Close
Small house by the private or enclosed area.

Cottage Garden
Small house with a garden.

Cottage Gate
Small house with an entrance way.

Cottage Grove
Small house in the small wood.

Cottage Vale
Small house in the valley.

Country Cottage
Small house in the countryside.

Country Estate
Large, stately home in the countryside.

Country Willows
Country willow trees.

Coventry
Tree by the cove; exclusion. *The phrase 'sent to Coventry' is believed to have come from the then unpopular English city of Coventry, where soldiers were billeted. It may also have originated from the English Civil War where*

Royalist prisoners were sent to the very Parliamentarian town of Coventry.

Coventry Cottage
Small house near the tree by the cove; small house of exclusion. (See Coventry)

Coventry Estate
Large, stately house near the tree by the cove; large, stately house of exclusion. (See Coventry)

Coventry Manor
Estate house near the tree by the cove; estate house of exclusion. (See Coventry)

Cowlea/Cowlee/Cowleigh/Cowley/Cowly
Cow meadow.

Creeks Bend Cottage
Small house by the creek bend.

Creekside
Small stream on the hillside.

Creekside Cottage
Small house with a small stream on the hillside.

Creekview/Creek View
Vista of the small stream.

Crescent Cottage
Small house in the curved street.

Crescentville
Curved street in the village.

Cressbrook/Cressbrooke
Small stream where cress grows.

Cresswell
Stream where cress grows.

Cresswell Cottage
Small house by the stream where cress grows.

Crestview
Summit vista.

Crookwell
Crooked stream or well.

Crookwell Cottage
Small house by the crooked stream or well.

Cross Cottage
Small house by the crossroads; the small house with a cross; small house with trees that cross over each other in a 'T', 'X' or a '+' pattern.

Crosslea/Crosslee/Crossleigh/Crossley/Crossly
Meadow with trees that cross over in a 'T', 'X' or a '+' pattern; meadow with a cross in it; meadow by the cross streets.

Cross Streets Manor
Estate house by the cross streets; estate house with a cross; estate house with trees that cross over each other in a 'T', 'X' or a '+' pattern.

Cross Trees
Where the trees cross each other in a 'T', 'X' or a '+' pattern.

Crosstree Cottage
Small house by the trees crossing over each other in a 'T', 'X' or a '+' pattern.

Crosswinds
Winds that cross over each other.

Crosswind Cottage
Winds that cross over each other at the small house.

Crosswinds Estate
Large, stately house with winds that cross over it.

Crosswood
Forest by the cross roads.

Crystal Creek Cottage
Small house by the clear and little stream.

Crystal Grove
Small wood of crystal; clear stream in the small wood.

D

Dale Brook/Dale Brooke
Small stream in the valley.

Dale Cottage
Small house in the valley.

Dale House
Valley home.

Dale Wood
Valley forest.

Dalelea/Dalelee/Daleleigh/Daley/Daly
Valley meadow.

Darkwood Cottage
Small house made of dark wood; small house in the dark forest.

Daydream Cottage
Small house of day dreams.

Deep Haven Woods
Place of refuge in the deep forest.

Denham
Comfortable room in the small village; hill farm; village on the hill.

Denstone Cottage
Small house with a comfortable room made from stones.

Dew Downes
Beads of moisture on the lower meadow.

Dimpledell
Small holes in the secluded valley.

Downland Manor
Estate house in the lower meadow.

Downside
Lower hills.

Driftwood
A piece of wood drifting in the water.

Driftwood Cottage
Small house where river wood can be found drifting near by.

Drycreek/Dry Creek
Arid brook.

Drylands Estate/Dryland Estate
Large, stately house on the dry fields.

Dryriver/Dry River
Arid stream.

Drysdale
Arid valley. *Sir Russell Drysdale (1912–81) was an Australian painter noted for his landscapes depicting the strong colours and harsh conditions of the Australian outback.*

Dusty Plains
Dusty meadows.

E

East Bay Cottage
Small house by the eastern bay.

East Bridge
Bridge to the east.

East Cliff/Eastcliff
Eastern summit.

East Cottage
Small house in the east.

East Fossil Manor
The estate house to the east of the old area.

East Pasture
Eastern meadow.

Eastbank
Eastern river or lake bank.

Eastlea/Eastlee/Eastleigh/Eastley/Eastly
Eastern meadow.

Eastside
Eastern hillside.

Eastville
Eastern village.

Eastwell Manor
Estate house with the eastern well or stream.

Eastwich
Eastern bay.

Eastwick/Eastwicke
Eastern village. The Witches of Eastwick *was a 1987 film starring Cher and Jack Nicholson about three women who have their wishes granted at a price.*

Eastwind Manor
Estate house in the path of the easterly wind.

Eastwood
Eastern forest.

Echo Bay
Inlet with repeated sound.

Eclipse Manor
Hidden estate house. *This house may be hidden behind something, a tree or a hill.*

Edgecott/Edge Cottage
Small house on the edge.

Edgehall
Hall by the edge of town.

Edgewater Estate
Large, stately house by the shore of a river, sea, ocean or lake.

Edgewood/Edge Wood
Edge of the forest.

Endeavour Cottage
Small house of those committed to trying. The Endeavour *was the ship in which Captain James Cook and his crew sailed to Australia in 1770.*

Endeavour House
Home of those committed to trying. (See Endeavour Cottage)

F

Fable Haven
Refuge that is spoken about in a moral story.

Fablewood/Fable Wood
Forest in moral story.

Fablewood Cottage/Fable Wood Cottage
Small house in the forest, spoken about in moral story.

Fablewood House/Fable Wood House
Home in the forest, moral story.

Fair Haven/Fayre Haven
Good refuge.

Fair Lawns/Fayre Lawns
Good grassy area; light-coloured grassy area.

Fair View/Fayre View
Good vista; light-coloured vista.

Fairbanks/Fayre Banks
Good shore; light-coloured shore.

Fairfield/Fayre Field
Good meadow; light-coloured meadow.

Fairford/Fayre Ford
Good, shallow river crossing; light-coloured, shallow river crossing.

Fairholme/Fayre Holme
Good home; light-coloured home; good hamlet or village; light-coloured, small inshore island; floodplain. *'Holm/holme' is also a form of 'hamlet' and used as alternative of 'home'.*

Fairthorne/Fayrethorn
Good prickle; light-coloured prickle.

Fairwater/Fayrewater
Good lake, sea or river; light-coloured lake, sea or river.

Fairways/Fayreways
Good cross roads; light-coloured cross roads. *Also a home for a keen golfer!*

Fairwinds/Fayrewinds
Good winds.

Faithful House
House of loyalty and beliefs.

Falling Star Cottage
Small house under the falling stars.

Faraway House
Remote home. *The Faraway Tree series of children's books by English writer Enid Blyton (1896–1968) has delighted several generations of young readers.*

Farmborough
The ranch in municipal or town.

Fenton
Marsh town; fenced town.

Five-Mile View
A vista that is five miles wide.

Flatford
Flat, shallow river crossing.

Flatford Cottage
Small house by the flat, shallow river crossing.

Flatford Estate
Large, stately house by the shallow, flat river crossing.

Flourishing Cottage
Small house of health and growth.

Flourishing Meadow
Healthy, growing field.

Ford House
Home by the shallow river crossing.

Forest Cottage
The small house in the woods.

Forest Edge
Edge of the woods.

Forest Gate
Entry to the woods; gate that leads into the woods.

Forest House
Home in the woods.

Forestlea/Forestlee/Forestleigh/ Forestley/Forestly
Wood meadow.

Forest View
Vista of the woods.

Forestville
Village in the woods.

Fountain Cottage
Small house with a water fountain or a spring.

Fountain Court
Home with a water fountain or a spring in the courtyard.

Fountain House
Home with a fountain or spring.

Fourwinds/Four Winds
Winds blowing from four directions.

Fourwinds Cottage
Small house where the wind blows from four directions.

Fourwinds Estate
Large, stately house where the wind blows from four directions.

Fourwinds House
Home where the wind blows from four directions.

Fourwinds Villa
Country house where the wind blows from four directions.

Freshwater
Fresh water stream or lake.

Freshwater Cottage
Small house by the fresh water stream or lake.

Frost House
Cold home.

Frosty Cabin
Cold lodge.

G

Gaiety Cottage
Small and happy home.

Gaiety House
Happy home.

Gate Bridge
Entrance by the bridge.

Gates Heath
Entrance to the heather.

Gatestone
Stone entrance.

Gentlewood
Gentle forest; the gentile's (pagan's) wood.

Gentlewood Cottage
Small house in the gentle forest; small house in the gentile's (pagan's) wood.

Glencotte/Glenncotte/Glen Cottage/ Glenn Cottage
Small cottage in the valley.

Godspeed
To wish success on a journey.

Goldwell
Well or stream containing gold; gold-coloured stream.

Good Cottage/Goode Cottage
Good, small house. *'Goode' is either an alternative spelling for 'goodwife', an archaic word used before the surname of a woman who is not of nobility; Goody.*

Good House/Goode House
Good home. (See Goode Cottage)

Gothic Manor
The estate house built or influenced by those built in the twelfth–sixteenth centuries. *This architecture is characterised by vaulting and pointed arches and large windows. Many churches are designed in this style.*

Grace Hall
Graceful hall.

Grandton
Great town.

Grandview
Great vista.

Granite Falls Cottage
Small cottage by the granite waterfalls.

Grapeview
Vista of the grape vines.

Grassmere/Grassymere
Grassy area by the lake.

Grassmere Cottage/Grassymere Cottage
Small house on the grassy area by the lake.

Grassy Hill
Grass growing on the hill.

Graycrest/Greycrest
Grey-coloured summit.

Graycrest Cottage/Greycrest Cottage
Small house on the grey-coloured summit.

Graystanes/Greystanes
Grey-coloured stones.

Graystanes House/Greystanes House
Home made from grey-coloured stones.

Graystone Cottage/Greystone Cottage
Small house made of grey-coloured stones.

Graystones/Greystones
The grey-coloured stones.

Grove Hall
The hall in the small wood.

H

Half Sovereign
A 'Half Sovereign', was a gold coin worth ten shillings.

Halfpenny House
Home where a halfpenny was found; a house bought for a small amount. *A halfpenny was a British bronze coin.*

Handsome House
Beautiful home.

Hardcastle
Fortified estate house.

Hardy Cottage
Small, strong house. *This name might also be chosen by admirers of any of several Australian Hardys: writer Frank, his comedian sister Mary, yachtsman Sir James or pioneer viticulturist, Thomas. Alternatively, the name could be in honour of American comedian Oliver Hardy of the famous Laurel and Hardy team, or the English writer Thomas Hardy.*

Hardy House
Strong house. (See Hardy Cottage)

Harmony Cottage
Small home of pleasing music or song; small house of agreement.

Harmony House
Home of pleasing music or song; house of agreement.

Harvest House
Home used at reaping time.

Haven Crest
Refuge on the summit.

Haven Pasture
Meadow of refuge.

Havenside
Hillside refuge.

Havenwood
Forest of refuge.

Heath Cottage/Heather Cottage
Small house in the field of heather or grass.

Heathmont/Heathermont
Heather on the mountain.

Heavenly Cottage
Small house of paradise.

High Banks
Tall shore.

High Breeze
High and gentle wind.

High Cloud Cottage
Small house set high in the clouds; small house on the high mountain.

High Ranges
High mountain area; high area were animals graze.

High View
Tall vista.

Highacres
Tall land. *A name for a property or house on a hill or mountain.*

Highbury Estate
High, large and stately home; large, stately house where berries grow on high bushes.

Highdale
High valley.

Highville
High village.

Highworth
High farm; property of great value.

Hill Brook Estate/Hill Brooke Estate
Large, stately home by the hill stream.

Hill House
Home on a hill.

Hillgrove
Small wood on a hill.

Hillside Manor
Estate house on the side of the hill.

Hilltop
Summit of the hill.

Hilltop Cottage
Small house on the hill summit.

Hilltop Estate
Large, stately home on the summit of the hill.

Hindmarsh
Property with a marshland at the rear.

Hindmarsh Estate
Large, stately home with a marshland at the rear.

Hindmarsh Manor
Estate house with a marshland at the rear.

Hinterland
An area inland from the coast or river.

Hollynook/Holynook
Holly growing in the secluded place; holy secluded place. *This nook would generally be located by a church.*

Hollywell/Holywell
Holly by the well or stream; holy stream or well. *This house would generally be located by a church.*

Hollywell Cottage/Holywell Cottage
Small house with holly growing by the well or stream; small house by the holy stream or well. *A church would generally be located by this house.*

Hollywood/Holywood
The holy forest; holly growing by the well or stream. *A name for those with a very glamorous looking home to consider. Hollywood in the USA is famed throughout the world for its movie making.*

Holm/Holme
Hamlet or village; small inshore island; floodplain. *'Holm/holme' is also a short-form of 'hamlet' and is sometimes used as an alternative of 'home'.*

Holm Cottage/Holme Cottage
Small house in the hamlet or village; small house on the inshore island; small house on the floodplain. (See Holm/Holme)

Holmelea/Holmelee/Holmeleigh/ Holmeley/Holmely
Meadow in the hamlet or village; meadow on the small inshore island; floodplain meadow. (See Holm/Holme)

Holm Wood/Holme Wood/ Holmewood/Holmwood
Home in the hamlet or village; home on the small inshore island; home on the floodplain. (See Holm/Holme)

Holmdale/Holmedale
Valley in the hamlet or village; valley on the small inshore island; valley near the floodplain. (See Holm/Holme)

Holmelea/Holmelee/Holmeleigh/Hol mley/Holmly
Meadow in the hamlet or village; meadow on the small inshore island; floodplain meadow. (See Holm/Holme)

Holmey House
Home in the hamlet or village; home on the inshore island; home on the floodplain. (See Holm/Holme)

Home Sweet Home
A house where one is comfortable and grateful to be there. *'Home Sweet Home' is also the title of a well-known song by Henry Bishop to words by John Payne. Australian soprano Dame Nellie Melba used to sing it in concerts when she returned to Australia. The Maori version of this famous saying is Kia-ora.*

Homelea Cottage/Homelee Cottage/ Homeleigh Cottage/Homeley Cottage/ Holmly Cottage
Small house on the meadow.

Homestone Cottage
Small house made from stone.

Homeward
In the direction of home.

Hope Cottage
Small house of faith, wishes or desires.

Hopewell
Stream of faith, wishes or desires; wishing well.

Howarth
High farm; hill farm.

Huntington Lake Cottage
Small house by the hunter's lake; small house by the lake of the hunters' town.

I

In The Forest
To reside in the woods.

In The Woods
In the forest. A name for a home or property situated in a forest area.

Into The Woods
To enter the forest. Into the Woods *won a Tony Award in 2002 for the Best Revival of a Musical. The show combines various fairytale characters such as Cinderella, Jack and the Beanstalk and Little Red Ridinghood with the story of a baker and his wife who are cursed with childlessness by a witch. They must perform various missions involving other fairy tale characters to break the spell.*

Ingham
Famous farm; famous village. *Also an English place name.*

Ingliswood
The English forest.

Isleton
Small island town.

J

Jolie House/Jollie House
Jolly home. French for pretty.

Jubilee House
Anniversary. *A name for a house celebrating its 25th, 50th or 60th anniversary of being built.*

K

Kentwood
The warrior's forest.

Kinderslea/Kinderslee/Kindersleigh/ Kindersley/Kindersly
The kind one's meadow; meadow containing firewood. *The name is also thought to be a variant of the English place name, 'Kinnersley', after Hugh de Kinardesleg.*

Kingscliff
The king's cliff.

Kingsmead/Kingsmeade
The king's meadow; the king's sweet, honey drink. *Mead is also a very sweet alcoholic drink made from honey, water, malt and yeast.*

Kingsmeadow
The king's field.

Kingston
The king's town.

Kingstone
The king's stone.

Kingswood
The king's forest.

L

Lake Hill
Hill over looking the lake.

Lake Side/Lakeside
Lake by the hillside; beside the lake.

Lakes Edge Manor
Estate house by the lakeshore.

Lakes Way/Lakesway
Lake path.

Lakewood Cottage
Small house by the forest lake.

Lament Cottage
Small house of grief.

Landwade
One who reaches the land by the water.

Langlea/Langlee/Langleigh/Langley/ Langly
Long meadow.

Lansdown/Lansdowne/Landsdown/ Landsdowne
Hill slope; the land below.

Landsdown Cottage/Landsdowne Cottage/Lansdown Cottage/ Lansdowne Cottage
Small house on the hill slope; small house on the downward slope.

Landsdown Estate/Landsdowne Estate/ Lansdown Estate/Lansdowne Estate
Large, stately house on the hill slope; large, stately house on the downward slope.

Landsdowne House/Landsdown House/Lansdown House/Lansdowne House
Home on the hill slope; home on the downward slope.

Landsdown Manor/Landsdowne Manor/Lansdown Manor/Lansdowne Manor
Estate house on the hill slope; estate house on the downward slope.

Lawn Manor/Lorn Manor/Lorne Manor
Estate house with a lawn.

Lea Hill/Lee Hill/Leigh Hill/Ley Hill
The meadow hill.

Leacroft/Leecroft/Leighcroft/Leycroft
Small meadow.

Leafy Glade/Leafyglade/Leafglade/ Leaf Glade
Leaf covered meadow.

Lea Farm/Lee Farm/Leigh Farm/ Ley Farm
Meadow ranch.

Lin Wood Estate/Linwood Estate
Large, stately house by the forest pond.

Little Bourn/Little Bourne/ Littlebourn/Littlebourne
Small stream.

Little Brook/Little Brooke
Small stream.

Little Brook Cottage/Little Brooke Cottage
Small house by the small stream.

Little Brook Manor/Little Brooke Manor
Estate house by the small stream.

Little Haven
Small refuge.

Little Haven Cottage
Small house of refuge.

Little River Cottage
Small house by the small river.

Lochlea/Lochlee/Lochleigh/Lochley/ Lochly
Lake meadow.

Lockslea/Lockslee/Locksleigh/Locksley/ Locksly
Lakes by the meadows.

Lonesdale
One meadow; lonely meadow.

Long Acre/Longacre
Long land.

Long Acres
Long land.

Long Lands/Longlands
Long fields.

Long Lane Cottage/Longlane Cottage
Small house on the long lane.

Long Meadows
Long fields.

Long Swamp
Long marshland.

Longlea/Longlee/Longleigh/Longley/ Longly
Long meadow.

Lorneville
Victorious village.

Lovall Cottage
Small house where the owner adores all.

Love Close
Adored road that is closed at the end.

Love Cottage
Small house of adoration.

Love Hamlet
Small village of adoration.

Love Manor
Adored estate house.

Love Nook/Lovenook
Adored, cosy and secluded place.

Lovecroft
Small, secluded woods of adoration.

Lovedale
Adored valley.

Lovewood
Adored forest.

Loveworth
Adored farm; valued adoration.

Lower Court
Lower courtyard.

Lowerdale
Lower valley.

Luckford
Fortunate, shallow river crossing.

Lucknow Cottage
Fortune is needed immediately in this small house.

Luckwell Cottage
Small house by the fortunate well or stream.

M

Madewood
Created forest.

Maiden Cottage
Small house owned by an unmarried woman.

Main Cottage
Small and most important house among other cottages. *This name was usually given to one house on a large farm or property. It was lived in by the chief farmer of the property. The owners would reside in an estate house.*

Maincreek Cottage
Small, important house by the brook; small house by the important brook.

Mainstreet Cottage
Small house on a major street.

Majestic Manor
Royal estate house.

Mandalay/Manderlay
Meadow worthy of love. *'Mandalay' is the name of the mansion in Daphne De Maurier's novel* Rebecca, *about a rich widower who marries a naïve young woman. She discovers that the memory of her husband's first wife still has a grip on her husband and even the servants. This novel was later turned into a movie directed by Alfred Hitchcock in 1940 and starred Laurence Olivier and Joan Fontaine.*

Mandalay Cottage/Manderlay Cottage
Small house in the meadow worthy of love. (See Mandalay).

Mandalay Estate/Manderlay Estate
Large, stately house in the meadow worthy of love. (See Mandalay)

Mandalay Manor/Manderlay Manor
Estate house in the meadow worthy of love. (See Mandalay)

Manorville
Estate house in the village.

Mansfield
The man's meadow. *Jane Mansfield (b. Vera Jayne Palmer 1933–67) was an American actor who was killed in a car accident.*

Mansion at the Oakes/Mansion at the Oaks
Estate house with oak trees growing near by.

Mansion at the River
Estate house by the river.

Mansion at the Stream
Estate house by the small river.

Mansion Brook/Mansion Brooke/ Mansionbrook/Mansionbrooke
Estate house by the small stream.

Mansion Hall
Estate house by the city hall.

Mansion Hill/Mansion on the Hill
Estate house on the hill.

Mansionlea/Mansionlee/Mansionleigh/ Mansionley/Mansionly
Estate house in the meadow.

Marsh House
Home on the marshland.

Marshgate Manor
Estate house at the beginning of the marshland.

Mayfair
Good, month of May; light-coloured may flowers; fete in May. *Mayfair is the most prestigious property in the board game, Monopoly. The Parker Brothers first marketed the game on a broad scale in 1935.*

Mead Hall/Meade Hall
Hall in the meadow; hall where the sweet honey drink is made. *Mead is also a very sweet alcoholic drink made from honey, water, malt and yeast.*

Meadow Cottage
Small house in the meadow.

Meadow Lea/Meadow Lee/Meadow Leigh/Meadowlea/Meadowlee/ Meadowleigh/Meadowley/Meadowly
Fields.

Meadow Marsh Manor
Estate house in the fields by the swampland.

Meadow View
Vista of the fields.

Meadow Vista
Vista of the fields.

Meadowdale
Field valley.

Meadowfoot
Lower field.

Meadowlake
Lake in the field.

Meadowlea Cottage/Meadowlee Cottage/ Meadowleigh Cottage/Meadowley Cottage/Meadowly Cottage
Small house in the fields.

Meadowlea House/Meadowlee House/ Meadowleigh Cottage/Meadowley House/Meadowly House
Home in the fields.

Meadowlea Manor/Meadowlee Manor/ Meadowleigh Manor/Meadowley Manor/Meadowly Manor
Estate house in the fields.

Meadowvale
Meadow valley.

Meadowville
Village in the fields.

Medieval House
Home from the middle ages.

Memory Cottage
Small house that contains memories.

Merrivale
Happy valley.

Merriville
Happy village.

Merry Fields
Happy meadows.

Middle Brook/Middle Brooke
Middle of the small stream.

Middle Cottage
Small house in the middle of two other cottages.

Middlethorne
Thorn bush in the middle of the property.

Middleton Estate
Large, stately house in the middle of town.

Middlewich
Middle of the bay; middle-most salt works.

Midlands Manor
Estate house in the middle of the meadows.

Mighty Oak/Might Oake
Estate house with mighty oak trees.

Mighty Oak Manor/Mighty Oake Manor
Estate house with mighty oak trees.

Mighty Oaks/Mighty Oakes
Strong oak trees.

Milefield
The mile long meadow.

Milestone Cottage
Small house by the milestone. *A milestone may also mark a major stage in one's life.*

Milestone Manor
Estate house by the milestone. (See Milestone Cottage)

Milford
Shallow river crossing by the mill.

Mill Wood/Millwood
From the mill in the forest.

Millbrook/Millbrooke
Mill by the stream.

Millgate
The entrance to the mill.

Misty Manor
Estate house in the light fog.

Misty Meadows
Light fog over the fields.

Misty Morning
Light fog in the morning.

Misty Mountain
Mountain covered in the light fog.

Mistymead/Mistymeade
Light fog over the fields. *Mead is also a very sweet alcoholic drink made from honey, water, malt and yeast.*

Moments Cottage
Small house.

Monarch Manor
One who reigns over the estate house.

Montrose Estate
Large, stately house where the mountain rose grows.

Moon Hill
Moon peaking over the hill.

Moorcourt
Courtyard by the marshlands.

Moorefield
Meadow marshland.

Moorview
Vista of the marshland.

Moreton
Marshland town.

Morningside
Hillside in the morning sun.

Morningside Cottage
Small house in the morning sun.

Mornington
Morning town.

Mornington Cottage
Small house in the morning town.

Morningvale
Morning valley.

Morningview
Vista of the morning.

Morton House
Home in the marshland town.

Moss Mews
Moss growing on a row of houses or stables.

Mount Hope
Mountain of faith.

Mount Pleasant
Nice mountain.

Mount Pleasant Cottage
Small house on the nice mountain.

Mountain Escape
Retreat on the mountain.

Mountain Hall
Hall on the mountain.

Mountain Home
House in the mountains.

Mountain House
Home in the mountains.

Mountain Lodge
Cabin in the mountains.

Mountain Rose Cottage
Small house with mountain roses growing nearby.

Mountain Valley
Dale between the mountains.

Mountain View
Vista of the mountain.

Mountain View Cottage
Small house with vistas of the mountain.

Mountainside
Beside the mountain.

Mountside
The mountainside.

Muddy Water Manor
Estate house by the muddy stream or river.

Myrtle Tree Cottage
Small house where myrtle trees grow.

N

Narrowlanding
Thin, level land.

Natura
Nature; natural.

Neutral Ground
Impartial land.

New Court
New courtyard.

New Field House
Home by the new meadow.

New Moor Estate
Large, stately home by the new marshland.

Newburn Estate
Large, stately house by the new stream.

Newell
New well or stream.

Newholme/Newholm
New home; new village. *'Holm/holme' is also a form of 'hamlet' and is contemporarily used as alternative of 'home'.*

Newholmewood
New home in the forest. (See Newholme)

Newington/Newton
New town.

Nine Wells
Property with nine wells or springs.

Noble Cottage
Small house where the respected one resides.

North Bay Cottage
Small house by the northern inlet.

North Bridge
Northern bridge.

North Cottage
Small house on the northern side.

North Glade
A northerly open space in the forest.

North Pasture
Northern meadow.

Northbank
Northern river or lake shore.

Northern Woods
Northern forest.

Northlea Cottage
Small house in the northern meadow.

Northlea/Northlee/Northleigh/ Northley/Northly
Northern meadow.

Northlea Estate/Northlee Estate/ Northleigh Estate/Northley Estate/ Northly Estate
Large, stately home in the northern meadow.

Northside
Northern hillside.

Northville
Northern village.

Northwell Manor
Estate house with a northern well or stream.

Northwind Manor
Estate house with a northerly wind.

Northwood
Northern forest.

Northwood Cottage
Small house in the northern forest.

Norwich
Northern farm; northern bay.

Norwich Cottage
Small house on the northern farm; small house by the northern bay.

Norwood
Northern forest.

O

Oak Grove/Oake Grove
Oak tree wood.

Oak Grove Cottage
Small house in the oak tree wood.

Oak Tree Cottage
Small house near the oak tree.

Oakemead/Oakemeade/Oakmead/ Oakmeade
Oak tree meadow; sweet honey drink by the oak tree. *Mead is also a very sweet alcoholic drink made from honey, water, malt and yeast.*

Oakehampton/Oakhampton
Proud oak tree town.

Oakehurst/Oakhurst
One who resides on the hill in the oak tree forest.

Oaklawn Manor
Large, stately home with oak trees growing on the lawn.

Oakelea/Oakelee/Oakeleigh/Oaklea/ Oaklee/Oakleigh
Oak tree meadow.

Oakelea Cottage/Oakelee Cottage/ Oakeleigh Cottage/Oaklea Cottage/ Oaklee Cottage/Oakleigh Cottage/
Small house in the oak tree meadow.

Oaklea Manor/Oaklee Manor/ Oakleigh Manor/Oakley Manor/Oakly Manor
Estate house by the oak tree meadow.

Oakevale/Oakvale
Oak tree valley.

Oakeville/Oakville
Oak tree village.

Old Charm Cottage
Old, charming and small house.

Oldfield
Old meadow.

Oldfield House
Home on the old meadow.

Oldfields
Old meadows.

Oldlea/Oldlee/Oldleigh/Oldley/Oldly
Old field.

Onetree
The place where one tree stands alone.

Orange Grove
Orange trees growing in the small wood.

Orchard House
Home with a fruit tree farm.

Orchard Mansion
Estate house with a fruit tree farm.

Orchard's End
Lower part of the fruit tree farm.

Our House
Home owned by those who reside in it.

Oval House
Oval shaped home; home by the playing field.

Over Water Estate
Large, stately house built over an underground spring; large, stately home with water views.

Overton
Over the town; a place with views over the town below it.

Overton Estate
Large, stately house that has views over the town.

Overwood Cottage
Small house with views over the forest.

Oxbridge
Oxford and Cambridge; bridge over the place where the oxen graze; bridge where the oxen pass over.

P

Packwood
Collection of firewood.

Paddington
Noble town. *Paddington Bear is the creation of the English author Michael Bond, whose story book,* A Bear Called Paddington, *was first published in 1958. Paddington wears a duffle coat, a hat and boots and his favourite food is marmalade.*

Paddington Cottage
Small house in the noble town. (See Paddington)

Painted View
Perfect vista; a vista worth painting.

Palestone Cottage
Small house made of light-coloured stones.

Palestone Manor
Estate house made with light-coloured stones.

Paradise Haven
Heavenly refuge.

Paradise Valley
Heavenly valley.

Paramount Manor
Supreme estate house; a name for a house situated on a high hill.

Park Haven
Recreation refuge.

Parklake
Recreation land with a lake.

Parklane
Small road by the recreational area. *Park Lane is the second most prestigious property in the board game Monopoly. The Parker Brothers first marketed the game on a broad scale in 1935.*

Parkside
Hillside recreational area.

Parkview
A vista of the recreational area.

Parkview Cottage
Small house with a vista of the recreational area.

Parkview Estate
Large, stately house with a vista of the recreational area.

Parkview Manor
Estate house with a vista of the recreational area.

Parkway
Path in the recreational area.

Peace Haven
Quiet refuge.

Peaceful Nook
Quiet, small and secluded place.

Pear Tree Cottage
Small house with pear trees growing nearby.

Petite House
Small house.

Pinnacle Cottage
Small house on the highest point; small house of the high achiever.

Pinnacle House
Home on the highest point; home of the high achiever.

Plainfield
Flat meadow.

Pleasance House
Nice house.

Plentiful Cottage
Small house that meets one's needs.

Ploughfield
The ploughed meadow.

Premier Lodge
The new and important cabin.

Pretty Hills
House on the attractive hills.

Prosperity Cottage
Small house of success.

Prosperity Estate
Large, stately home of success.

Prosperity House
Home of success.

Prosperity Manor
Estate house of success.

Providence
Destiny or divine guidance.

Providence Cottage
Small house of destiny or divine guidance.

Providence House
Home of destiny or divine guidance.

Q

Quaint Acres
Pleasant land; small, old-fashioned land.

Quaint Cottage
Pleasant, little house; small, old-fashioned house.

Quaintville
Pleasant, little village; old-fashioned village.

Queensberry
Where the queen's berries grow; the queen's shire or castle.

Queenscliff
The cliff by the queen's residence.

Queensland
The queen's land. *Queensland is a state in Australia known as 'The Sunshine State', due to its tropical climate.*

Queenswood
The queen's forest.

R

Rainham/Rainhamlet
Rain on the farm; rainy village.

Rainwell Court
Courtyard by the small stream that appears in the rain.

Remembrance Cottage
Small house of memories; memory of a loved one. *A dedication to those who have passed over, especially those who died in war and are remembered in Remembrance Day ceremonies.*

Remembrance Estate
Large, stately house of memories; memory of a loved one. (See Remembrance Cottage)

Restdownes
Place of relaxation in the lower hills.

Ridgeway
Path by the ridge.

Ripple Cottage
Small house by the rippling water.

Ripple Cove
Ripples in the bay.

Rippleside Cottage
Small house beside the rippling water.

Riven Cottage
Small house split apart.

River Cottage
Small house by the river.

River Dale
River by the valley.

River Haven
Refuge by the river.

River Stone/Riverstone
River stone.

River View Cottage
Small house with a vista of the river.

River Vista/Rivervista
View of the river.

River Walk Cottage
Small house near the river path.

River Wind Cottage
Small house by the windy river.

Riverdell
River in the valley.

Riverdell Cottage
Small house by the river in the secluded valley.

Riverdell Manor
Estate house by the river in the valley.

Riverhouse
Home by the river; house on the river. *This would be a perfect name for a houseboat.*

Riverland
Where the river crosses through the land.

Riverlea/Riverlee/Riverleigh/Riverly
River meadow.

Rivers End/Riversend
The end of the river.

Riverside Cottage
Small house by the river.

Riverslea/Riverslee/Riversleigh/Riversley/Riversly
River meadow.

Riverslea Cottage/Riverslee Cottage/Riversleigh Cottage/Riversley Cottage/Riversly Cottage
Small house by the river meadow.

Riverswood/Rivers Wood
River forest.

Riverview
Vista of the river.

Riverwood
River forest.

Riverwood Cottage
Small house by the river forest.

Roadside Cottage
Small house by the side of the road.

Rock Field/Rockfield
Rocky meadow.

Rock Ledge/Rockledge
Rocky ledge.

Rockland
Rocky fields.

Rocklea/Rocklee/Rockleigh/Rockley/Rockly
Rocky meadow.

Rocklea Cottage/Rocklee Cottage/Rockleigh Cottage/Rockley Cottage
Small house by the rocky meadow.

Rockstones
Rocks and stones.

Rockwell
Rocky well or stream.

Rockwell Cottage
Small house by the rocky well or stream.

Rolling Hills
Flowing hills. *'Rolling Hills' always conjures up a vision of softly flowing hills and would be a perfect name for a property that matches this description. The mansion*

property that featured in the novels by V.C. Andrews is called 'Rolling Hills'.

Rookwood
A maze made of trees in the forest. *'Rookwood Cemetery' in Sydney, Australia, is the largest cemetery in the Southern Hemisphere. Approximately one million people have had their final resting place within the 300-hectare boundaries.*

Rosary Cottage
Small house where the rosary is recited. *Catholics use 'Rosary Beads' in prayer.*

Rosary Lodge
The cabin where the rosary is recited. (See Rosary Cottage)

Roughwoods
The coarse forest.

Round Hill House
Home on the round hill.

Runnymeade/Runnymede
Wet meadow. *Mead is also a very sweet alcoholic drink made from honey, water, malt and yeast. In 1215 King John signed the Magna Carta at Runnymede in Surry.*

Rutherglen/Rutherglenn
Castle in the valley.

Rutherglen Cottage/Rutherglenn Cottage
Small castle cottage in the valley.

Rutherglen Estate/Rutherglenn Estate
Large castle in the valley.

Rutherglen House/Rutherglenn House
Castle in the valley.

Rutherglen Manor/Rutherglenn Manor
Castle in the valley.

Ryegate
Rye grass by the gate or entrance.

S

Sacred Cottage
Holy and small house.

Sacred Heart
The holy centre. *This name is often given to churches as it describes the holy centre of the community.*

Sacred Heart Cottage
Small house with a holy centre. (See Sacred Heart)

Salvation Cottage
Small, safe home of deliverance. (See Salvation House)

Salvation House
Safe home; home of deliverance. *'The Salvation Army' is a famous international Christian organisation that gives aid, spiritual guidance and assistance to people in over 100 countries.*

Sanctuary
Refuge; a holy altar area in a church; a place of worship.

Sanctuary Cottage
Small house of refuge. (See Sanctuary)

Sandalwood
Wood of the sandalwood tree. *The sandalwood tree is used not only for its wood but also for its oil which is used in soaps and perfumes.*

Sandalwood Cottage
Small house by the sandalwood tree or forest. (See Sandalwood)

Sandy Hills
Sand dunes.

Savage Lands
Uncivilized fields.

Scotney Cottage
Small house where the Scotsman resides.

Scottcott
Small house where the Scotsman resides.

Sea View/Sea Vista/Seaview/Seavista
Vista of the sea.

See View/See Vista/Seeview/Seevista
See the view.

Sellers Wood
One who sells products in the forest.

Selwyn Estate
Blessed friend who resides in the manor house.

Sentry House
Guarded house.

Serenity Cottage
Quiet, relaxing house.

Serenity Estate
Quiet, relaxing, large and stately home.

Serenity Gate
Quiet and relaxing entrance to the house.

Serenity House
Quiet and relaxing house.

Serenity Manor
Quiet and relaxing estate house.

Serenity Vale/Serenityvale
Quiet and relaxing valley.

Serenityville
Quiet and relaxing village.

Seven-Mile Creek
Seven-mile long stream.

Shadow Corner
Shadowy corner.

Shadow Cottage
Small, shadowy house.

Shadowland
Shadow field.

Shady Nook
Shady, small and secluded place.

Shady Pines
The shade of the pine trees.

Shakespeare Cottage
Small house inspired by or named after William Shakespeare. *Shakespeare (1564-1616) was born in Stratford-upon-Avon. He is often claimed to be the greatest English playwright, with such plays as* The Tempest, Midsummer Night's Dream *and* Macbeth, *to name just a few.*

Shallowdale
Shallow valley.

Sharingham/Sharing Hamlet
The shared farm; shared village.

Sheffield Cottage
Small house by the crooked meadow.

Sheltered Cottage
Small, protected house.

Sherbrook/Sherbrooke
Bright stream.

Sherwood Forest
Bright woods. *Sherwood Forest in Nottinghamshire, England, is famed as the home of the legendary Robin Hood.*

Shield Hill
Property where shields were made; protective hill.

Silent Grove
Small, quiet wood.

Silent Valley Grove
Small, quiet forest in the valley.

Sizemore
Property by the large marshland.

Sky House
High home.

Sky Lodge
High cabin.

Slade
Valley.

Sladen
One who resides in the valley.

Sladen Cottage
Small house in the valley.

Sladenville
Village in the valley.

Smallholm/Smallholme
Small house; small inshore island; flat low-lying river land.

Snow Dale Cottage
Small house in the snow valley.

Snow Hill/Snowy Hill
Snow on the hill.

Snow Lodge/Snowy Lodge
Cabin used only when it snows.

Snow Summit Cabin
Lodge at the top of a snowy hill.

Snow Village
Small, snowy settlement.

Snowball
A ball of snow. *A snowball is a mass of pressed snow rolled together into a ball and thrown. Snowball fights are common in snowy areas.*

Snowden
Snowy lair.

Snowdrop Cottage
Small house where snow drops fall.

Snowvale
Snow valley.

Snowville
Snow village.

Snowy Summit
Snow covered top.

Sodbury
Muddy borough; muddy castle.

Sol Cottage
Small house of the sun; small house of soil.

Somerset/Sommerset/Summerset
Summer place. *'Somerset' is the name of a county in England and a town in Tasmania, Australia.*

Somerton
Summer town.

Somerton Cottage
Small house in the summer town.

Sommerville
Summer village.

Sonnet Grove/Sonnetgrove
Poetic, small wood.

Sonnet Inlet
Poetic bay.

Sonnetwood
Poetic forest.

South Bank/Southbank
Southern shore.

South Bay Cottage
Small house by the southern inlet.

South Bridge
Southern bridge.

South Cottage
Small house on the southern hillside.

South Croft
Small, southern pasture.

South Pasture
Southern meadow.

South View
Southern vista.

South Winds Estate
Large, stately house in the path of the southern wind.

South Wood/Southwood
Southern forest.

Southden House
Home in the southern valley.

Southlea/Southlee/Southleigh/Southley/Southly
Southern meadow.

Southside
Southern hillside.

Southvale
Southern valley.

Southville
Southern village.

Southwell Manor
Estate house with a well or stream in the south.

Southwich
Southern bay.

Southwind Estate
Large, stately home in the path of the southern wind.

Southwind Manor
Estate house in the path of the southern wind.

Sovereign Cottage
Small house where the monarch resides.

Sovereignville
The monarch's village.

Springbank
Shore of the stream.

Springbank Estate
Large, stately home by the shore of the stream.

Spring Cottage
Small house by the small stream.

Spring Farm
Ranch with a stream.

Spring Haven
Springtime refuge.

Spring Hill
Small stream on the hill.

Spring Manor
Estate house by the stream.

Springhill Cottage
Small house on the hill with a stream.

Springtime
The spring season.

Springtime Cottage
Small house used in the springtime.

Springvale
Stream in the valley.

Springvale Cottage
Small house by the valley stream.

Springville Cottage
Small house in the village by the stream.

Springwell
The streams.

Springwood
Stream in the forest. *Springwood is also a town in the Blue Mountains of NSW, Australia.*

Springwood Cottage
Small house in the forest by the stream.

Springwood Mansion
Estate house in the forest by the stream.

Stable Cottage
Small house with a stable.

Still Meadows
The still fields.

Stillwater
Still lake or pond. *'Still Water' was the name of the band in the 2000 movie,* Almost Famous*, starring Kate Hudson.*

Stockwell
Well or stream where the animals drink.

Stoneacre
Stones on the measured land.

Stonebank
Stones on the shore.

Stonecrop Meadow
Stones on the agricultural field.

Stonehead
Stone at the front or beginning of a property.

Stonehenge
Ritual stone monument consisting of a circular structure of posts and lintels. *Stonehenge is a famous and mysterious stone structure near Salisbury, England. It is believed to have been built in 3100 BC.*

Stoneholme
House made of stone; stone hamlet or village; small, stoney inshore island; stoney floodplain. *'Holm/holme' is also a form of 'hamlet'.*

Stonelea/Stonelee/Stoneleigh/Stonley
Stone meadow.

Stoneridge
Stoney ridge.

Stoneton
Stone town.

Stoney End
Stoney end of the land or road.

Stoney Ford
Stoney and shallow river crossing.

Stoneycroft
Stone covered small pasture.

Storm Haven
Refuge from the storm.

Stormbound
To be delayed by a storm.

Stormside
Hillside storm.

Stormside Cottage
Small house on the stormy hillside.

Stormy Skies
Grey/gray skies; a sky about to storm.

Strawbridge
Straw by the bridge.

Strawdale
Straw valley.

Streamside
Stream on the hillside.

Streamside Cottage
Small house by the stream.

Sugar Hill
Sweet hill.

Summer Breeze Cottage
Small house where the warm wind blows. *A perfect name for a summerhouse.*

Summer Cottage
Small house used in the summertime. *A perfect name for a summerhouse.*

Summer Fields/Summerfields
Summer meadows; warm meadows.

Summer Haven
Summer refuge. *A home used to escape the heat of the summer or to enjoy the hot weather.*

Summer Holme/Summer Home
Home used during summer time; summer hamlet or village; small, summer inshore island; summer floodplain. *'Holm/holme' is also a form of hamlet. Today the name is sometimes used as an alternative spelling of 'home'. A perfect name for a summerhouse.*

Summer House
Home used during summer. *The perfect name for a holiday home.*

Summerhill
Summer hill; warm hill. *'Summerhill' is the name of the famous school founded in England by educationist A.S. Neill, a pioneer of the free schools movement.*

Summerlea/Summerlee/Summerleigh/ Summerley/Summerly
Summer meadow.

Summertime Cottage
Small house used in the summer time. *This house would generally be used in the warmer months. 'Summertime' is the title of a well-known song from the 1935 musical,* Porgy and Bess *by George Gershwin.*

Summertime Manor
Estate house in the summer.

Summerton
Summer town.

Summertops
Summer summit.

Summervale
Summer valley.

Summerwood
Summer forest.

Sun Cottage
Small house in the sun.

Sunbeam Cottage
Small house where the rays of the sun can be seen and possibly equipped with kitchen appliances of a well-known brand.

Sunblessed Cottage
Small house with plenty of sun.

Sunbound
Moving toward the sun.

Sunburst Cottage
Small house in the sunshine.

Suncliff
Sunshine cliff.

Suncliff Cottage
Small house on the sunshine cliff.

Suncliff House
House on the sunshine cliff.

Sundial House
Home with a sundial.

Sundowner
An evening drink; the sun going down.

Sunkist Cottage
Small house with plenty of sunshine.

Sunningdale
Sunshine valley.

Sunny Corner
Sunshine in the corner block.

Sunnybrae
Sunshine on the hillside.

Sunnycroft
Sunny and small pasture.

Sunnydale
Sunshine in the valley. *Sunnydale was the town Buffy fought evil in, in the television series* Buffy the Vampire Slayer.

Sunnydale Cottage
Small house in the sunshine valley.

Sunny Downes/Sunnydownes
The sunshine on the lower meadows.

Sunny Hill
Sunshine on the hill.

Sunny Meadows/Sunnymeadows
Sun shining over the meadow.

Sunny Ridge
Sunshine on the ridge.

Sunnyholm/Sunnyholme/Sunnyhome
House of sunshine; sunshine hamlet or village; sunshine on the inshore island; floodplain of sunshine. *'Holm/holme' is also a form of 'hamlet'. Today the name is sometimes used as an alternative spelling of 'home'.*

Sunnylea/Sunnylee/Sunnyleigh/ Sunnyley/Sunnly
Sunny meadow.

Sunnymead/Sunnymeade
Sunny meadow. *Mead is also a very sweet alcoholic drink made from honey, water, malt and yeast.*

Sunnyside
Sunny hillside.

Sunny Valley
Sunny dale.

Sunray Flats
The sun's rays are shining on the meadows.

Sunrise Cottage
Small house with the vista of the dawn.

Sunset Cottage
Small house with a vista of the setting sun.

Sunset Cove
Dusk over the bay.

Sunset Fields
Dusk on the meadows.

Sunset Heads
Dusk on the source of the river.

Sunset Moors
Dusk on the marshland.

Sunset Place
Place where the sun sets.

Sunstone Cottage
Small stone house of sunshine.

Sutherlands
Southern fields.

Sutton House
House in the southern town.

Sweetwater
Clean, sweet spring or well.

Tanglewood
Twisted branches in the forest.

Templeston/Templestone
Temple stone.

Templeton
Temple town.

Tender Haven
Soft, comfortable place of refuge.

The Abbey
Religious building; the church.

The Acreage
Land measured in acres.

The Alpine
High mountains.

The Alpine Village
Small town in the high mountains.

The Ancient Gate
Very old entrance.

The Borough
The municipal.

The Boundary Stone
Stone that signifies a fence line or acreage.

The Brass Bell Cottage
Small house with a brass bell. *The bell was an important form of communication in the Middle Ages. It warned of fire, flood,*

invasion or other catastrophes. The person who resided closest to the bell had the job of ringing it when it was needed.

The Bridge House
Home by the bridge.

The Brook/The Brooke
Small stream.

The Byway
Small road that is seldom used.

The Castle Tower
Castle tower.

The Chimes
House with bells that chime. (See Bell)

The Clock Tower
A building with a clock in its tower.

The Corner House
Home on the corner.

The Cosy Cabin
Comfortable cabin.

The Cottage
Small House. *This name features high on the list of most popular house names in the USA, UK and Australia.*

The Country House
A home in the countryside. *This name features high on the list of most popular house names in the USA, UK and Australia. The name may suggest that the owners have a town house as well and are therefore rich.*

The Courtyard
Enclosure containing a garden by a building.

The Cove
Bay. *In colloquial Australian English, 'cove' is a not very respectful term for a man, especially a boss, sheepstation manager or convict overseer.*

The Creek
Small stream. *The name might be used jocularly for an old house that needs restumping or that has creaky doors.*

The Crossing
Crossroad; ford.

The Crossroads
The place where two roads meet.

The Dell
Secluded valley.

The Echoes
Rebounding sound. *A name for a home situated in a valley or on a cliff where echoes can be heard.*

The Falls
Waterfalls.

The Fancy Cottage
Small and decorated home.

The Fancy House
Decorated home.

The Fields
The meadows.

The Four Seasons
An area that experiences summer, autumn/fall, winter and spring. The Four Seasons *is a well-known orchestral piece by Italian composer Antonio Vivaldi (1680–1741).*

The Glade
Open place in a forest.

The Hamlet
The small village. Hamlet *is also a play by William Shakespeare.*

The Happy House
House of joy.

The Haven
Refuge.

The Hay Farm
Hay ranch.

The Heads
Mouth of the river.

The Heartland
The centre; where one's heart belongs.

The Hideaway
The retreat. *The hideaway has traditionally been a peaceful retreat that invigorates the mind, body and spirit.*

The High House
Home that is set high.

The High Woods
High forest.

The Highlands
High mountain land. *A mountainous region in central and northern Scotland, famous for its beauty and Scottish/Gaelic culture.*

The Highside
The upper hillside.

The Hills
Knolls.

The Homestead
Farm house.

The Homestead Cottage
Small farmhouse.

The House Meadow
Home in the fields.

The Ideal House
The perfect house.

The Infield
Inner meadow.

The Island House
Home on the island.

The Isle House
Home on the small island.

The Knoll
The hill.

The Lake
The lake.

The Lake Cottage
Small house by the lake.

The Lake House
Home by the lake.

The Lamp Post/The Lampe Post
Old-fashioned streetlight.

The Last Post
The last fence pale marking out the end of a property. The second of two bugle calls used at the hour, for retiring a military group; a bugle call used for a military funeral or tattoo.

The Little Cottage
Small house.

The Little Estate
Small, stately house.

The Little Grove
Small, secluded wood.

The Little House
Small home.

The Little Manor
Small estate house.

The Lodge
The cabin. *'The Lodge' is the name of the official residence reserved for the Australian Prime Minister. It is located in Canberra.*

The Loft
Elevated living quarters.

The Long Barn
The long building used for storing animal feed, farm machinery or grain.

The Low Path
The lower pathway.

The Low Woods
Lower forest.

The Manor
Estate house. *'The Manor' is a popular name for the larger style of house resembling especially an older English style of house where a lord once resided.*

The Manor House
Estate house. (See The Manor)

The Marsh
Marshland or swamp.

The Meades
The meadows. *Mead is also a very sweet alcoholic drink made from honey, water, malt and yeast.*

The Mews
A row of apartments or homes.

The Mineral Springs
Water that is rich in minerals. *Some Mineral Springs are believed to have healing properties.*

The Mission
The ministry.

The Moors
Marshland.

The Nook
Small, secluded place.

The Old Cottage
The aged, small house.

The Old House
The aged home.

The Old Mansion/The Olde Mansion
The old estate house. (See The Mansion)

The Old Western Cottage
Small, aged house in the west; or possibly a house after the style of those seen in old cowboy movies.

The Orchard
Fruit tree pasture.

The Palace
Royal estate house.

The Park Meadows
The recreational fields.

The Pasture
The meadow.

The Pathway
A path.

The Peak
The summit.

The Plains
Treeless fields.

The Pretty Place
An attractive area.

The Priory
The religious place. *This is a popular name for large homes or those that are bed and breakfasts. Traditionally however, a priory was a religious building and often the name stayed with the building to reflect its history.*

The Reeds
Tall, grassy area in a marsh or pond.

The Reeds Cottage
Small house near the reeds.

The Regency
Exercising ruling power in place of the sovereign. *A period of rules or style relating to furniture or dress in 1811–20, when a regent (later to become George IV) effectively ruled Britain in place of George III, who was considered mad and therefore incapable.*

The Rest
Place of relaxation.

The Retreat
A place of refuge or relaxation. *'The Retreat' is a popular house name used for a holiday home in a peaceful place that invigorates the mind, body and spirit.*

The River
River.

The Rock
Rock. *This name would suit a property with a large rock on it that could be used as a landmark.*

The Rock Pool
Rocky pond.

The Rocks
Rocks. *The Rocks is an old area of Sydney, NSW, Australia, built on rocky land close to Circular Quay. It is now a popular area for tourists to shop for souvenirs.*

The Sanctuary
Holy place; refuge.

The Secret Hideaway
Place hidden from knowledge and view.

The Shadows
Shady.

The Shelter
Refuge.

The Shore
The beach shoreline.

The Small House
Cottage.

The Springs
Small streams.

The Springs Cottage
Small house by the streams.

The Stable
Horse stable.

The Station
Transport station. *'The Station', in Australia and New Zealand is a huge farm or ranch, usually raising cattle or sheep.*

The Stones
Stones. *Also a nickname for the English rock band, The Rolling Stones.*

The Swamp
Marshland.

The Terrace
A planted or paved area.

The Upper Path
High pathway.

The Valley
Dale.

The View
Vista.

The Vines
House surrounded with vines. *A perfect name for a home with grape vines or other vines growing near it.*

The Water Hole
Where animals go to drink.

The Waterside
Water by the hillside.

The Weir
Dam by the stream.

The Well Cottage
Small house by the well or stream.

The Western Manor
Western estate house.

The Wetlands
Marshland.

The Willows
Willow trees.

The Winter House
House used in the wintertime.

The Winter Place
Place used in the wintertime. *This is also the name of the palace at Luxor in Egypt, used by the Egyption royal family as a winter retreat during the colonial period. It was used as a location in the film of Agatha Christie's murder mystery* Death on the Nile. *After the making of this film, the name became popular for cinema houses.*

The Woods
The forest.

This Old House
An aged home. An affectionate name for an old home.

Thistlelea Cottage
Small house by the thistle meadow.

Thorlea/Thorlee/Thorleigh/Thorley/Thorly
Prickly meadow.

Thorlea Manor/Thorlee Manor/ Thorleigh Manor/Thorley Manor/ Thorly Manor
Estate house in the prickly meadow.

Thorn Hill
Where prickles grow on the hill.

Thornhill
Prickly hill.

Thornlea Cottage/Thornlee Cottage/ Thornleigh Cottage/Thornley Cottage/ Thornly Cottage
Small house in the prickly meadow.

Thornlea Estate/Thornlee Estate/ Thornleigh Estate/Thornley Estate/ Thornly Estate
Large, stately home in the prickly meadow.

Thornlea House/Thornlee House/ Thornleigh House/Thornley House/ Thornly House
Home in the prickly meadow.

Thornlea Manor/Thornlee Manor/ Thornleigh Manor/Thornley Manor/ Thornly Manor
Estate house in the prickly meadow.

Three Bells
Three bells. *The bell was an important form of communication in the Middle Ages. It warned of fire, flood, invasion or other catastrophes. The person who resided closest to the bell had the job of ringing it when it was needed.*

Three Chimneys
The house with three chimneys.

Three Corners
The property with three corners; triangular shaped land.

Three Hills Estate
Large, stately home on three hills.

Top Ridge
Summit of the ridge.

Topview
The best vista; vista from the summit.

Towerbank
The tower by the shore.

Townhead House
The home where the head of the town resides; the mayor's house.

Townsend
The end of the town.

Tradewinds
The wind that blows in the direction of the equator.

Tranquil Woods
Peaceful forest.

Tranquility Cottage
Small, peaceful house.

Trickle Brook
Small, softly flowing stream.

Trinity Cottage
Three fold small house; small house of the Father, the Son and the Holy Spirit.

Tudor House
A house in the Tudor period style (1485–1603).

Tumbling Water
White-water stream.

Turnlea/Turnlee/Turnleigh/Turnley
Meadow that changes direction.

Twelve Mile Estate
Large, stately house that is twelve miles long or wide.

Twelve Oakes/Twelve Oaks
Where 12 oak trees grow.

Twin Oakes Estate/Twin Oaks Estate
Two of the same oak trees on the property.

Two Stone Cottage
Small house with two stones. *This house may have two large stones that are used as a landmark.*

Two Stones
Two Stones. *This house may have two large stones that are used as a landmark.*

U

Under The Stars
The property under a star-studded sky.

Undercroft
Below the small pasture.

Underwood
Below the forest.

Underwood House
House built below the forest.

Uppark
Higher end of the recreational area.

Upper Court
Higher courtyard.

Upperdale
Higher valley.

Upperdale Cottage
Small house in the high valley.

Upperford
Shallow river crossing by the high field.

Upton House
House in the high section of town.

V

Valley View
Vista of the valley.

Valley View Cottage
Small house with the vista of the valley.

Valley View Estate
Large, stately house with the vista of the valley.

Victorian Cottage
The small, Victorian house. *A name for a Victorian-style (1837–1901) house. An affectionate name for an old house.*

Villawood
Country house in the forest.

Vista Cottage
Small house with a view.

W

Wallingford
Wall by the shallow river crossing.

Wallington
Wall by the town.

Water Gate/Watergate
Spring or small stream by the entrance. *The Watergate scandal occurred during the 1972 presidential election campaign. Five people employed by President Richard Nixon's re-election campaign were caught breaking into the Democrat headquarters in the Watergate building in Washington.*

Waterbank
River or lakeshore.

Waterfall Cottage
Small house by the waterfall.

Waterfall House
Home by the waterfall.

Waterfall Manor
Estate house by the waterfall.

Waterford
Shallow water crossing. *'Waterford' is also the name of a county in Ireland, and of its county town, noted for its beautiful glassware.*

Waterford Cottage
Small house by the shallow river crossing.

Watering Field Manor
Estate house by the meadow waterhole.

Waterside Cottage
Small house beside the water.

Waterside House
House beside or near the water.

Watersmeet
Where the waters meet; river mouth.

Waterwheel Creek
Rotating wheel actioned by water to run machinery.

Waverlea/Waverlee/Waverleigh/ Waverley/Waverly
Quivering meadow.

Waverlea Cottage/Waverlee Cottage/ Waverleigh Cottage/Waverley Cottage
Small house in the quivering meadow.

Waverlea Estate/Waverlee Estate/ Waverleigh Estate/Waverley Estate
Large, stately house in the quivering meadow.

Waverlea House/Waverlee House/ Waverleigh House/Waverley House
Home in the quivering meadow.

Waverlea Manor/Waverlee Manor/ Waverleigh Manor/Waverley Manor
Estate house in the quivering meadow.

Welcome Cottage
Small and welcoming house.

Welcome Estate
Large, stately and welcoming house.

Welcome Lodge
Welcoming cabin.

Welcome Manor
Welcoming estate house.

Welcome Valley
Welcoming dale.

Welcomeville
Village of greetings.

Wellbrook/Wellbrooke
Well by the stream.

Wellcombe Cottage
Welcoming, small house.

Wellpark Manor
Stream in the recreational area of the estate house.

West Bay Cottage
Small house by the western inlet.

West Bridge
Western bridge.

West Cottage
Small, western house.

West Lodge
Western cabin.

West Pasture
Western meadow.

West Wind Cottage
Small house in the path of the western wind.

Westbank
From the western shore.

Westbank Cottage
Small house on the western shore.

Westbury
Western berry bush; western stream.

Westbury Cottage
Small house with a berry bush in the west; small house with a western stream.

Westlea/Westlee/Westleigh/Westley/Westly
Western meadow.

Westlea Cottage/Westlee Cottage/Westleigh Cottage/Westley Cottage/Westly Cottage
Small house in the western meadow.

Westlea Estate/Westlee Estate/Westleigh Estate/Westley Estate/Westly Estate
Large, stately house in the western meadow.

Westlea Manor/Westlee Manor/Westleigh Manor/Westley Manor/Westly Manor
Estate house in the western meadow.

Westside
Western side.

Westville
Western village.

Westville Cottage
Small house in the western village.

Westward Manor
Estate house facing west.

Westwell Manor
Estate house with a western well or stream.

Westwich
Western inlet; western village.

Westwind Manor
Estate house in the path of the western wind.

Westwood
Western forest.

Whispering Pines
Pine trees rustling in the breeze.

White Lace Cottage
Small house with white lace work (a decorative trim to usually a veranda, made from iron); small house where the lace worker resides.

Wide View
Broad vista.

Wild River
Hard and fast flowing river.

Wild Wind Estate
Large, stately house in the path of the harsh wind.

Wilderness Cottage
Small house in the wild.

Wilderness Farm
Wild ranch.

Wilderness House
Home in the forest.

Wilderness Lodge
Wild cabin.

Wildfire Estate
A property that had a bush-fire.

Wildlands/Wyldlands
Wild fields.

Winderhall
Windy hall.

Windermere
Windy lake. *Lady Windermere is a character in Oscar Wilde's comedy* Lady Windermere's Fan *about a blackmailing divorcée who is driven by maternal love to sacrifice herself for the sake of a younger woman whose reputation is about to be ruined.*

Windlands
Windy fields.

Windmill Cottage
Small house by the windmill.

Windmill House
Home by the windmill.

Windrain Cottage
Small house in the wind and the rain.

Windrush Cottage
Small house where wind hurries by.

Windside
Hillside wind.

Windsor
Bank with a windlass. *Windsor is a town in Berkshire, England. The British royal family and close relatives anglicised their surnames during World War I. 'Guelph' became 'Windsor' in 1917 and 'Battenberg' became 'Mountbatten'. 'Windsor' remains the surname of the Queen of England.* (See Windsor Castle)

Windsor Castle
The fortress or castle by the bank with a windlass. *Windsor Castle is an official residence of the Queen of England. It is the largest occupied castle in the world and has been a royal palace for over 900 years.*

Windsor Cottage
Small house by the bank with a windlass.

Windstay Cottage
Small house in the continuing wind.

Windswept Cottage
Small house in the windy area.

Windville
Windy village.

Windward
In the path of the wind.

Windward Cottage
Small house in the path of the wind.

Windy Cliff/Windycliff
Wind on the cliff.

Windy Gully
Windy trench with water running in it.

Windy Hill
Wind on the hill.

Windy Ridge/Windyridge
Wind on the ridge.

Windy Valley
Wind in the valley.

Windyroad Cottage
Small house on the windy road.

Winfield/Wynfield
The winter meadow; friendly meadow.

Wingrove/Wyngrove
Small, secluded and friendly wood.

Wingrove Cottage/Wyngrove Cottage
Small house in the little and friendly wood.

Winstone/Wynstone
The friend's stone.

Winter Cottage/Wynter Cottage
Small house used in the wintertime. *This cottage might be used in the ski or snow season.*

Winter Cove/Wynter Cove
Winter bay.

Winter Garden Cottage/Wynter Garden Cottage
Small house with a winter garden.

Winter Haven/Wynter Haven
Winter refuge.

Winter Park/Wynter Park
Winter recreational area.

Winterfields/Wynterfields
Winter meadows.

Winterford/Wynterford
Shallow river crossing that is used in winter.

Winterhall/Wynterhall
Winter hall.

Winterstone/Wynterstone
Winter stone.

Winterwood/Wynterwood
Winter forest.

Winton/Wynton
Friendly town; winning town. *A house bearing this name could be named for award-winning Australian novelist Tim Winton, whose novels include* Cloudstreet, The Riders *and* Dirt Music.

Winworth/Wynworth
The friend's farm. *As an element in Old English place names, 'worth', 'worthig' and 'worthign' all denote an enclosure.*

Wishing Well Cottage
Small house by the hope well; small house by the wishing well or stream.

Wishington Manor
Estate house by the wishing town.

Wishton
Desired town.

Wishwell Estate
Large, stately house with a wishing well.

Wiston
Wish town.

Wood Bridge/Woodbridge
Wooden bridge; bridge in the forest.

Wood Cove/Woodcove
Forest by the bay.

Wood Haven/Woodhaven
Forest refuge.

Wood Hole/Woodhole
Ditch or hole in the forest.

Woodburn
Forest by the small stream.

Woodcroft
Small pasture in the forest.

Woodfield Cottage
Small house in the forest meadow.

Woodford
Shallow river crossing in the forest.

Woodgate House
Home with a wooden gate or entryway.

Woodland Cottage
Small house in the forestland.

Woodland Gardens
Garden in the forest.

Woodlands
Forest fields.

Woodlane
Forest lane.

Woodlea/Woodlee/Woodleigh/Woodley/Woodly
Forest meadow.

Woodlea Cottage/Woodlee Cottage/Woodleigh Cottage/Woodley Cottage/Woodly Cottage
Small house in the forest meadow.

Woodrow
Path in the forest.

Woodside
Hillside forest.

Woodslea/Woodslee/Woodsleigh/Woodsley/Woodsly
Forest meadow.

Woodslea Cottage/Woodslee Cottage/Woodsleigh Cottage/Woodsley Cottage
Small house in the forest meadow.

Woodsong
Song of the forest; sounds of the forest.

Woodstock
Forest stockyard. *This name may also be inspired by the huge 1969 rock concert held at Woodstock Bethel in upstate New York. Woodstock was also a character in the comic strip 'Peanuts', created by Charles M. Schultz on 2 October 1950.*

Woodvale
Forest valley.

Woodville
Village in the forest.

Woodwich
Forest by the bay or village.

Woolston
Wool town.

Woolston Cottage
Small house in the wool town.

Woolthorpe
Wool village.

Y

Yearnville
Wishing village.

Yew Tree Cottage
Small house by the yew trees.

CHAPTER 6

GARDEN GARNERED

Gardens are bursting with inspiration to be used in your search for a house name. Beautiful flowers, trees, bushes, animals, birds and insects can enkindle a beautiful nature name for your home. Flowers such as roses, wisteria, lilies and orchids can give a romantic ambience and inspire names such as 'Rose Cottage', 'Wisteria Cottage', and 'Orchid Nook'.

A

A Place To Grow
English
A place to learn and grow.

Acacia Cottage
Latin/Old English
Small house where the acacias grow.

Acorn Oaks
Old English/English
Acorns from the oak trees.

Alder Tree House
Old English
Home by the alder tree.

Alder Trees
Old English
Alder trees.

Almond Tree Estate
Old English
Large, stately house where the almond trees grow.

Aloe House
Old English/English
Home where aloe grows.

Alpine Lodge
Norse/English
Cabin in the snow regions.

Alpine Violet Cabin
Norse/Old English
Alpine violets growing by the lodge.

Ambrosia Lodge
Old English/English
Ambrosia trees by the cabin.

Apple Croft Cottage
Old English
Small house by the small apple orchard.

Apple Garth
English/Scandinavian
Apple tree enclosure.

Apple Tree Cottage
Old English
Small house by an apple tree.

Apricot Cottage
Latin/French/Old English
Apricot trees by the small house. Apricot-coloured house.

Arosa Cottage/Arosia Cottage
Italian/Old English
Small house with roses.

Ash Glen/Ashglen
Old English/Scottish
Ash tree valley.

Ash Glen Cottage/Ashglen Cottage
Old English/Scottish
Small house in the ash tree valley.

Ash Glen Grove/Ashglen Grove
Old English/Scottish
Small wood of ash trees in the valley.

Ash Hill
Old English
Ash tree hill.

Ashcosy
Old English
Ash trees nearby.

Ashdell
Old English
Ash trees in the valley.

Asherton
Old English
Ash tree town.

Asherton Valley
Old English
The ash tree, valley town.

Ashfield
Old English
Ash tree meadow.

Ashlea Cottage
Old English
Small house in the ash tree meadow.

Ashlyn
Old English
Ash trees by the pool or pond.

Ashlyn Woods/Ashlynwoods
Old English
Ash trees by the forest pond.

Ashton Estate
Old English
Large, stately house by the ash tree town.

Ashwell
Old English
Ash trees by the well or stream.

Ashwell Cottage
Old English
Small house by the ash tree stream or well.

Ashwood
Old English
Ash tree forest.

Ashwood Cottage
Old English
Small house by the ash tree forest.

Aspen Tree Cottage
Old English
Small house by the aspen tree.

B

Bamboo Gardens
Malaysian/Old English
Bamboo growing in the garden. *A great name for an Asian inspired garden.*

Banksia Cottage
Latin/Old English/Australian English
Small house by the banksia tree. *The banksia is so named in honour of explorer and botanist Sir Joseph Banks (1743–1820), who accompanied Captain James Cook to New Zealand and Australia on* The Endeavour.

Barkley
Old English
Bark in the meadow.

Beech Tree Cottage
Old English
Small house by the beech tree.

Berry Cottage
Old English
Small house with berry trees.

Big Creek Pines
Old English/Middle English
Pine trees by the large stream.

Biggletree/Biggoltree
Old English
Big, old tree. The Air Adventures of Biggles *was a popular Australian children's radio serial during the decade following World War II. Scripts were based on the books by Captain W.E. Johns about the adventures of fictional aviation hero Squadron Leader James Bigglesworth, affectionately known as 'Biggles'.*

Big Timber/Bigtimber
Old English
Tall and wide timber.

Big Timber Lodge
Old English
Cabin made from tall and wide timber.

Birch Corner
Old English
Birch tree in the corner of the property.

Birch Tree Cottage
Old English
Small house with a birch tree.

Bird Of Paradise House
Old English/English
Home where the bird of paradise plant grows or where the bird of paradise lives.

Black Heath/Blackheath
Old English
Black heather. *Blackheath is in the township of The Blue Mountains and is well known for its Rhododendron Festival held annually in November.*

Bloomfield
Old English
Flowers blooming in the meadow.

Blossom Cottage
Old English
Small, flowering house.

Blue Bell Brae
Old English/Scottish
Blue-bell flowers growing on the hillside.

Blue Gum Cottage/Bluegum Cottage
Australian/Old English
Small house by the blue gum trees.

Blueberry Cottage
Old English
Small house where the blueberries grow.

Boronia House
Latin/Old English
Home where boronias grow.

Botany Bay
Latin/Old English
Flora on the inlet. *The First Fleet arrived at Botany Bay, Australia in 1788, marking the beginning of European settlement. Botany Bay was originally named 'Stingray Harbour' by Captain James Cook. The name was later changed to 'Botany Bay' due to the flora botanist Sir Joseph Banks collected there. Captain Cook wrote about the fertile land that had been found there and this information convinced the British government that it would be the perfect place to establish a penal colony.*

Botany Cottage
Latin/Old English
Small house of plants.

Botany House
Latin/English
Home of plants.

Bramble/Brambles
Old English
Secluded place; blueberry shrub.

Briar
French/Latin/Gaelic
Heather; wild rose.

Briar Estate
French/Latin/Gaelic/Old English
Large, stately house by the wild rose forest.

Briarbank/Briar Bank
French/Latin/Gaelic/Old English
Wild rose riverbank.

Briarwood Cottage
French/Latin/Gaelic/Old English
Small house in the wild rose forest.

Broad Gardens
Old English
Wide gardens.

Broad Oaks/Broad Oakes/ Broadoakes/Broadoaks
Old English
Wide oak trees.

Broadway
Old English
The wide way. *Broadway is an avenue in New York famed for its musicals and large plays.*

Bud Meadows/Budmeadows
Old English/English
Fields of budding flowers.

Bushgrove
English/Australian/Old English
Small, secluded bushland

Bushgrove Cottage
Australian English/Old English
Small house in the small, secluded bushland.

Buttercup Cottage
Old English
Small house where buttercup flowers grow. *Buttercup is also a character in Gilbert and Sullivan's* HMS Pinafore. *She reveals a terrible secret about a baby swap, so that Josephine can marry her beloved Ralph (because he's really the captain), while Captain Corcoran must become a lowly sailor as befits his true station.*

Buttercup Lodge
Old English
Cabin where buttercup flowers grow.

C

Cactus Cottage
Latin/Greek/Old English
Small house where cactus grow.

Camellia Court
Latin/Old English
Camellias growing in the courtyard. *Camellias owe their Latin botanical name and their English name derived from it to Moravian Jesuit missionary G.J. Kamel (1661–1706), who described the flower.*

Canola Cottage
Latin/Old English
Small house near the canola plants; the yellow coloured house.

Canola Fields
Latin/Old English
Meadow where the canola grows; yellow-coloured meadow.

Cedar Falls
Latin/Greek/French/Middle English/Old English
Cedar trees by the waterfalls.

Cedar Grove
Latin/Greek/French/Middle English/Old English
Cedar trees growing in the small wood.

Cherry Blossom Cottage
Old English
Small house by the flowering cherry trees.

Cherry Tree Cottage
Old English
Small house where cherry trees grow.

Cherry View/Cherryview
Old English
Vista of the cherry trees.

Chestnut Cabin
Old English
Lodge where chestnuts can be found near by.

Chestnut Cottage
Old English
Small house where chestnut trees grow.

Clover Cottage
Old English
Small house with clover.

Clover Dale/Cloverdale
Old English
Clover valley.

Clover Fields
Old English
Clover meadows.

Clover Hill
Old English
Clover growing on the hill.

Clover Leaf Manor
Old English
Estate house with clover.

Clover Moore
Old English
Clover growing on the marshland. *Clover Moore is Lord Mayor of Sydney, Australia.*

Clover Woods
Old English
Clover forest.

Cloverlea/Cloverlee/Cloverleigh/ Cloverley/Cloverly
Old English
Clover meadow.

Cloverlea Cottage/Cloverlee Cottage/ Cloverleigh Cottage/Cloverley Cottage/ Cloverly Cottage
Old English
Small house in the clover meadow.

Cloverlea House/Cloverlee House/ Cloverleigh House/Cloverley House/ Cloverly House
Old English
Home in the clover meadow.

Coconut House
English/Old English
Home where coconut palms or trees grow.

Coconut Tree Cottage
English/Old English
Small house where the coconut palms or trees grow.

Conifer Cottage
Greek/Latin/Old English
Small house where the conifer tree grows.

Cosy Oaks
Old English
Close to the oak trees.

Cottage Vines
Old English
Small house with vines.

Cottonwood Estate
Old English
Large, stately house with cottonwood trees.

Country Gardens
Old English
Garden in the country; country style garden. Country Gardens *is a well-known piano piece by Australian composer Percy Grainger (1882–1961).*

Country Pines
Old English
Country area where pine trees grow.

Cranberry Cottage
Old English
Small house where cranberries grow; red/pink-coloured house.

Cresswell
Old English
Watercress growing by the stream or well.

Cypress House
Latin/Greek/French/Middle English/Old English
House made of cypress; house by the cypress trees.

D

Daffodil Cottage
Latin/Greek/French/Dutch/Old English
Small house where daffodils grow; yellow-coloured house.

Daffodil Downs/Daffodil Downes
Latin/Greek/French/Dutch/Old English
Daffodils growing on the rolling, country hills.

Daffodil Flats
Latin/Greek/French/Dutch/Old English
Daffodils growing on a flat field.

Dahlia Manor
Old English
Estate house where dahlias grow.

Daisy Brook/Daisy Brooke
Old English
Daisy flowers by the small stream.

Daisy Chain Cottage
Old English
Small house where the daisy flowers are linked into a decorative chain.

Daisy Cottage
Old English
Small house where daisies grow.

Daisy Dale
Old English
Daisy flower valley.

Daisy Fields
Old English
Daisy flower meadows.

Daisy Flats
Old English
Daisy flower meadows.

Daisy Hills
Old English
Daisies growing on the hill.

Dancing Laurels
Old English
Laurel trees swaying in the wind.

Dancing Willows
Old English
Willow trees swaying in the wind.

Dandelion Estate
Old English
Large, stately house where dandelions flowers grow.

Daphne Chateau
Latin/Greek/English/French
Daphne bushes growing by the castle.

Daphne Downes
Latin/Greek/English/French
Daphne bushes growing on the flowing hills.

Darkwood/Darkwoods
Old English
Dark forest; black forest.

Delahaye
French
House surrounded by a hedge.

Dove Tree Cottage
Old English
Small house where the dove tree grows; small house where the doves nest in the tree.

Elm Court
Old English
Elm trees in the courtyard.

Elm House
Old English
Home with elm trees.

Elm View/Elmview
Old English
Vista of the elm trees.

Elmcott
Old English
Elm trees by the cottage.

Elms Cottage
Old English
Small house by the elm trees.

Elmscott
Old English
Cottage by the elm trees; Ilman's cottage. *Emlscott is a hamlet in Devon and was originally called 'Yelmscot'.*

Elmswell
Old English
Elm trees by the well or stream.

English Rose Cottage
Old English
Small house where the English rose grows.

Eucalypt Cottage
Greek/Latin/Australian/Old English
Small house by the eucalypt tree.

Eucalyptus Hill
Greek/Latin/Australian/Old English
Eucalypt tree hill.

Fallen Tree
Old English
Felled tree.

Fern Brook/Fern Brooke/Fernbrook/Fernbrooke
Old English
Ferns by the small stream.

Fern Gully
Old English
Fern valley.

Fern House
Old English
Home where ferns grow.

Fern Leaf House/Fernleaf House
Old English/Middle English
Home where the ferns grow.

Fern Leaf Gully/Fernleaf Gully
Old English/Middle English
Fern valley.

Fern Side Cottage /Fernside Cottage
Old English
Ferns growing beside the small house; ferns growing by the small house on the hillside.

Fern Tree Gully/Ferntree Gully
Old English/Middle English
Fern trees growing in the valley.

Fernbank
Old English
Ferns growing by the shore.

Ferndale
Old English
Fern valley.

Fernlea//Fernleah/Fernlee/Fernleigh/ Fernley/Fernly
Old English
Fern meadow.

Fernleaf Cottage
Old English
Small house where the ferns grow.

Fernleaf House
Old English
Home where the ferns grow.

Ferntree Cottage
Old English
Fern trees growing by the small house.

Ferntree Estate
Old English
The fern trees growing by the large, stately home.

Ferntree Gully
Old English
Fern trees growing by the channel cut by running water after heavy rain. *Ferntree Gully is an outer suburb of Melbourne, Australia, named for the ferntrees that are native to the area.*

Ferntree House
Old English
Fern trees growing by the home.

Ferntree Manor
Old English
Fern trees growing by the estate house.

Fernydale
Old English
Fern valley.

Fig Tree/Figtree
Old English
Fig tree.

Fig Tree Cottage/Figtree Cottage
Old English
Small house where fig trees grow.

Fig Tree Estate/Figtree Estate
Old English
Large, stately house where the fig trees grow.

Fig Tree House/Figtree House
Old English
Fig tree home.

Fig Tree Mews/Figtree Mews
Old English
Fig trees in a row.

Fig Tree Row/Figtree Row
Old English
Fig trees in a row.

Figlea/Figlee/Figleigh/Figley/Figly
Old English
Meadow of fig trees.

Figtreelea/Figtreelee/Figtreeley/ Figtreely
Old English
Fig tree meadow.

Figtree Manor
Old English
Fig tree estate house.

Firbank
Old English
Fir trees growing by the shore.

Firefern Manor
Old English
Estate house where the fire fern grows.

Firewood
Old English
Wood to make a fire.

Firwood Estate
Old English
Large, stately, forest house where fir the trees grow.

Flame Tree Cottage
Old English
Small house where the flame trees grow.

Flaxen Cottage
Old English
Small house where the flax grows.

Fleur
French
Flower.

Fleur Cottage
French/Old English
Small house of flowers.

Fleur Hamlet
French/Old English
Flowers growing in the small village.

Fleur Haven
French/Old English
Flower refuge.

Fleur Meadows
French/Old English
Flower fields.

Fleurette
French
Little flower.

Fleurette Chalet
French
Small house with little flowers.

Fleurette Chateau
French
Little flower castle.

Fleurette Cottage
French/Old English
Small house with little flowers.

Flora
Latin
Flowers; plants.

Flower Cottage
Old English
Small house where the flowers grow.

Flower Palace
Old English
Flower castle or stately home.

Flower Place
Old English
Where flowers grow.

Flower Valley
Old English
Flower dale.

Flowerdale
Old English
Flower valley.

Flowerville
Old English
Flower village.

Forest Cottage
Old English
The small house in the woods.

Forest Court
Old English
Courtyard in the woods.

Forest Dale/Forestdale
Old English
Wood valley.

Forest Edge
Old English
Edge of the woods.

Forest Gate
Old English
Entry to the woods; gate that leads into the woods.

Forest Glen/Forest Glenn/ Forestglen/Forestglenn
Old English/Scottish
Wood valley.

Forest House
Old English
Home in the woods.

Forest View
Old English
Vista of the woods.

Forestlea/Forestlee/Forestleigh/ Forestley/Forestly
Old English
Wood meadow.

Forestlyn/Forestlin
Old English
Wood pond or pool.

Foreston
Old English
Town in the woods.

Forestville
Old English/French
Village in the woods.

Forget Me Not Cottage
Old English
Unforgettable small house; cottage where the forget-me-not flower grows.

Foxglove Cottage
Old English
The small house where the foxglove plants grows.

Freesia House
Latin/German/Old English
Home where the freesia flowers grow.

G

Garden Gables
Old English
Triangular section near the roof over the garden.

Garden Gate Cottage
Old English
Small house by the garden entrance.

Gardenia Gables
Latin/Old English
Gardenia shrubs growing by the gables (the triangular section of a roof). *The gardenia owes its Latin botanical name, from which its English name is derived, to the US physician, Dr Alexander Garden (1730–91).*

Gardenia Gardens
Latin/Old English
Gardenia shrubs growing in the garden.

Gardenia House
Latin/Old English
House where the gardenia shrub/tree grows.

Garland Cottage
Old English/Old French
Small house with a wreath of flowers. A garland may also be an anthology of short literary pieces, poems or ballads.

Garland Estate
Old French/Old English
Large, stately house with a wreath of flowers. (See Garland Cottage)

Garland House
Old English/Old French
Small house with a wreath of flowers; small house on the triangular land; battle land. (See Garland Cottage)

Geranium Hamlet
Old English
Geraniums growing in the small village.

Glen Elm/Glenn Elm/Glenelm/ Glennelm
Scottish/Old English
Elm trees in the valley.

Glen Garland/Glengarland
Scottish/Old French
Valley with a flower wreath. (See Garland)

Glen Iris/Gleniris
Greek/Latin/Middle English/Scottish
Valley where the iris flowers grow.

Glen Laurel/Glenn Laurel/Glenlaurel/ Glennlaurel
Scottish/Latin/English
Valley of laurel trees; valley of victory.

Glen Maple
Scottish/English
Valley of maple trees.

Golden Weeping Willows
Old English
The golden, weeping willow trees.

Goninan
Cornish
Hedge made from ash trees.

Grand Pines
Old English
The great pine trees.

Grassmere/Grassymere
Old English
Small, grassy area; grassy lake.

Grassmere Cottage/Grassymere Cottage
Old English
Small house in the grassy area; small house by the grassy lake.

Green Lawn/Greenlawn
Old English/ Middle English
House with green grass.

Green Trees Estate/Greentrees Estate
Old English
Large, stately house where the green trees grow.

Gumnut Cottage
Old English
Small house by the gum tree. *A name inspired by Australian writer and illustrator May Gibbs's* Gumnut Babies *(1916).*

Gypsy Rose Cottage
Old English
Small house where the gypsy with the rose resides. *'Gypsy Rose Lee' was the stage name of Rose Louise Hovick (1911–70), who rose to fame as a singer-dancer and became a featured burlesque entertainer in New York. She later pursued a career as a film actor and fiction writer.*

H

Hazeldene
Old English
Hazel tree valley.

Haselhurst/Hazelhurst
German/Old English
Hazel tree grove.

Hasham
Old English
Hazel tree farm; hazel tree village.

Hazelnut Estate
Old English
Large, stately house by the hazelnut trees.

Hazelwood
Old English
Hazelnut tree forest.

Heath Cottage/Heather Cottage
Old English
Small house where the heather grows.

Heather House
Old English
Heather home; home on the heather.

Heatherlands
Old English
Heather meadows.

Heathmont/Heathermont
Old English/French
Heather on the mountain.

Hedgelea/Hedgelee/Hedgeleigh/ Hedgeley/Hedgely
Old English
Hedged meadow.

Hibiscus Glen/Hibiscus Glenn
Latin/Greek/Scottish
Hibiscus valley.

Hibiscus Nook
Latin/Greek/Old English
Hibiscus growing in the small, secluded wood.

High Hedge
Old English
Property with a high hedge.

High Woods
Old English
Upper forest.

Holly Grove
Old English
Holly growing in the small wood; small, holy wood.

Holly House
Old English
Holly growing by the house; holy house.

Holly Tree
Old English
The holly tree; holy tree.

Hollywood
Old English
The holy forest; holly growing by the well or stream. *A name for those with a very glamorous looking home to consider. Hollywood in the USA is famed throughout the world for its movie making.*

Honeysuckle Cottage
Old English
Small house where the honeysuckle vine grows.

Huckleberry Cottage
North American/Old English
The small house where blueberries grow. The Adventures of Huckleberry Finn *by Mark Twain was first published in America in January 1885. Since the first publication of this favourite American classic, it has inspired movies and television series based on the character of Huckleberry Finn and his best friend, Tom Sawyer.*

Hyacinth View
Latin/Greek/Old English
Vista of the hyacinth flowers. *Hyacinth Bucket is a character in the Brittish BBC television show* Keeping up Appearances *(1990) starring Patricia Routledge as the toffee-nosed Hyacinth Bucket (she insisted it be pronounced 'Bouquet') and Clive Swift as her long-suffering husband Richard.*

I

Impatiens Cottage
Old English/Latin
Small house where the impatiens grow.

In The Garden
Old English
One who can be found in the garden; property in the middle of a garden.

Iris Downs/Iris Downes
Greek/Latin/Middle English/Old English
Iris growing on the flowing hills.

Iris Glen/Iris Glenn/Irisglen
Greek/Latin/Middle English/Old English/Scottish
Iris flower valley.

Iris Waters
Greek/Latin/Middle English/Old English
Iris flowers growing by the lake or river.

Irislea/Irislee/Irisleigh/Irisley/Irisly
Greek/Latin/Middle English/Old English
Iris flower meadows.

Ironbark Cottage
Australian/Old English
Small house where the ironbark trees grow; strong bark; eucalyptus tree. The Man from Ironbark *is a famous poem by the Australian poet, A.B. 'Banjo' Patterson, 1892. He was one of Australia's great icons and had a romantic view of the bushman's life.*

Ivy Bank/Ivybank
Old English
The ivy vine growing by the shore.

Ivy Bridge/Ivybridge
Old English
The ivy vine growing over the bridge.

Ivy Cottage
Old English
Small house covered in ivy.

Ivy House
Old English
The ivy vine, growing over or near the home.

Ivy Rose Cottage
Old English
Small house where the ivy vine and roses grow.

Jacaranda Cottage
Latin/Portuguese/Old English
Small house by the jacaranda tree. *A tree with soft lavender blue-coloured flowers.*

Jacaranda Grove
Latin/Portuguese/Old English
Jacaranda tree growing in the small wood. *A tree with soft lavender blue-coloured flowers.*

Jacaranda Tree
Latin/Portuguese/Old English
A tree with soft lavender blue-coloured flowers. Jacaranda Tree *was written by Bates and published in 1994 and a novel with the same name was written by Rebecca Brandewyne in 1996.*

Jasmine Chalet
Arabic/Persian/French
Jasmine growing by the small house.

Jasmine Cottage
Arabic/Persian/French/Old English
Small house where the jasmine grows.

Jasmine Grove
Arabic/Persian/French/Old English
Jasmine growing in the small wood.

Jasmine Knoll
Arabic/Persian/French/Old English
Jasmine hill.

Jonquil Downs/Jonquil Downes
French/Spanish/Latin/Old English
Jonquil flowers growing on the flowing hills.

Juniper Lodge
Latin/Middle English/Old English
Cabin by the juniper tree. *This name might also be chosen by owners who enjoy a gin and tonic.*

Kangaroo Paw Cottage
Australian Aboriginal/Old English
Small house where the kangaroo paw (a native plant that resembles the paws of a kangaroo) grows.

Karri
Australian Aboriginal
Eucalyptus tree.

Kauri
Maori
Where the kauri (a New Zealand tall tree conifer) grows.

Kava Cottage
Latin/Old English
Small house where the shrubby pepper plant (a native Australian plant) grows.

Kinnikinnick
Native American
Mixture of bark and leaves and was sometimes smoked by the Native Americans (Algonquians).

Knapweed Cottage
Middle English/Old English
Small house where the knapweed (a thistle-like plant related to the daisy family) grows.

Knot Garden
Old English
Formal garden with plants shaped into knot-like pattern displays.

L

Lady Fern Court
Old English
Soft fern growing in the courtyard.

Laurel Bank
Latin/Old English
Laurel trees growing by the shore; victorious shore.

Laurel Cottage
Latin/Old English
Victorious, small house; laurel trees growing by the small house.

Laurel Gables
Latin/Old English
Laurel trees growing by the gables of the house (the triangular section of a roof); the victorious gables.

Laurel Manor
Latin/Old English
Laurel trees growing by the estate house; the victorious estate house.

Laureleigh/Laurelea/Laurelee/Laureley/Laurellea/Laurellee/Laurelleigh/Laurelley
Latin/Old English
Laurel trees growing in the meadow; the victorious meadow.

Le Thorne
French/Old English
The prickle.

Lea Cottage
Old English
Small house in the meadow.

Leafy Glade/Leafyglade/Leafglade/Leaf Glade
Old English
Leaf covered meadow.

Lemon Tree Court
Arabic/Persian/Old French/Middle English/Old English
Lemon tree courtyard.

Lilac Cottage
Arabic/Persian/Sanskrit/Old English
Small house where the lilac tree grows.

Lilac Fields
Arabic/Persian/Sanskrit/Old English
Lilac flower meadow.

Lilac House
Arabic/Persian/Sanskrit/Old English
Home where the lilac trees grow.

Lilac Park
Arabic/Persian/Sanskrit/Old English
Lilac trees growing in the recreational area.

Lilli Bank/Lillibank/Lilly Bank/ Lillybank/Lily Bank/Lilybank
Old English
Lilies growing on the lake or river shore.

Lily Chalet
Old English/French
Small house with lilies.

Lily Cottage
Old English
Small house where lilies grow.

Lily Of The Valley
Old English
Lilies growing in the valley. *'Lily-of-the-valley' is the common name for Convallaria majalis, which is prized for its delicate, drooping, white, bell-shaped flowers and its strong fragrace.*

Lily Rock/Lilyrock
Old English
Lilies by the rock.

Lily Vale Cottage/Lilyvale Cottage
Old English
Small house in the lily valley.

Lily Valley
Old English
Lilies growing in the valley.

Lily Waters
Old English
Lilies growing by the river or lake.

Lime Cottage
Spanish/French/Old English
Small house where lime trees grow; lime-coloured, small house. *'Lime' signifying limestone or slaked lime is derived from Old English, but the name of the fruit tree and its fruit comes to us from French via the Spanish 'lima'.*

Linden Cottage/Lynden Cottage
Old English
Small house by the linden tree. *The linden tree is better known today as a lime tree.*

Linden Lea Cottage/Lindenlea Cottage/ Lynden Lea Cottage/Lyndenlea Cottage
Old English
Small house by the linden tree meadow. *'Linden Lea' is a song by English composer Ralph Vaughan Williams to words by William Barnes.* (See Linden Cottage)

Linden Wood/Lindenwood/ Lynden Wood/Lyndenwood
Old English
Linden tree forest. (See Linden Cottage)

Liquid Amber House/ Liquidamber House
Australian/Old English
Home where the liquidamber tree grows. *'Liquid amber' is a colloquial Australian name for beer, so this house name might also be chosen by a homeowner who enjoys beer.*

Little Glen/Little Glenn
Old English/Scottish
Little valley.

Little Grove
Old English
Little wood.

Little Heather
Old English
Small heather.

Little Lea Cottage/Little Lee Cottage/ Little Leigh Cottage/Little Ley Cottage
Old English
Small house in the little meadow.

Lobelia Cottage
Latin/Old English
Small house where the lobelia flower grows.

Low Woods
Old English
The forest below.

M

Macadamia Meadows
Australian/Old English
Macadamia trees growing in the fields.

Magnolia Cottage
Latin/French/Old English
Small house where the magnolia trees grow.

Magnolia Estate
Latin/French/Old English
Large, stately house with magnolia trees.

Magnolia House
Latin/French/Old English
Home where the magnolia trees grow.

Magnolia Vale
Latin/French/Old English
Magnolia tree valley.

Mallow Estate
Old English
Large, stately house where the mallow grows.

Mango Tree Mountain
Old English
Mangoes growing on the mountain.

Maple Hill
Old English
Maple tree hill.

Maple Tree Cottage
Old English
Small house where maple trees grow.

Maple Tree Manor
Old English
Estate house with maple trees.

Mapleton
Old English
Maple trees growing in the town.

Marigold Manor
Old English
Estate house where marigolds grow.

Marigold Moor
Middle English/Old English
Marigold flowers growing in the marshland.

Marshmallow Cottage
Old English
Small house where the marshmallow plant grows.

Melrose
Latin/Greek/Old English
Sweet rose; roses growing by the mill. *Melrose is a burgh in Scotland, on the River Tweed. It is known for the ruins of a famous abbey.*

Melrose Cottage
Latin/Greek/Old English
Small house of the sweet rose; roses growing by the small house near the mill.

Melrose Estate
Latin/Greek/Old English
Large, stately house of the sweet rose; roses growing by the large, stately house near the mill.

Melrose House
Latin/Greek/Old English
Home of the sweet rose; roses growing by the home near the mill.

Melrose Manor
Latin/Greek/Old English
Estate house of the sweet rose; roses growing by the estate house near the mill.

Melrose Place
Latin/Greek/Old English
Area with the sweet rose; roses growing by the area near the mill. Melrose Place *was a soap opera from 1992–9, starring Heather Locklear. It was about the love lives, dramas and scandals of the tenants in an apartment complex named 'Melrose Place'.*

Memory Gardens
Old English
Garden of memories.

Moonflower Cottage
Old English
Small house where the moonflower grows.

Moss Valley
Old English
Moss growing in the gully; green gully.

Mountain Ebony House
Old English
Home where the mountain ebony tree grows; home on the black mountain.

Mountain Laurel
Old English/Latin
Victory mountain; mountain laurel trees.

Mulberry
Old English
The mulberry tree.

Mulberry Cottage
Old English
Small house where mulberry tree grows.

Narcissus Garden
Latin/Old English
Daffodil garden (a species with pale petals and an orange iris).

Nardoo
Australian Aboriginal
Nardoo or Nardu is an Australian species of mud-loving and aquatic ferns, the sporocarps of which are ground into flour.

Native Garden
Old English
A garden that consists of plants, bushes or trees from the native country they are planted in.

Navel Orange Orchid
Old English
Seedless oranges grown on a fruit tree farm.

Nectar Garden
Greek/Old English
Garden where the flowers secrete a sweet liquid and is collected by bees and some types of birds.

Nectarine Cottage
Greek/Old English
Small house where nectarine trees grow.

Nettle Knoll
Old English
Hill where the stinging plant (Urtica dioica) grows.

Night Garden
Old English
A garden developed to be especially pleasing in the evening, perhaps with the addition of lighting and lit water features.

Nocturnal Garden
Latin/Old English
A garden developed to be especially pleasing in the evening, perhaps with the addition of lighting and lit water features.

Noontide Garden
Old English
A garden that is especially pleasing in the middle of the day when all the flowers are out.

Novice Garden
Latin/Old French/Old English
The beginner's garden.

Nymph Garden
Latin/Greek/Old French/Old English
Garden of the female nature spirits.

Oak Knoll
Old English
Oak tree hill.

Oak Tree
Old English
The oak tree.

Oaklawn
Old English/English
Oak tree lawn.

Oaklea/Oaklee/Oakleigh/Oakley/Oakly
Old English
Oak tree meadow.

Oakmead/Oakmeade
Old English
Oak meadow. *Mead is also a very sweet alcoholic drink made from honey, water, malt and yeast.*

Oakvale
Old English
Oak tree valley.

Oakville
Old English
Oak tree village.

Oakwood
Old English
Oak tree forest.

Oakwood Estate
Old English
Large, stately house in the oak tree forest.

Oakwood Manor
Old English
Estate house in the oak tree forest.

Olive Branch Cottage
Latin/Greek/Middle English/Old English
Small cottage of friendship; small house where the olive trees grow.

Olive Dale/Olivedale
Latin/Greek/Middle English/Old English
Olive tree valley.

Orange Blossom Cottage
Old English
Small house where orange blossoms bloom.

Orange Tree Orchard
Old English
Orange tree pasture or farm.

Orangewood Estate
Old English
Large, stately house by the orange orchard or forest.

Orchid Cottage
Latin/Old English
Small house where orchid flowers grow.

Orchid Nook
Latin/Old English
Small and secluded fruit tree farm.

Orrick
Old English
One who resides by the oak tree.

P

Palm Court
Latin/Old English
Palm tree courtyard.

Palm Grove/Palmgrove
Latin/Old English
Small wood of palm trees.

Palm Springs
Latin/Old English
Palm trees growing by the streams. *Palm Springs is a town in California.*

Palm Tree Cottage
Latin/Old English
Small house with palm trees.

Pansy Cottage
Old English
Small house where the pansy flowers grow.

Petal Cottage
Old English
Small house of flower petals.

Pine Crest
Old English
Pine tree summit.

Pine Grove/Pinegrove
Old English
Small wood of pine trees.

Pine Grove Cottage/Pinegrove Cottage
Old English
Small house by the small pine tree wood.

Pine Haven
Old English
Pine tree refuge.

Pine Ridge
Old English
Pine tree ledge.

Pine Top Estate/Pinetop Estate
Old English/English
Large, stately home with pine trees growing on the summit near by.

Pine Tree Estate
Old English
Large, stately home with pine trees.

Plum Tree Cottage
Old English
Small house where plum trees grow.

Poinsettia Cottage
Old English
Small house where the poinsettia grows.

Poppy Cottage
Old English
Small house where poppies grow.

Poppy Creek
Old English
Poppy flowers growing by the small stream.

Poppy Hall
Old English
Poppies growing by the town hall.

Poppy Manor
Old English
Poppies growing at the estate house.

Posy Cottage
Old English
Small house with posies.

Pressed Petals
Old English
Pressed flower petals.

Primrose Nook
Old English
Primrose growing in the small, secluded place.

Quaint Gardens
Latin/Middle English
Attractive and unusual gardens.

Queen Plums
Old English
A Brazilian palm with plum-coloured leaves.

Quiet Gardens
Latin/Middle English/French/Old English
Peaceful gardens.

Quince Gardens
Latin/Greek/Old English
Garden where the quince trees (a pear-shaped fruit usually used for jams) grow.

Quivering Gardens
Middle English/Old English
Trembling gardens. A garden may give the impression of quivering when the wind blows gently through it.

Rain Lily Cottage
Old English
Small house where the rain lily grows.

Rainforest Cottage
Old English
Small house in the tropical woodland. *Rainforests are sometimes called 'The Earth's Lungs', as they help provide us with oxygen. They also contain a huge biodiversity and are home to over half the Earth's plant and animal species, even though they are only six percent of the Earth's ground surface and are diminishing rapidly.*

Red Cedars Cottage
Latin/Greek/French/Middle English/Old English
Small house by the red cedar trees.

Red Clover Cottage
Old English
Small house by the red clover field.

Red Rose Manor
Old English
Estate house where the red roses grow. *The red rose is known as a symbol of true love.*

Red Gum Cottage/Redgum Cottage
Australian/English/Old English
Small house where red gums grow.

Redwood Estate
Old English
Large, stately house where redwood trees grow.

Ring O' Rose/Ring O' Rosie
Old English
Ring of roses. *Ring o'rosie is a children's game in which children form a ring and chant a rhyme.*

Ringrose
Old English
Roses growing in a round area; ring of roses.

Rhododendron
Latin/Greek
Shrub with clusters of pink, red, purple or white flowers.

Rosalea Cottage/Roselee Cottage/ Roseleigh Cottage/Roseley Cottage
Old English
Small house with roses in the meadow.

Rosarium
Latin
Rose garden.

Rose Bay
Old English
Roses by the inlet. *Rose Bay is a suburb of Sydney, Australia, known for being close to tourist attractions.*

Rose Bay Estate/Rosebay Estate
Old English
Large, stately house by the rose inlet.

Rose Chalet
Old English/French
Roses growing by the small house.

Rosecliff
Old English
Roses by the cliff.

Rose Cottage
Old English
Small house with a garden of roses. *'Rose Cottage' is by far the most popular house name in Australia, Britain and the USA. It is a prevalent name as roses grow in many different regions throughout the world. In Gilbert and Sullivan's* Ruddigore, *'Rose Cottage' was the name of the house in which Rose Maybud lived with her Aunt Hannah.*

Rose Court
Old English
Rose courtyard.

Rose Garden
Old English
Garden of roses.

Rose Lodge
Old English
Rose cabin.

Rose Manor
Old English
Roses growing by the estate house.

Rose Pink Villa
Old English/Italian
Country house with pink roses.

Rose Ridge
Old English
Roses growing on the cliff.

Rose Wood Estate
Old English
Large, stately house with a rose forest.

Rosebank
Old English
Roses growing by the shore.

Rosebud Cottage
Old English
Small house with rose buds.

Rosebud Court
Old English
Rosebuds growing in the courtyard.

Rosedale
Old English
Rose valley.

Roseland/Roselands
Old English
Rose fields.

Roselea/Roselee/Roseleigh/Roseley/ Rosely
Old English
Rose meadow.

Roselea Cottage/Roselee Cottage/ Roseleigh Cottage/Roseley Cottage/ Rosely Cottage
Old English
Small house in the rose meadow.

Roselle Cottage
Old English/Greek/French
Rose in the small house.

Rosemead/Rosemeade
Old English
Rose meadow. *Mead is also a very sweet alcoholic drink made from honey, water, malt and yeast.*

Rosemont
Old English/French
Rose mountain.

Rosemont Cottage
French/Old English
Small house on the rose mountain.

Rosemoor/Rosemoore
Old English
Roses growing on the marshland.

Rosemoor Cottage
Old English
Small house with roses, by the marshland.

Rosemount
Old English
Rose mountain.

Rosemount Cottage
Old English
Small house on the rose mountain.

Rosemount Estate
Old English
Large, stately house on the rose mountain.

Roseneath Cottage
Old English
Small house where roses grow below it.

Rosette Cottage
Spanish/Old English
Small cottage with little roses.

Rosewhite Cottage
Old English
Small house of the white roses.

Roswell/Rothwell
Old English
Roses by the well or stream.

Rosewood
Old English
A reddish wood.

Rosewood Estate
Old English
Large, stately house by the rose forest.

Rosy Close
Old English
Roses growing at the closed end of the road.

Rotherwood
Old English
Rose wood.

Rotherwood Manor
Old English
Large, stately house by the rose wood.

Row O' Trees
Old English
Row of trees.

Rowan Tree Estate
Old English
Large, stately house where rowan trees grow.

Royal Oak/Royal Oake
Old English
Royal oak tree.

Royal Oak Cottage/Royal Oake Cottage
Old English
Small house by the royal oak trees.

Royal Oak Estate/Royal Oake Estate
Old English
Large, stately house by the royal oak trees.

Royal Oak Manor/Royal Oake Manor
Old English
Estate house by the royal oak trees.

Royal Oakes/Royal Oaks
Old English
Royal oak trees.

Rozelle Cottage
Old English/Greek/French
Rose in the small house.

Seven Oakes/Seven Oaks
Old English
Place with seven oak trees.

She Oak Estate/Sheoak Estate
Australian/Old English
Large, stately house where the she oaks grow.

Silky Oak Estate
Old English
Large, stately house where silky oaks grow.

Silver Oaks
Old English
Silver oak trees.

Silver Trees
Old English
Silver-coloured trees.

Silver Wattle Cottage
Old English
Small house where the silver wattle tree grows. *The 'Silver Wattle' is one of many different kinds of wattle tree that grow throughout areas of Australia. It features silver leaves and a small, fluffy mass of yellow flowers.*

Snapdragon Estate
Old English
Large, stately house where snapdragon flowers grow.

Spruce Tree Estate
Old English
Large, stately house with spruce trees.

Sugar Gum Cottage
English/Old English
Small house by the sweet gum tree.

Summer Garden
Old English
Summertime garden.

Summer Rose
Old English
Roses that grow during the summertime.

Sunflower Cottage
Old English
Small house by the sunflowers.

Sunflower Manor
Old English
Estate house with sunflowers growing near by.

Sunflowers
Old English
Sunflowers.

Sweet Violets
Old English
Sweetly scented violet flowers.

Sweet Pea Cottage
Old English
Small house where the sweet peas grow.

Sycamore House
French/Latin/Greek/Old English
Home where the sycamore trees grow.

Sycamore Knoll
French/Latin/Greek/Old English
Sycamore trees growing on the hill.

T

Tall Timbers
Old English
Tall trees.

Tall Trees
Old English
Tall trees.

Tanglewood
Old English
Forest with crossing vines and trees.

Tea Rose Cottage
Chinese/Old English
Small house where the tea roses grow.

Tea Tree Cottage
Chinese/Old English
Small house where the tea-tree grows. *Tea Tree is a shrub native to Australia and New Zealand. It is grown both for its aromatic oil and for its ornamental pink, white or red flowers. It is so named because colonial settlers used its leaves as a substitute for tea.*

The Acorn
Old English
The acorn.

The Alpine Rose Estate
Norse/Old English
Large, stately house where the alpine rose grows in the snowy region.

The Ash Bungalow
Old English/Hindi
Ash trees by the small house.

The Bay Tree Manor
Old English
Estate house with trees near the inlet.

The Blackberry Manor
Old English
Estate house where blackberries grow.

The Botanical Garden
Latin/Old English
Grand garden with specimens of different kinds of plants. *Many towns and cities have botanical gardens for people to visit and marvel at the beauty and diversity of nature.*

The Botanicals
Latin
The plants.

The Cedar Cottage
Latin/Greek/French/Middle English/Old English
Small house where cedar trees grow.

The Cedars
Latin/Greek/French/Middle English/Old English
Where cedar trees grow.

The Cherry Trees
Old English
Cherry trees.

The Conifers
Greek/Latin/Old English
Conifer (pine) trees.

The Elms
Old English
Elm trees.

The English Rose
Old English
The English rose. *A style of rose that is believed to have originated when Henry Tudor challenged the monarchy for the throne and in doing so, split England in two opposing sides—The House of Lancaster (symbolised by a red rose) and the loyalist House of York (symbolised by a white rose). Tudor married the daughter of the Duke of York to try and unify the two sides and in doing so created a new emblem of the English rose, a red rose (Lancaster) with a white heart (York). Madeleine Carroll (1906–87) was a 1930s movie star who appeared in films such as Hitchcock's* The 39 Steps *(1935) and* The Secret Agent *(1936), and was known as the* 'English Rose'.

The Eucalypt Cottage
Greek/Latin/Australian/Old English
Small house where the eucalypt tree grows.

The Eucalyptus Cottage
Greek/Latin/Australian/Old English
Small house where the eucalyptus trees grow.

The Forest
Old English
The wood.

The Forest Trees
Old English
The trees in the wood.

The Fronds
Old English
Ferns; palm trees.

The Garden House
Old English
Home in the garden.

The Garden of Eden
Old English
Paradise. *The Garden of Eden was the original home of Adam and Eve, according to the Book of Genesis in* The Bible.

The Garden Pond
English
Small lake in the garden.

The Garden River
Old English
Garden by the river.

The Garden Wall
Old English
Garden with a wall.

The Gardens
Old English
Place where flora grow.

The Golden Maple
Old English
Gold-coloured maple tree.

The Great Oakes/The Great Oaks
Old English
Large, tall oak trees.

The Gums
English/Australian English
A place where the gum trees or eucalyptus trees grow.

The Hay Loft
Old English
Where hay is stored on an upper level, usually in a barn.

The Hedge
Old English
Property with a hedge.

The Hedges
Old English
Property with hedges.

The Hollies
Old English
Place where the holly grows; holy place.

The Lemon Tree
Arabic/Persian/Old French/Middle English/Old English
The lemon tree.

The Lilac Tree
Arabic/Persian/Sanskrit/Old English
The lilac tree.

The Limes
Spanish/French/Old English
The lime trees; linden trees.

The Little Trees
Old English
Property with small trees or saplings.

The Magic Garden
Old English
Magical garden.

The Mayflower
Old English
A springtime flower. The Mayflower *was a ship in which the pilgrims sailed from England to Massachusetts, USA, in 1620.*

The Mighty Oak/The Mighty Oake/The Mighty Oakes/The Mighty Oaks
Old English
The great oak tree.

The Mulga
Australian English
The bush land. *Mulga Bill was a character written by A.B. 'Banjo' Patterson in his ode 'Mulga Bill's Bicycle', which was published in the Sydney Mail newspaper in 1896.*

The Old Orchard/The Olde Orchard
Old English
The old orchard.

The Orchard
Old English
Fruit tree farm.

The Palms
Greek/Latin/Old English
Palm trees.

The Pear Tree
Old English
The pear tree.

The Pines
Old English
Pine trees. *This a popular property or house name especially in the USA.*

The Pines Cottage
Old English
Small house with pine trees growing nearby.

The Poplars
Old English
The poplar trees. *A popular house or property name in Australia and the United Kingdom.*

The Poppies
Old English
The poppy flowers.

The Rockery
Old English
The home with a feature garden made of rocks and plants.

The Rose Garden
Old English
Rose garden. *This is a popular house name with rose lovers.*

The Rose Garden Cottage
Old English
Small house with a rose garden.

The Rose Garden Estate
Old English
Large, stately house with a rose garden.

The Rowan Trees
Old English
Property with rowan trees.

The Royal Oakes/The Royal Oaks
Old English
The oak trees planted on the royal estate.

The Saplings
Old English/English
Small, young trees.

The Scented Rose
Old English
Where the scented roses grow.

The Sculpture Garden
Latin/Middle English
A garden with art made from, traditionally, stone or wood.

The Secret Garden
Old English
Secluded, hidden garden.

The Shrubbery
English
Many shrub trees.

The Silk Tree Estate
Old English
Large, stately house where silk trees grow.

The Silver Birch
Old English
Silver Birch tree.

The Silver Firs
Old English
The silver fir trees.

The Sunflower
Old English
The sunflower.

The Swaying Elms
Old English
Elm trees, swaying in the wind.

The Timbers
Old English
The forest.

The Tree House
Old English
Home surrounded by trees; high home.

The Tree Plains
Old English
Trees on the flat meadows.

The Water Gardens
Old English
Gardens by the waters edge; the lily gardens.

The Wind In The Willows
Old English
Willow trees, swaying in the wind. The Wind in the Willows *is a book by Kenneth Grahame, published in 1908. It is one of the most beloved children's books of all time. It is set in the English countryside and concerns the adventures of Rat, Mole, Badger and Mr Toad.*

The Yew Tree Cottage
Old English
Small house with yew trees near by. *The fine-grained wood is prized for its elasticity and has long been used for making shooting bows.*

Thistleton
Old English
Town where the thistle grows.

Thornton
Old English
Thorn town; prickly town.

Three Firs
Old English
Three fir trees.

Three Leaf Clover
Old English
Luck. *The three-leaf clover is associated with good luck as is believed to be a symbol for the Holy Trinity. The shamrock is also the national emblem of Ireland. The superstition of the four-leaf clover is believed to have originated with the Druids, who believed that the shamrock helped them to see evil spirits giving them time to hide. It is also used to protect both humans and animals from evil spells and bad luck.*

Timbertop Estate
English/Old English
Large, stately house where the timber grows on the summit.

Timberwood
Old English
Timber forest.

Ti-Palm Cottage/Ti-Tree Cottage
Polynesian/Old English
Small house where the ti-palm (or ti-tree) grows. *The ti-palm (or ti-tree) is a tropical palm-like tree native to New Zealand and Polynesia.*

Trewick
Cornish/Old English
Tree house; tree village.

Tulip Cottage
Old English
Small house where tulip flowers grow.

Tulip Mews
Old English
Tulip flowers in a row.

Tulip Terrace
Old English
Tulip flowers growing in the planted or paved area.

Twin Oaks/Twin Oakes
English/Old English
Two oaks that are alike.

Two Willows Estate
Old English
Large, stately house with two willow trees.

U

Umbrella Tree
Latin/Italian/Old English
An American magnolia tree; any tree that takes on an umbrella-shape.

Upper Garden
Old English
The higher garden.

Urban Garden
Latin/Old English
City garden.

V

Villa Gardenia
Italian/Latin/English
Country house with a garden. (See Gardenia Gables)

Viola Manor
Old English
Estate house where the viola flowers grow.

Violet Cottage
Old English
Small house where violet flowers grow; purple house.

Violet Oasis
Latin/Old English
Violet flowers growing in a fertile area in a desert or dry area.

Violet Vista
Old English/Italian
Purple-coloured view; view of violet flowers.

W

Walnut Tree Cottage
Old English
Small house where the walnut tree grows.

Waterlily Cottage
Old English
Water lilies growing by the small house.

Waterlily Estate
Old English
Water lilies growing at the large, stately house.

Wattle Brae/Wattlebrae
Old English/Scottish
Shelter on the hill; wattle trees growing on the hill. *The wattle tree grows throughout areas of Australia. It features silver leaves and a small, fluffy mass of yellow flowers.*

Wattle Tree Cottage
Australian/English
Small house with wattle trees growing nearby. (See Wattle Brae)

Wattlegrove
Old English
Shelter in the small wood; wattle trees growing in the small wood. (See Wattle Brae)

Wattlemere
Old English
Shelter by the lake; wattle trees growing by the lake. (See Wattle Brae)

Weedmore
English/Old English
Weeds on the marshland; more weeding of this property is needed.

Weeping Figs
Old English
Weeping fig trees.

Weeping Willow Manor
Old English
Estate house with weeping willow trees.

Weeping Willows
Old English
Where the weeping willow trees grow.

Welcome Cottage
Old English
Small, welcoming house.

Welcome Manor
Old English
Welcoming estate house.

Whispering Pines
Old English/English
Wind rustling through the pine trees.

White Rose Cottage
Old English
Small house where white roses grow.

Wild Flower/Wildflower
English/Old English
Flowers growing in the wild.

Wild Rose Cottage
Old English
Small house where the wild roses grow.

Wild Rose Manor
Old English
Estate house where the wild roses grow.

Wildberry House
Old English
Home where wild berries grow.

Willow Brook/Willow Brooke
Old English
Willow trees growing by the small stream.

Willow Dale/Willowdale
Old English
Willow valley.

Willow Downs/Willow Downes
Old English
Willow trees on the flowing hills.

Willow Farm
Old English
Willow tree ranch.

Willow Glen/Willow Glenn/ Willowglen/Willowglenn
Old English/Scottish
Willow tree valley.

Willow Grove/Willowgrove
Old English
Willow trees growing in the small wood.

Willowsmere
Old English
Small willow trees; willow trees growing by the lake.

Wisteria Cottage
Old English
Small house where wisteria grows. *This is a very popular house name in Australia. Wisteria is also the hair colour favoured by Barry Humphries' alter ego Dame Edna Everage.*

Wisteria House
Old English
Home where wisteria grows. (See Wisteria Cottage)

Woodbine Way
Old English/Middle English
Path where the honeysuckle grows.

Wythe
Middle English
Willow tree.

X

Xerophyte Garden
Latin/Old English
A garden of plants (especially cactus) that are structured to adapt to arid conditions.

Y

Yarrow Cottage
Old English/Middle English
Small house where yarrow is grown. *Yarrow is used as a tonic and astringent.*

Youngwoods
Old English
New forest.

Z

Zen Garden
Mahayana (Buddhist)/Old English
Garden of enlightenment and meditation. *Zen affirms that enlightenment occurs through meditation and intuition rather than faith.*

Zesty Garden
French/Old English
Citrus garden; garden of keen enjoyment. *The zest (peel) of a citrus fruit can be used as flavouring.*

Zigzag Garden
German/Old English
A garden that has lines that move in one direction then turn in another direction. *Zigzags can especially be used in a hedge garden design.*

Herbal infusion

Herbs and spices play an important part in our daily life, whether in cooking, aromatherapy, medicine, or in providing us with a relaxing cup of herbal tea. Herbs and spices can also provide you with inspiration for your house name. *All herbal remedies should only be administered as directed by a doctor or herbalist.*

Alfalfa House
Spanish/Arabic
Home where the alfalfa grows. *One of the most nutritious plants with leaves rich in calcium, magnesium, potassium, beta-carotene, vitamins A, B12, C, D, E and K*

Aloe vera
Latin
Plant related to the lily family used to treat burns, skin conditions, sunburn and insect bites. It is a common ingredient in cosmetics.

Angelica Cottage
Medieval Latin/Old English
Angelica plant by the small house.

Aniseed Croft
Middle English/Old English
Aniseed growing in the small wood.

Basil Cottage
Middle English/French/Latin/Old English
Small house where basil grows.

Bay Leaf Hamlet
Old English
Small village where bay leaves grow.

Black Pepper Cottage
Old English
Small house where black pepper is ground.

Camomile Cottage/Chamomile Cottage
Old English
Small house where chamomile grows. *Chamomile is well known as a soothing herb, especially when made into hot tea.*

Caraway House
Middle English/Arabic/Old English
Home where caraway seeds are grown.

Cardamom Estate
Latin/Greek/Old English
Large, stately house where cardamom grows.

Cayenne Manor
Old French English
Estate house where cayenne peppers are grown.

Chervil Cottage
Greek/Old English
Small house where the chervil (a herb closely related to the carrot family) grows. *Dandelion, watercress and chervil were combined by the ancient Greeks as a tonic to ward off winter illnesses due to lack of vitamins and minerals. It is still used today as a tonic.*

Chilli Pepper Cottage/Chili Pepper Cottage
Spanish/Old English
Small house where chilli peppers are grown.

Chive Cottage
Middle English/French/Latin/Old English
Small house where chives grow.

Cinnamon Cottage
Latin/Greek/Middle English/Old English
Small house where cinnamon is grown.

Clove Cottage
Middle English/French/Latin/Old English
Small house where cloves are grown.

Cocoa Cottage
Spanish/Old English
Small house where cocoa is made.

Coriander Cottage
Middle English/French/Latin/Old English
Small house where coriander grows.

Curry Cottage
Tamil-MalayOld English
Small house where the curry leaf plant is grown; home where curry or powder ingredients for curry are prepared.

Dill Cottage
Old English
Small house where dill grows.

Echinacea Estate
Latin/Old French/Middle English
Large stately house where echinacea is grown. *Echinacea is native to America. It is used medicinally to strengthen the immune*

system, purify the blood and in the treatment and prevention of colds and flu.

Eucalyptus Cottage
Greek/Latin/Australian/Old English
Small house where the eucalyptus trees grow. *Eucalyptus is a traditional Australian Aboriginal remedy used for its antiseptic properties and to relieve coughs and colds.*

F

Fennel Cottage
Latin/Old English
Small house where fennel is grown or where its seeds are collected.

Fenugreek Farm
Latin/Old English/French/Middle English
Land where fenugreek is cultivated.

G

Galangal Glade
Latin/Old English
Open space where the galngal grows. *Also known as 'aromatic ginger', galangal is a rhizome of the ginger family, used medicinally in China as well as in Thai and other Southeast Asian cuisine.*

Garlic House
Old English
Home where garlic grows. *Garlic is used both medicinally and gastronomically and was believed to keep vampires away.*

Ginger Cottage
Old English
Small house where ginger is grown. *Ginger Rogers (Virginia Katherine McMath, 1911–95) was a US film actor and dancer, who rose to fame for her performances in musicals, particularly dancing with Fred Astaire. Ginger Meggs was the red-headed boy hero of the popular comic strip of the same name, created by Australian cartoonist Jimmy Bancks. Bancks began the comic strip in 1922 and continued it until his death in 1952.*

Ginseng
Chinese
Aromatic root used as a tonic known as far back as the first century AD, when ginseng was described in a document as 'enlightening and increasing wisdom'. *Russian folklore suggests that ginseng is a stimulant and boosts immunity. Today it is still used to promote endurance and to reduce stress and regulate blood sugar.*

H

Hemlock House
Old English
House where hemlock grows. *Hemlock is a poisonous European plant that is a member of the parsley family. It was known to the ancient Greeks, who used it in small quantities as a sedative and in larger quantities as a means of execution. When the philosopher Socrates was condemned to death, he was given a cup of hemlock to drink.*

Herb Cottage/Herbal Cottage/ Herbe Cottage
Old English
Small house where herbs are grown, collected or stored.

J

Jasmine Cottage
Persian/Old English
Small house where jasmine grows. *Jasmine is mainly used for its beautiful perfume although it has in the past been used (in tea form) to soothe coughs and to rinse sore eyes and wounds.*

L

Lavender Cottage
Old English
Small house where lavender grows; lavender-coloured, small house. *A very popular house name throughout Australia, the United Kingdom and the United States due to lavender being so hardy and able to grow in many countries.*

Lavender Fair/Lavender Fayre
Old English
Lavender exhibition; good lavender.

Lavender Flower Cottage
Old English
Small house where lavender flowers grow.

Lavender Grove
Old English
Small wood where lavender grows.

Lavender Mews
Old English
Rows of lavender.

M

Marjoram Estate
Middle English/French/Latin/Old English
Large, stately house where marjoram grows.

Mint Cottage
Old English
Small house where mint grows.

Mustard Manor
Latin/Old French/Middle English
Estate where mustard is grown.

N

Nigella Cottage
Latin/Old English
Small house where nigella (black cumin) is grown. *Nigella Lawson (aptly named after the spice) is a food writer with her own cooking programs. She is author of several cook books.*

Nutmeg Cottage
Old English
Small house where the nutmeg tree grows.

Nutmeg Hamlet
Old French/Old English
Small village where nutmeg trees grow.

O

Oregano Downes
Spanish/Latin/Greek/Old English
Oregano growing on the flowing hills.

P

Paprika Dell
Greek/Old English
Paprika growing in the secluded valley.

Parsley Cottage
Old English
Small house where parsley grows.

Parsley House
Old English
Home where parsley grows.

Pepper Cottage
Old English
Small house where pepper is made or ground.

Peppermint Cottage
Old English
Small house where peppermint is grown.

Poppy Seed Manor
Latin/Old English
Estate house where poppies are grown.

Primrose Cottage
Old English
Small house where primrose grows.

R

Rosemary Cottage
Old English
Small house where rosemary grows. *Rosemary is used in cooking and in skin and hair care products as well as symbolically for remembrance days. 'Rosemary' is also a woman's name.*

Rosemary Hamlet
Old English
Rosemary growing in the small village.

S

Saffron House
Old English
Home where saffron grows.

Sage Cottage
Middle English/French/Latin/Old English
Small house where sage grows.

T

Tarragon Turrets
Arabic/Spanish/Old French/Middle English
Place with small towers where tarragon is grown.

Tea Tree Cottage
Old English
Small house by the tea trees. *Tea trees are native to Australia and their oil is used for its antiseptic properties.*

The Old Thyme Garden
Old English
Old garden where thyme grows.

Thyme Cottage
Old English
Small house where thyme grows.

Turmeric Manor
Old English
Estate house where turmeric grows.

V

Valerian Vale
Medieval Latin/Middle English/Old French
Valley where valerian grows. *Valerian is used medicinally as a sedative and antispasmodic.*

Vanilla Cottage
Spanish/Old English
Sweetly scented house; a sweet flavouring; small, beige-coloured house.

W

Witch-Hazel
Old English
The witch-hazel plant. *Witch-hazel is native to North America. Its bark and leaves are used medicinally to treat inflammation and bruising. It is also used in skincare products.*

Wormwood Way
German/Old English
Path where the wormwood grows. *Wormwood is a bitter, aromatic herb, used medicinally and in the preparation of some alcoholic beverages, such as absinth and vermouth. Sprigs of wormwood are sometimes place in cupboards and drawers to repel pests such as borers and silverfish.*

Ylang-ylang House
Malayan/Old English
House of the essential oils. *Ylang-ylang is distilled from the fragrant flowers of the Malayan tree and is used in aromatherapy (as a sedative) and in perfumery.*

CHAPTER 7

IT'S TRADITION

The United Kingdom has a vast number of historical buildings, castles and homes of nobility, each of which can serve as a source of house names. First names, surnames, places, wealth and status provide some foundations for the house names that appear in this section.

A

Abels
German/Latin
Poplar tree grove with white or shimmering leaves.

Abercrombie
Scottish
One who resides by the river mouth.

Aberdeen
Scottish
Mouth of the river.

Abernathy
Celtic
Where the rivers meet.

Ackroyd
Old English
Oak grove.

Acres
Old English
A measurement of land. *This name is usually used in conjunction with a prefix such as 'Green Acres'.*

Adelaide
German/Old English
Noble. *'Adelaide' is the capital city of South Australia and is renowned for its beautiful architecture.*

Affleck
Gaelic
Field with flat stones. *Ben Affleck (b. 1972) is an American actor best known for starring in* Good Will Hunting *(1997) which he also co-wrote with Matt Damon. It won an Academy Award for Best Original Screenplay.*

Ahrens
Swedish
Tenant farmer.

Aisling
Gaelic
Visionary or dreamer.

Akehurst
Old English
Oak forest.

Akerman
Old English
Plougher of fields; farmer.

Alcott
Old English
Old cottage.

Aldersea
Old English
Small island or land in a marshland area; from the old sea.

Alston
Old English
Old stone.

Altman
Old English
Old man.

Amity
Old French
Friendship. *Amity was the town featured in the 1975 movie* Jaws, *directed by Steven Spielberg and starring Roy Schneider and Richard Dreyfuss.*

Andrewartha
Cornish
Home on high ground.

Appleby
Old English
Home by the apple tree orchard.

Arwen
Welsh
Muse. *In the movie trilogy,* The Lord of the Rings, *based on the novels of J.R.R. Tolkien, the character of Arwen was played by Liv Tyler.*

Ashbolt
Old English
House by the ash tree grove.

Ashlea/Ashlee/Ashleigh/Ashley/Ashly
Old English
Ash tree meadow.

Ashmore
Old English
Ash trees by the marshland; ash trees by the lake; ash trees by the fence or boundary line.

Aspen
Old English
Poplar trees. *Poplar trees are tall trees that are along a boundary often used as windbreaks on a property.*

Aspinall
Old English
Poplar trees by the stream. (See Aspen)

Aspland
Old English
Poplar tree field. (See Aspen)

Assell
Old English/German
Noble.

Astle
Old English
Eastern hill.

Athol
Old English
Hollowed area; Gaelic, from Ireland. *The people who reside in this house are Irish or have an Irish ancestry.*

Atlee/Atlea/Atleigh/Atley/Atly
Old English
At the meadow.

Atwell
Old English
At the stream or well.

Aurora
Latin
The golden beauty of the dawn. *An aurora is caused by electrically charged particles from the sun accelerating along magnetic fields into the earth's upper atmosphere. As they collide with gas atoms they give off light. The cumulative effect of these collisions is a spectacular display of moving bands of light. The aurora of the Northern Hemispere is called 'aurora borealis' or 'northern lights'; that of the Southern Hemisphere is called 'aurora australis' or 'southern lights'.*

Avonia
Old English
River. *Stratford-upon-Avon was the place where William Shakespeare was born. He was also known as 'The Bard of Avon'.*

Axford
Old English
Shallow river crossing by the ash tree grove.

Aylward
German
Guardian or protector.

B

Bainbridge
Old Norse/Old English
Straight river running through the small town; straight bridge.

Baisden
Old Norse/Old English
Cow barn in the valley.

Bamford
Old English
Shallow river crossing by the tree trunks.

Barclay
Old English
Birch tree meadow.

Bauman
German
Tennant farmer.

Beacham
Old French
Fair farm; fair village.

Beachlea/Beachlee/Beachleigh/Beachley/Beachly
Old English
Beach meadow.

Beaulieu
Old French
Beautiful place.

Beaumont
Old French
Beautiful hill.

Bede
Old Celtic
Life.

Bedwell
Old English
Small stream in the valley.

Beecroft
Old English
Small pasture where bees are kept.

Bellamy
French/Latin
Beautiful friend.

Bellevue Terrace
French/Old English
Beautiful view of the planted or paved area; view of the bell.

Bellgard
French/German
Beautiful guardian or protector.

Belmont
Old English/French
Bell on the mountain; beautiful mountain.

Belmont Cottage
French/Old English
Small house by the beautiful mountain.

Benneworth
Old English
House with a boundary fence or wall.

Bianca
Italian
White.

Bichel
German
One who resides on the hill.

Birnbaum
German
One who resides by the pear tree.

Blackburn/Blackbourn/Blackbourne
Old English
Dark or black stream.

Blackthorn/Blackthorne
Old English
Dark or black prickles.

Blakely
Old English
Black meadow.

Blandford
Old English
Light-coloured river crossing.

Bloomfield
Old English
Flowering meadow.

Blunden
Old French/Old English
White valley.

Bonfield
Old French/Old English
Good meadow.

Bonnyfields
Old French/Old English
Good meadows.

Boorne
Old English
Stream.

Boreham
Old English
Village that farms pigs; pig farm.

Bormann
German
One who resides by the stream.

Bornholtz
German
One who resides by the stream in the forest.

Bosch
German
Bush.

Boulton
Old English
House in the settlement town.

Bradbury
Old English
Broad house.

Bradford
Old English
Broad river crossing.

Braithwaite
Old English
Broad clearing.

Bramble/Brambles
Old English
Secluded place; blueberry shrub.

Bransgrove
Old English
Raven grove.

Braveheart
Old English
Brave of heart. *This name became popular when the movie of the same name was*

released in 1995 staring Mel Gibson. Braveheart *is about William Wallace who united the thirteenth century Scots in their battle to overthrow English rule.*

Bretherton
Old Norse/Old English
The brother's town.

Brighton
Old English
Bridge town; sunny town.

Brimicombe
Old English
Secluded place in the narrow valley.

Brindley
Old English
Burning meadow.

Broadhurst
Old English
Wide, forested hill.

Brock
Old English
Stream.

Bruggenham
German
One who resides by the bridge over the reeds; bridge village; bridge on the farm.

Brylei
Gaelic/Old English
Hill meadow.

Budden
German
Farm marshland.

Burford
Old English
Shallow river crossing by the thorny area.

Burrow
Old English
Municipal or fortified town.

Butterfield
Old English
The butter maker's meadow. Butterfield 8, *directed by Daniel Mann and based on the novel by John O'Hara, won Elizabeth Taylor her first Oscar for best actress for her portrayal of Gloria Wondrous in 1969.*

C

Calcroft
Old English
Cold, small pasture.

Caldcott
Old English
Cold cottage.

Caldwell
Old English
Cold stream or well.

Cassell
Italian/Old English
One who lives in the important house.

Castle
French/Latin
Fortified estate house.

Caulfield
Old English
Cold meadow.

Cavalier
Italian/French
Knight.

Cawton
Old English
Cow town.

Cazaly
French
One who resides in a small house. *Roy Cazaly (1893–1963) was a famous Australian Rules Football player.*

Ceinwen
Welsh
Beautiful friend.

Chahine
Old Gaelic
A circular-shaped, fortified stone house.

Chinnery
French/Latin
One who resides in the oak tree forest.

Chittleborough
Old English
Valley hamlet; valley municipal or fortified town.

Clayfield
Old English
Meadow of clay.

Clement
Latin
Merciful.

Clennell
Old English
Hill that is free from weeds.

Cleveland
Old English
Cliff land.

Cleveland House
Old English
House by the cliff.

Clewett
Old English
One who resides by the cliff.

Cleworth
Old English
Hamlet or village on the cliff.

Clifford
Old English
Shallow river crossing by the cliff.

Cluff
Old English
One who resides by the cliff.

Clooney/Clunies/Cluny
Scottish
Meadow resting place. *George Clooney (b. 1961) is an American actor best know for the television series* ER *and for such movies as* The Perfect Storm *and* Ocean's Eleven. *George is also the nephew of singer Rosemary Clooney (1928–2002).*

Compton
Old English
Farm in the small valley.

Coniber
Old English
Rabbit grove.

Copeland
Old English
Hilltop meadow.

Coplea/Coplee/Copleigh/Copeley/Coply
Old English
Hilltop meadow.

Cordeaux
French
Kind hearted.

Cotrell
Old French
One who resides in a cottage.

Country Villa
Old English/Italian
Country house.

Coventry
Old English
Tree by the cove; exclusion. *The phrase 'sent to Coventry', is believed to have come from the then unpopular English city of Coventry, where soldiers were billeted. It may also come from the English Civil War where Royalist prisoners were sent to the very Parliamentarian town of Coventry.*

Cracknell
Old English
Crow by the well or stream. *Ruth Cracknell (1925–2002) starred as Maggie Beare in the Australian television series* Mother and Son. *Ruth also appeared in many movies including* The Chant of Jimmy Blacksmith *(1978).*

Cragside
Scottish/English
Rocky hills.

Crampton
Old English
Farm on the river bend.

Cranston
Old English
The town with cranes.

Craven
Old English/Gaelic
Crow or raven; garlic.

Crawford
Old English
Crow by the shallow river crossing.

Cresswell
Old English
Watercress growing by the stream or well.

Croft
Old English
Small pasture. *The character of Lara Croft in the movies* Tomb Raider *(2001) and* The Cradle of Life *(2003) was played by Angelina Jolie (b. 1975).*

Crossing
Old English
Road or river crossing place.

Crosslea/Crosslee/Crossleigh/Crossley/Crossly
Old English
Road or river crossing in the meadow.

Cuddlepie
Australian English/Old English
Sweet as pie and inspires affection. *'Cuddlepie' is the name of a character in Australian writer and illustrator May Gibbs's* Gumnut Babies *(1916) and* Snugglepot and Cuddlepie *(1918). The 'Gumnut' characters have been much loved by generations of Australian children and were further popularised through Gibbs's long-running comic strips.*

Cutcliff
Old English
Cottage on the cliff.

D

Daintree
Old English
The World Heritage listed Daintree Rainforest is situated in Northern Queensland, Australia. It is one of the most diverse and beautiful rainforests on earth and is home to a large array of plants and animals all in an area of approximately 1200 square kilometres.

Darlea/Darlee/Darleigh/Darley/Darly
Old English
Deer meadow.

De Haven
French/Old English
Place of refuge.

Debenham
Old English
Village by a dark, deep river; farm by the dark, deep river.

Delahaye
French
House surrounded by a hedge.

Dell
Old English
Valley.

Dellis
Latin
Delightful.

Denham
Old English
Valley farm; valley village.

Denmead
Old English
Valley meadow.

Denton
Old English
Valley town.

Devaux
French
One who resides in the valley.

Dingle
Old English
One who resides in the deep valley.

Doorely
Irish/Gaelic/Old English
Dark meadow.

Drysdale
Old English
Arid valley. *Sir Russell Drysdale (1912–81) was an Australian painter noted for his landscapes depicting the strong colours and harsh conditions of the Australian outback.*

Dunton
Old English
Dark town.

E

Easson
Old English
Eastern son.

Easterbrook/Easterbrooke
Old English
Small, eastern stream.

Edelweiss
German
Mountain flower. *'Edelweiss' was a song that featured in* The Sound of Music *(1965) starring Julie Andrews. It was a song dedicated to the mountain flower and Austria. Bill Lee actually sang the song, dubbing Christopher Plummer's voice.*

Edelweiss Cottage
German/Old English
Mountain flowers growing by the small house. (See Edelweiss)

Edelweiss House
German/Old English
Home by the mountain flowers. (See Edelweiss)

Eden
Latin/Greek/Hebrew
Paradise. *'The Garden of Eden' was the original home of Adam and Eve according to the Book of Genesis in* The Bible.

Eden Cottage
Latin/Greek/Hebrew/Old English
Small house of paradise. (See Eden)

Eden House
Latin/Greek/Hebrew/Old English
Home of paradise. (See Eden)

Edencroft/Eden Croft
Latin/Greek/Hebrew/Old English
Small pasture paradise. (See Eden)

Edenview/Eden View
Latin/Greek/Hebrew/Old English
The vista of paradise. (See Eden)

Ekmann
German
Man who resides on the corner.

Eldercott
Old English
The old one's cottage; the old cottage.

Elmcott
Old English
Elm trees by the cottage.

Endicott
Old English
Cottage at the end of the street or row.

Engelbrecht
German
Bright angel.

Englehart
German
Strong angel.

Erin
Celtic
Western island; peace. *'Erin' is also another name for Ireland.*

Evangeline
Latin/Greek
Good news, messenger.

Evol
English
Love. 'Evol' is 'love' spelt backwards.

F

Faery
Irish/Celtic
Fairy. An old spelling variant of 'fairy'.

Fahey
Gaelic
Foundations.

Fairclough
Old English
Beautiful valley.

Fawlea/Fawlee/Fawleigh/Fawley/Fawly
Old English
Hay meadow.

Featherstone
Old English
Stone monument; feather-shaped stones.

Federation House
Older style house; the union or league house. *Federation architecture is a distinctive architectural style popular in houses built at the time of Australia's Federation (1901), typically using local sandstone.*

Fernlea/Fernlee/Fernleigh/Fernley/Fernly
Old English
Meadow of ferns.

Field
Old English
Meadow; pasture land.

Finnemore
Old French
Fine love; fine marshland.

Finucane
Irish
Beautiful.

Fishborne/Fishburn/Fishburne
Old English/Scottish
Fishing stream.

Fishlock
Old English
Fishing stream.

Fleur
French
Flower.

Flora
Latin
Flowers; plants.

Folklore Cottage
Small house of traditional beliefs.

Folklore House
Home of traditional beliefs.

Ford/Forde
Old English
Shallow river crossing. *The Ford Motor Company was founded by Henry Ford and 11 investors in 1903 and by 1908 the Model T was born.*

Forrester
Old English
One who resides or works in the forest. *Forrester Creations is the name of the fashion house in the soap* The Bold and the Beautiful *(debut 1987).*

Freeborne/Freeburn/Freeburne
Old English
Free flowing stream; one who is born into freedom.

G

Gainsford
Old English
Straight, shallow river crossing.

Gala Hall
Large, community building where festive gatherings are held.

Gala House
The home where festive gatherings are held.

Gamertsfelder
German
One who resides on the cliff farm.

Garland
Old French/Old English
Triangular land; battle land; small house with a wreath of flowers. *A garland may also be an anthology of short literary pieces, poems or ballads.*

Garioch
French
One who resides by the oak tree grove.

Gatfield
Old English
Goat field; gate field.

Gemmell
Celtic
Old.

Geschwind
German
Fast, quick.

Gilbourne
Old Norse/Scottish/Old English
Valley stream.

Gladstone
Old English
Bird stone; happy stone.

Glen/Glenn/Glyn/Glynn
Scottish
Valley

Glenhaven
Scottish/Old English
Valley refuge.

Glenlach/Glenloch/Glennlach/Glennloch
Scottish
Valley lake.

Glenlach Cottage/Glennlach Cottage
Scottish/Old English
Small house by the valley lake.

Glenmore/Glenmoore/Glennmoore
Scottish/Old English
Valley marshland.

Glenrock/Glennrock
Scottish/Old English
Valley of rocks.

Glenside
Scottish/Old English
Hillside valley.

Goninan
Cornish
Hedge made from ash trees.

Grandville
Old English
Great village.

Granville
Old English
Great village.

Grassy Plains
English/Northern American
Grass covered open fields.

Greenway
Old English
Green path.

Grice
German
Grey.

Grove
Old English
An area with trees or shrubs.

H

Hackett
Scottish/English
Crooked. *A name for a home on a crooked block of land.*

Hadfield/Hadley
Old English
Open meadow.

Hainsworth
Old English
Old farm.

Hall
Old English
Large building of importance. *A Hall was usually the main meeting place in a village or town and therefore held a great deal of importance for the community.*

Halfwegg
Dutch/German
Halfway.

Hallam
Old English
Nook.

Halliwell
Old English
Holy stream. *The television series* Charmed *features the Halliwell sisters, Phoebe, Paige and Piper, as witches who right wrongs and protect the innocent.*

Halstead
Old English
Hall by the homestead; hut on a site. *This is used to name a small shelter where one may live while building a house.*

Hamilton
Scottish/Old English
Enclosed village.

Hamlet
Old French
Little home; village. Hamlet *was written by William Shakespeare in 1600.*

Hampton
Old English
Farm village; proud village; proud farm.

Hanbury
Old English
High, fortified building.

Hanford
Old English
High and shallow river crossing.

Hanging Rock
English/Old English
Rock overhanging a ledge or a cliff. Picnic at Hanging Rock *is an Australian movie made in 1975, based on Joan Lindsay's 1967 novel of the same title. The movie is about three students and a schoolteacher from Appleyard Cottage who disappear on an excursion to Hanging Rock. The movie is fictional although it is widely thought to be based on a true story. Hanging Rock is an actual place near Mount Macedon in Victoria, Australia.*

Hanging Rock Chalet
English/Old English/French
Small house near to the rock that overhangs a ledge or a cliff. (See Hanging Rock)

Hanlea/Hanlee/Hanleigh/Hanley/Hanly
Old English
High meadow.

Happy Valley
Old English
Joyous dale. *'Happy Valley' is a popular place name in Britain, USA and Canada. Australia and New Zealand also have their own Happy Valleys near Adelaide and Wellington respectively. Hong Kong has a famous race course called Happy Valley.*

Harcourt
Old English
Hawker's cottage.

Hardy
Old French/Middle English
Bold; daring. *This name might also be chosen by admirers of any of several Australian Hardys: writer Frank, his comedian sister Mary, yachtsman Sir James or pioneer viticulturist, Thomas. Alternatively, the name could be in honour of American comedian Oliver Hardy of the famous Laurel and Hardy team, or the English writer Thomas Hardy.*

Hargreaves
Old English
Grove of hares.

Harley/Harlea/Harlee/Harleigh/Harly
Old English
Wooded hare meadow.

Harmsworth
Old English
Farm with hares.

Hartford
Old English
The deer's shallow river crossing.

Hartlea/Hartlee/Hartleigh/Hartley/Hartly
Old English
The deer's meadow.

Hartop
Old English
Hares on the hill summit.

Hartwell
Old English
Deer stream.

Hartwood
Old English
Deer forest.

Haselhurst/Hazelhurst
German/Old English
Hazel tree grove.

Hasham
Old English
Hazel tree farm; hazel tree village.

Hasluck
English
To be fortunate.

Haswell
Old English
Hazel wood stream or well.

Hatfield
Old English
Meadow of heather.

Hathaway
Old English
Heather path.

Hatherlea/Hatherlee/Hatherleigh/Hatherley/Hatherly
Old English
Heather meadow.

Haven
Old English
Refuge.

Hawlea/Hawlee/Hawleigh/Hawley/Hawly
Old English
Hedged meadow.

Haylea/Haylee/Hayleigh/Hayley/Hayly
Middle English
Hay in the meadow.

Hazelton
Old English
Hazel wood town.

Heathcliff/Heathcliffe
Old English
Heather growing on the cliff. *'Heathcliff' is also the name of the hero of Emily Brontë's only novel* Wuthering Heights.

Heathcott
Old English
Cliff cottage by the heather.

Heemskerk
Dutch
One who resides by the church in the village.

Heritage
Latin/Old French
Inherited property.

Heritage House
Latin/Old French/Old English
Protected house. *Statutory Heritage Listings or registers protect and manage the places and objects that we, as a community, want to keep. Heritage Councils also manage the approval of major changes so that heritage significance is retained, not diminished. (Check with your local Heritage Council for more information).*

Hetherington
Old English
Heather settlement town.

Highland
Old English/Scottish
From the high mountain land.
The Highlands is a mountainous region in central and northern Scotland, famous for its beauty and Scottish/Gaelic culture.

Highlander
Scottish/English
Person from the high mountain land.
A 'Highlander' is someone who resides in the mountainous region of central and northern Scotland, famous for its beauty and Scottish/Gaelic culture.

Hillton/Hilton
Old English
Hill town. *The Hilton Hotel empire was founded by Conrad Hilton who purchased his first hotel in Cisco, Texas in 1919. Today there are over 500 Hilton Hotels throughout the world. Paris and Nicole Hilton are Conrad Hilton's socialite granddaughters, famous for being famous.*

Hinchcliff
Old English
Steep cliff.

Hocklea/Hocklee/Hockleigh/Hockley/Hockly
Old English
High meadow.

Hocknull
German/Old English
High hill.

Hofsteede
German
Enclosed farm.

Holborrow
Old English
Hill municipal; fortified hill town.

Holbrook/Holbrooke
Old English
Hollow by the small stream. *Holbrook is a town in southern New South Wales, Australia. It has had many previous names including Ten Mile Creek (1838) and German Town (1876) and changed to its current name in 1914, named after Submarine Commander Norman Douglas Holbrook.*

Hole
Old English
Hollow.

Holforth
Old English
Deep river crossing.

Hollamby
Old English
Home by the valley in the corner.

Hollingsworth
Old English
Holy, settlement farm.

Hollow
Old English
Hole.

Holm
Old English
Home; hamlet or village; inshore island; floodplain. *'Holm/holme' is also a form of 'hamlet'. Now the name is sometimes used as alternative spelling of 'home'.*

Hookway
Old English
Bend in the path.

Hoplea/Hoplee/Hopleigh/Hopley/Hoply
Old English
Meadow valley.

Hopwood
Old English
Valley forest.

Houghton
Old English
Grey-coloured town on the steep bank.

Huegel/Huegill
German
Hill.

Hull
Old English
Hill.

Hullston
Old English
Hill town.

Huntsdale
Old English
The hunter's valley.

Huntingdon
Old English
The hunter's hill.

I

Iddles
Old English
Unused or vacant land.

Iredell
Old English
Irish valley.

J

Johnstone
Old English
John's town; John's stone; God's gracious town; God's gracious stone.

Jovi/Jovia/Jovie/Jovy
Latin
Happy.

K

Keelan
Gaelic
Islander.

Keelea/Keelee/Keeleigh/Keeley/Keely
Irish/Old English
Beautiful meadow.

Keir
Gaelic
Dark.

Kenton
Old English
The king's town.

Kemp
Old English
Open meadow.

Kernaghan
Gaelic
Victory. *Lee Kernaghan is an Australian country music singer known for songs such as 'Boys From the Bush' and 'The Outback Club'. He also raised a massive $250,000 in his Pass the Hat Around tour in 1998, which he donated to struggling country towns that arranged the concerts.*

Keywood
Old English
Important forest.

Kilduff
Old English
Black forest.

Kilea/Kilee/Kileigh/Kiley/Kily
Old English
Narrow land.

Kingsford
Old English
The king's shallow river crossing.

Kingslea/Kingslee/Kingsleigh/Kingsley/Kingsly
Old English
The king's meadow.

Kingston
Old English
The king's town.

Kingswell
Old English
The king's stream or well.

Kininmouth
Scottish
The start of the king's land or stream.

Kinnard
Irish
The king's hill.

Kinnear
Scottish
Western headland.

Kio-ora
Irish
Home, sweet home. *Kio-ora is a very popular house name in Australia used by those with Irish roots.*

Kirkham
Old English
Church farm; church village.

Kirkland
Old English
Churchland.

Kirklea/Kirklee/Kirkleigh/Kirkley/Kirkly
Old English
Church meadow.

Kirkwood
Old English
Church forest.

Kirrilea/Kirralee/Kirrileigh/Kirriley/Kirrily
Irish
Dark.

Klein
German
Small.

Kleinberg
German
Small mountain.

Kleinburg/Klineburg
German
Small castle; small fortress.

Klinge
German
Loud stream in a gorge.

Knightlea/Knightlee/Knightleigh/Knightley/Knightly
Old English
The knight's meadow.

Knill
Old English
Hill.

Knoll
Old English
Hill.

Knowland
Old English
Hilly field.

Knowles
Old English
Grassy sloping hills.

Knox
Scottish
Rounded hill.

Kopenberg
Dutch/Afrikaans/German
Isolated hill; rocky mountain.

Kopenburg
Dutch/Afrikaans/German
Fortress on the isolated hill; fortress on the rocky hill.

Krumlin
German
One who resides by the curvy road.

Ky/Kyle
Gaelic
From the strait.

Kyloe
Old English
Meadow of cows.

L

Lachlan/Lochlan
Scottish
Land of lakes.

Lagan
Gaelic
Nook.

Laing
Old English
Long.

Lamont
French
The mountain.

Lander
Old English
Grassy plain owner.

Landon
Old English
Open land.

Lane
Old English
Small street.

Langford
Old English
Long, shallow river crossing.

Langlea/Langlee/Langleigh/Langley/Langly
Old English
Long meadow.

Langston
Old English
Long town.

Langworth
Old English
Long farm.

Lanslea/Lanslee/Lansleigh/Lansley/Lansly
Celtic/Old English
Church meadow.

Lasalle
French
Hall.

Lawford
Old English
Low, shallow river crossing.

Lea/Leah/Lee/Leigh/Ley
Old English
Meadow.

Legrand
Old French
The great one.

Leif
Scottish
Broad river.

Leland/Leyland
Old English
The meadow.

Lennox
Gaelic
Grove of elm trees.

Letherby
Old English
The sloping farm.

Leyton/Leiton
Old English
Meadow town.

Lias
Old English
Rock.

Liddon
Old English
Shelter.

Lige
Old English
Meadow.

Lillea/Lillee/Lilleigh/Lilley/Lilly
Old English
Lilies in the meadow.

Lilly White/Lillywhite/Lily White/ Lilywhite/Lily Whyte/Lilywhyte/
Old English
White lilies.

Lin/Lyn/Lynn
Old English
Pool or pond.

Linc
Old English
Pond.

Linden
Old English
Linden or lime trees.

Lisle
Old English
Island.

Locklea/Locklee/Lockleigh/Lockley/ Lockly
Old English
Enclosed meadow.

Lockslea/Lockslee/Locksleigh/ Locksley/Locksly
Old English
Enclosed meadows.

Logan
Irish
Hollow.

Longlen/Longlenn
Old English/Scottish
Long valley.

Longmuir
Old English/Scottish
Long marshland.

Loudon
German
Low valley.

Lundy
Scottish
Grove on an island.

Lyndon
Old English
Linden or lime tree hill.

Lytton
Old English
Town by the rapids.

M

Maldon
Old English
Meeting place in the hollow. *'Maldon' is also the name of a former gold rush town in Victoria, Australia.*

Malvern
Welsh
Bare hill.

Markham
Old English
Fenced farm; fenced village.

Marlow/Marlowe
Old English
Lake by the hill.

Marquis
French
Boundary or fence.

Marsh
Old English
Wet land.

Marwood/Marshwood
Old English
Marsh forest.

Mead/Meade
Old English
Meadow. *Mead is also a very sweet alcoholic drink made from honey, water, malt and yeast.*

Medbury
Old English
Fortified town in the meadow.

Melbourne
Old English
Mill stream. *Melbourne is the capital city of Victoria and the second largest city in Australia. It is renowned for its arts, food, wine and shopping.*

Merivale
Old English
Pleasant valley.

Merryweather/Merriweather
Old English
Bright, clear weather.

Merton
Old English
Town by the sea or lake.

Middendorf
German
One who resides in the middle of the town.

Middlecombe
Old English
Middle valley.

Middlefarm
Old English
Middle farm.

Middleton
Old English
Middle town.

Milborough
Old English
Mill municipal or fortified town.

Milburn
Old English
Mill by the stream.

Milford
Old English
Shallow river crossing by the mill. *Milford Sound, New Zealand, also known as Piopiotahi to the Maoris, features a stunning narrow inlet of the sea between steep cliffs and glaciers. It is located in the three million acres of Fiordland National Park and is one of New Zealand's most popular tourist destinations.*

Millhouse
Old English
House by the mill. *Millhouse is Bart's bumbling friend in* The Simpsons. *Richard Millhouse Nixon was America's 37th President. Nixon is best known for the so-called Watergate scandal, stemming from a break-in at the Democratic National Committee offices in 1972, which was traced to the Committee to Re-elect the President.*

Millington
Old English
Settlement in the mill town.

Millyn
Old English
Mill pool or pond.

Milton
Old English
Mill town.

Millward
Old English
Guardian of the mill.

Minster
Old English
Monastery church.

Mitford
Middle English
Large river crossing.

Monford
Old English
The monk's river crossing.

Montague
Old French
Pointed mountain.

Monteath
Scottish
Mountain river pasture.

Moorecroft
Old English
Small pasture in the marshland.

Mooreland
Old English
Marshland.

Moorewood
Old English
Forest in the marshland.

Mountain Heritage
Old English
Inherited mountain property. *Statutory Heritage Listings or registers protect and manage places that we, as a community, want to keep. Heritage Councils also approve major changes so heritage significance is retained. (Check with your local Heritage Council for more information).*

Morey
Irish/Old English
Marshland.

Morley/Morlea/Morlee/Morleigh/Morly
Old English
Meadow marshland.

Mort
Middle English
Stump.

Morton
Old English
Marsh town.

Mugglesdon
Old English
Pasture hill. *In J.K. Rowling's Harry Potter series of novels 'muggles' are humans with no magic powers.*

Muir
Scottish
Marsh.

Muirhead/Moorehead
Scottish/Old English
The beginning of the marshland. *Agnes Moorehead played Samantha's meddling mother Endora in the television series* Bewitched *(1967–1972).*

N

Nairn
Scottish
River.

Nayland
Old English
One who resides on the island.

Nerville
French/Irish
Sea village.

Nesbit
Old English
River bend.

Nethercliff
Old English
Home built at the foot of a cliff.

Nettleton
Old English
Town of nettle (stinging plant).

Neville
Old English
New village.

Newell
Old English
New well or stream. *The Newell Highway New South Wales is the main inland road link between Victoria and Queensland. It was named after the head of the NSW Government Main Roads Department in the 1930s.*

Newlyn
Old English
New pool or pond.

Norcliffe
Old English
Northern cliff.

Northcliff
Old English
Northern cliff.

Northrop
Old English
Northern farm.

Norton
Old English
Northern town.

Norville
Old English
Northern village.

Norward
Old English
Northern guardian.

Norwell
Old English
Northern stream or well.

Norwood
Old English
Northern forest.

Notley
Old English
Nut tree meadow.

Nowles
Old English
Hills.

Nye
Old English
Islander.

O

Oakes/Oaks
Old English
Oak trees.

Oaklea/Oaklee/Oakleigh/Oakley/Oakly
Old English
Oak tree meadow.

Ockerby
Old English
Old home.

Ogden
Old English
Oak tree valley. *Ogden is a city in Utah, USA.*

Ogilvie
Welsh
High plain; peak.

Oldfield
Old English
Old meadow.

Onilwyn
Welsh
Friend from the ash tree grove.

Ord
Old English
Point.

Orford
Old English
Upper, shallow river crossing.

Orlan
Old English
Pointed land.

Orrick
Old English
One who resides by the oak tree.

Orrin
Old English
River.

Orton
Old English
Riverside town.

Overington
Old English
The upper town.

Overton
Old English
High town.

Owles
Old English
Owl; one who loves the night.

Oxbrow
Old English
Where oxen are kept on the hill.

Oxford
Old English
Shallow river crossing used by oxen. *The University of Oxford is the oldest English-speaking university in the world and lays claim to at least nine centuries of teaching. It developed rapidly after 1167, when Henry II banned English students from attending the University of Paris.*

Oxenham
Old English
The ox village or farm.

Oxlea/Oxlee/Oxleigh/Oxley/Oxly
Old English
Meadow of oxen.

Oxton
Old English
Ox town.

P

Parker
Old English
One who resides in the woods.

Parkin
Old English
Little stone.

Paxton
Latin/Old English
Peaceful town.

Payne
Latin
From the countryside.

Peak
Old English
Pointed hill.

Pemberton
Old English
Barley farm, in town on the hill.

Pendle
Old English
Hill. *In the legend of the Pendle Witches, two old women (Demdike and Chattox Device) lived below Pendle Hill. They were accused of witchcraft and sent to Lancaster for trial. Extensive court documents were made on the case and together with the book written about how to uncover evidence of witches,* Daemonologie, *written by King James 1, they were the basis for Matthew Hopkins' career as the Witchfinder General. For the Quaker movement Pendle Hill also has significance as George Fox had a vision there in 1652, which led to the foundation of the movement.*

Penley/Penlea/Penlee/Penleigh/Penly
Old English
Enclosed or fenced meadow.

Pettigrew
Scottish/Old English
Small growth.

Pickford
Old English
Shallow river crossing by the pointy hill. *'Mary Pickford' was the screen name of Gladys Louise Smith (1893–1979) who with Douglas Fairbanks and Charlie Chaplin found the United Artists film studio in 1919.*

Picton
Old English
Town on the pointed hill.

Platt
Old French
Flat land.

Potthurst
Old English
Small, mountain lake.

Prescott
Old English
The priest's cottage.

Presley
Old English
The priest's meadow. *Elvis Presley (1935–77) was born in Mississippi, USA. He was famed for his beautiful voice and good looks and has sold over a billion albums worldwide, more than anyone else in the world. The first of his 33 films was* Love Me Tender *(1956).*

Preston
Old English
The priest's town.

Puddy
Old English
Bulge; puddle.

Putnam
Old English
One who resides by the pond.

Putt
Cornish/Old English
Hollow.

Quennel/Quenelle
German/French
One who resides by the oak tree. *Quenelles are meatballs or fishballs.*

Quenton
Old English
The queen's town.

Quiglea/Quiglee/Quigleigh/Quigley/Quigly
Old English
The queen's meadow.

Quimby
Old English
One who resides near the queen's estate.

Radburn
Old English
Red stream.

Radcliff/Radcliffe
Old English
Red cliff.

Radlea/Radlee/Radleigh/Radley/Radly
Old English
Red meadow.

Radnore
Old English
Red shore.

Ramsden
Old English
The ram's valley.

Ransford
Old English
The raven's shallow, river crossing.

Ranslea/Ranslee/Ransleigh/Ransley/Ransly
Old English
The raven's meadow.

Rashlea/Rashlee/Rashleigh/Rashley/Rashly
Old English
One who resides by the ash tree meadow.

Rawdon
Old English
Rough hill; roe-deer hill.

Rawlea/Rawlee/Rawleigh/Rawley/Rawly
Old English
Rough meadow; roe-deer in the meadow.

Rayburn
Old English
Roe-deer stream.

Raydon
Old English
Rye hill; roe-deer on the hill; river hill.

Rayfield
Old English
Rye meadow; stream in the meadow; roe-deer meadow.

Rayford
Old English
Shallow river crossing; rye by the shallow river crossing; roe-deer by the shallow river crossing.

Reddell
Old English
Red valley; reedy valley.

Redford
Old English
The red, shallow river crossing; reedy, shallow river crossing.

Redlea/Redlee/Redleigh/Redley/Redly
Old English
Red meadow; reedy meadow.

Remington
French/English
The raven's town.

Renaissance Manor
French/Old English
Estate house with the classical influences or features of the Renaissance. *A movement that occurred in Europe from the fourteenth to the seventeenth centuries, the Renaissance focused on the 'rebirth' of learning and marked the transition from the mediaeval to the modern era.*

Renfrew
Old English
Still river; the raven's river.

Renshaw
Old English
Raven's forest.

Renton
Old English
Raven's town.

Rexford
Old English
The king's ford.

Rexton
Old English
The king's town.

Rhidian
Welsh
One who resides by the river crossing.

Rhydwyn
Welsh
Friend from the white-river crossing.

Reichenbaeck
German
Marshland stream.

Reteif
French
Still.

Rhinda
Scottish
Pointed ridge.

Ridesdale
Old English
Reedy valley; red valley.

Ridge
Old English
Steep rocks.

Ridgelea/Ridgelee/Ridgeleigh/Ridgeley/Ridgely
Old English
Steep rocks in the meadow.

Rilea/Rilee/Rileigh/Riley/Rily
Old English
Rye meadow.

Ringwood
Old English
Forest with a circular boundary or fence.

Ringrose
Old English
Roses growing in a round area; ring of roses.

Rislea/Rislee/Risleigh/Risley/Risly
Old English
Brushwood meadow.

Riston
Old English
Brushwood town.

River
Latin
Large stream.

Riverina
Latin/English
River area.

Roan/Rowan
Old English
Rowan tree.

Robotham
Old English
Rough farm.

Roch/Roche
Old French
Rock.

Rochester
Old French/Old English
Stone camp.

Rockford
Old French/Old English
Stoney, shallow river crossing. *The* Rockford Files *(1974–80) was a television series about a private investigator and starred James Garner.*

Rockland
Old English
Stoney land.

Rockledge
Old English
Stoney ledge.

Rocklea/Rocklee/Rockleigh/Rockley/Rockly
Old English
Stoney meadow.

Rockwell
Old English
Stoney stream or well.

Rodden
Old English
Roe-deer valley.

Roebuck
Old English
Deer; female and male deer.

Roland
Old German
Famous land.

Romain/Roman/Romeo/Romy
Latin/French
From Rome in Italy.

Romney
Welsh
Curvy river.

Roslin/Roslyn/Rosslin/Rosslyn
Old English
Rose by the pool or pond. *The village of Roslin in Scotland is famed for its extraordinary Rosslyn Chapel (circa 1404–80). It has an outstanding variety of stone carvings inside, covering almost every square inch, of human figures, animals and plants.*

Roswell/Rothwell
Old English
Roses by the well or stream.

Rough
Scottish
Rock.

Rowell
Old English
Roe-deer spring or well.

Rowland
Old English
Roe-deer field.

Rowlea/Rowlee/Rowleigh/Rowley/Rowly
Old English
Overgrown meadow.

Roxbury
Old English
Castle fortress; rocky stream.

Royd
Old English
Clearing in the woods.

Royden
Old English
Rye hill.

Ruck
Old English
Rook; rock.

Ruford
Old English
Red, shallow, river crossing.

Rugby
Old English
Rock fortress; a football game. *Rugby is a town in Warwickshire, England, famous for the public school of the same name and for the football game that originated at the school.*

Rutherford
Old English
Castle river crossing.

Rutherglen/Rutherglenn
Old English
Castle in the valley.

Rutlea/Rutlee/Rutleigh/Rutley/Rutly
Old English
Red meadow.

Rycroft
Old English
Small, rye pasture.

S

Saddington
Old English
Settlement town.

Safford
Old English
Willow trees by the shallow, river crossing.

Salisbury
Old English
Fort by the willow tree stream. *'Salisbury' in England is famed for the Neolithic monument Stonehenge.*

Saltmarsh
Old English
Marshland by the sea.

Salton
Old English
Hall in the manor town; willow tree town.

Sambrook/Sambrooke
Old English
Small, sandy stream.

Sandborn
Old English
Sandy stream.

Sandford
Old English
Sandy, shallow river crossing.

Sanditon
Old English
Sandy or beachside town.

Santon
Old English
Beach or sandy town.

Schoen/Schon
German
Beautiful.

Schoenbrun/Schonbrun
German
Beautiful well; beautiful spring. *'Schönbrun' is the name of a famous palace in Vienna, now used as a museum.*

Scoville
Old French/Old English
Scottish village.

Seabert
Old English
Shining sea.

Seabrook/Seabrooke
Old English
Sea stream.

Seaton
Old English
Sea town.

Sedglea/Sedglee/Sedgleigh/Sedgley/Sedgly
Old English
Sword-shaped grass on the meadow.

Sedgwick
Old English
Sword-shaped grass on the dairy farm.

Seedhouse
Old English
Home where seed is sold.

Seeley/Seelea/Seelee/Seeleigh/Seely
Old English
Blessed, happy meadow; sea meadow; vista of the meadow.

Sefton
Old English
Town in the rushes.

Selby
Old English
House by a farm. *Selby (full name Selby Aloysius Trifle) is a talking dog written about by author Duncan Ball in his series of novels.*

Seldon
Old English
House on a hill.

Selth
German
Shelter.

Sewell
Old English
Stream by the sea.

Seymour
French
Marshland by the sea.

Shae/Shaye/Shay
Irish
Fairy palace.

Shallows
Old English
Low-level of water.

Shannon
Irish
Old one; river; small.

Shaw
Old English
One who resides by the grove; shore.

Sheffield
Old English
Crooked meadow.

Shelby
Old English
By the shells.

Sheldon
Old English
Shell hill.

Shellea/Shellee/Shelleigh/Shelley/Shelly
Old English
Shell meadow. *This house name might also be chosen by an admirer of English poet, Percy Bysshe Shelley (1791–1822) or his wife, writer Mary Wollstonecraft (Godwin) Shelley (1797–1851), author of* Frankenstein.

Shelpy
Old English
Sheep meadow.

Sheplea/Sheplee/Shepleigh/Shepley/Sheply
Old English
Sheep meadow.

Sherborne
Old English/Scottish
Clear stream.

Sherill
Old English
Shire on the hill.

Sherwood
Old English
One who resides at the bright woods. *Sherwood Forest is famed as the home of the legendary Robin Hood. Sherwood Forest can be found in Nottinghamshire, England.*

Shiplea/Shiplee/Shipleigh/Shipley/Shiply
Old English
Sheep meadow.

Silvan/Silvanu
Latin
One who resides in the forest.

Skene
Irish
Bush.

Slade/Sladen
Old English
Valley.

Smedlea/Smedlee/Smadleigh/Smedley/Smedly
Old English
Meadow.

Snedden
Old English
Snow valley.

Snodgrass
Scottish
Smooth grass.

Snowden
Old English
Snow valley.

Snowhill/Snow Hill
Old English
Snow on the hill.

Sol
Latin/Old English
Sun; soil.

Solea/Solee/Soleigh/Soley/Soly
Old English/Latin
Muddy meadow; sunny meadow.

Somerset
Old English
Summer place.

Somerville
Old English
Summer village.

Southee
Old English
From the south.

Sprecklea/Sprecklee/Spreckleigh/Spreckley/Spreckly
Old English
Twiggy meadow.

Springham
Old English
Farm by the stream; village by the spring.

Springmore
Old English
Stream by the marshland.

Springsteen
Old English
Stream of stones. *Bruce Springsteen is an American singer-songwriter, born in New Jersey 1949. He is best known for his* Born in the USA *album, released in 1984.*

Stamford
Old English
Stoney, shallow river crossing.

Stanbury
Old English
Stone fortress.

Stancliff/Stancliffe
Old English
Stoney cliff.

Standfield
Old English
Stoney meadow.

Standwood
Old English
Stoney forest.

Stanhope
Old English
Stoney hollow.

Stanlea/Stanlee/Stanleigh/Stanley/Stanly
Old English
Stoney meadow.

Stanmore
Old English
Stoney marshland.

Stannard
Old English
Hard stone.

Stanway
Old English
Stone path.

Stanwick
Old English
Stone village; stone farm.

Stanwood
Old English
Stoney forest.

Stein
German
Stone.

Stockdale
Old English
Stock in the valley.

Stocklea/Stocklee/Stockleigh/Stockley/Stockly
Old English
Stock in the meadow.

Stockwell
Old English
Well or stream by the stump; stream or well where the stock drink from.

Stone
Old English
Small rock.

Stratford
Old English
Street by the shallow, river crossing. *Stratford-upon-Avon, England, is the birthplace of William Shakespeare.*

Stratton
Old English/Scottish
River town.

Strom
German
River.

Stroud
Old English
Thicket.

Sturt
Old English
Hill.

Styles
Old English
One who resides by the stock enclosure or yard.

Suffield
Old English
Southern meadow.

Sully
Old English
Southern meadow.

Summit
Old English
Mountain peak.

Sutherland
Old English
Southern field.

Suttcliff
Old English
Southern ridge.

Sutton
Old English
Southern town.

Swalea/Swalee/Swaleigh/Swaley/Swaly
Old English
Crooked stream in the meadow.

Swindel
Old English
Pigs in the valley.

Swinford
Old English
Shallow river where the pigs cross over.

T

Tab/Tabbener
Gaelic
Spring.

Tafy
Old English
River.

Tain
Gaelic
Stream.

Talbert
German
Bright valley.

Talcott
Old English
Tall cottage.

Tanton
Old English
Quiet and still river by the town.

Teasdale
Old English
River valley; tea growing in the valley; tea trees growing in the valley.

Templeton
Old English
Temple town.

Terran
Latin
Earth.

Thackaray/Thackeray
Old English
Thorny or reedy nook. *This name might be chosen by an admirer of British novelist, William Makepeace Thackeray (1811–63), author of the satirical novel* Vanity Fair.

The Grange
Middle English/Latin
Large house with smaller buildings surrounding it. *An affectionate name for an old Victorian-style house.*

The Grange House
Middle English/Latin
Large house with smaller buildings surrounding it. *An affectionate name for an old Victorian-style house.*

The Manor
Estate house. *'The Manor' is a popular name for a larger house, especially one resembling an older English style of house where a lord once resided.*

The Manor House
Estate house. (See The Manor)

The Mansion
Middle English/French
The manor house. *The mansion is considered to be the ultimate in owning a home. It is a large, expensive and imposing residence that makes a statement about the wealth and importance of its owner. 'Mansion' may also be used to describe a large building divided into flats or apartments.*

The Oaks Ranch
Old English
Farm with oak trees. *'The Oaks' is also the name of a famous horserace, run annually at Epsom Downs, England. The race was founded in 1779, and some former British colonies have an 'Oaks' race in celebration of the English tradition.*

The Old Mansion/The Olde Mansion
The old estate house. (See The Mansion)

The Outback
English/Australian
Remote, rural area. *The 'Outback' of Australia conjures up images of red dirt and blue sky.*

The Southern Cross
Latin/Old English
Crossing in the south. *The 'Southern Cross' is a star constellation most famous in southern skies. It is depicted on the Australian and New Zealand flags.*

The Southern Cross Cottage
Latin/Old English
The small house by the crossing in the south. (See The Southern Cross)

Thistlewait/Thistlewaite
Old English
Thistle meadow.

Thorlea/Thorlee/Thorleigh/Thorley/Thorly
Old English
Thorny meadow.

Thornlea/Thornlee/Thornleigh/Thornley/Thornly
Old English
Thorny meadow.

Thornton
Old English
Thorny town.

Thorpe
Old English
Village home. *This name might also be chosen by an admirer of champion Australian swimmer, Ian Thorpe.*

Thunderhead
Middle English/Old English
Thick thunderclouds overhead.

Thurlow
Old English
Gapped hill; lower thorns.

Tilden
Old English
To cultivate the fertile valley.

Tilton
Old English
Hill town.

Tingwell
Old English
Home by the stream. *A home bearing this name might also be named in honour of Australian actor Charles ('Bud') Tingwell (b. 1923).*

Top Of The World
Old English
The highest summit.

Topper
Old English
One who resides at the top of the hill. *'Topper' is also a nickname for a top hat.*

Torbert
Old English
Rocky hill with a bright or sunny peak.

Tormod/Tormond
Scottish
Northerner.

Torn
Irish
Small, round hill.

Townlea/Townlee/Townleigh/Townley/Townly
Old English
Town in the meadow.

Townsend
Old English
At the end of the town.

Trafford
Old English
Shallow river crossing in the valley.

Travers
French
Crossroads.

Traytown
Old English
Tree town; three towns.

Tremain
Scottish
Big farm with trees; big farm with three trees.

Trevor
Welsh
Large village home.

Trewick
Cornish/Old English
Tree house; tree village.

Trot
Old English
Trickling stream. *'Trot' was also the nickname of David Copperfield's beloved aunt, Betsy Trotwood in Charles Dickens' novel* David Copperfield.

Trowbridge
Old English
Row of trees by the bridge.

Twin Mountains
Old English
Two mountains that are alike.

Twin Peaks
English/Old English
Two peaks that are alike. Twin Peaks *is a postmodernist TV series created by Mark Frost and David Lynch. The series was set in the fictional US town of Twin Peaks and concerned the puzzle of who killed Laura Palmer, a homecoming queen. ('She's dead. Wrapped in plastic.') The series screened in Australia in 1990–1.*

Twyford
Old English
Two shallow river crossings.

Ty/Tye
Old English
Enclosure.

Tyree
Scottish
Island dweller.

U

Udell
Old English
Yew tree valley.

Ultan
Old German
Noble stone.

Underwood
Old English
Lower forest.

Upcroft
Old English
Higher pasture.

Upton
Old English
High town.

Upwood/Upwoods
Old English
High forest.

Urban
Latin
Of the city.

V

Vada
Latin
Shallow, river crossing; ford.

Vail
Old English
One who resides in the valley.

Vale
Old English
Valley.

Van
Dutch
From.

Vance
Middle English
High place.

Varde
Old French
Green hills.

Varndale
Old English
Fern valley.

Vaughan
Celtic
Small.

Vause/Vaux
Old French
Valley.

Venn
Old English
Marsh.

Vienna Cottage
Hebrew/Latin/Old English
Graceful house. *Vienna is the capital city of Austria.*

Viewmont
Old English/French
Vista of the mountain.

Viewmont Cottage
English/French/Old English
Small house with a vista of the mountain.

Villa Grove
Italian/Old English
Country house in the small, secluded forest.

Vitus
French
Forest. *St Vitus was a legendary martyr known for his gift of healing.*

Von
German
From.

W

Wade
Old English
Water dweller.

Wadlea/Wadlee/Wadleigh/Wadley/Wadly
Old English
Water dweller from the meadow.

Wadsworth
Old English
Estate with a wading pool.

Wakefield
Old English
White meadow.

Waklea/Waklee/Wakleigh/Wakeley/Wakly
Old English
White meadow.

Walby
Old English
Place by a wall.

Walcott
Old English
Cottage near the wall.

Wallingford
Old English
Shallow river crossing by the wall.

Wayland
Old English
Path way; highway.

Waylon
Old English
Land by the highway or pathway.

Welbourn/Welbourne/Wellbourn/Wellbourne
Old English/Scottish
Well by the stream.

Weldon/Welldon
Old English
Spring in the valley. *This name might also be chosen by an admirer of writer Fay Weldon, whose novel* The Life and Loves of a She-Devil *was made into a television series. Weldon published her autobiography,* Auto da Fay *in 2002.*

Welford/Wellford
Old English
Shallow stream crossing.

Welton
Old English
Spring town; town with a well.

Wescott
Old English
Western cottage.

Weslea/Weslee/Wesleigh/Wesley/Wesly
Old English
Western meadow. *John Wesley (1703–91) is remembered as the founder of Methodism. His brother Charles was also a Methodist preacher and wrote many hymns.*

Westlea/Westlee/Westleigh/Westley/Westly
Old English
Western meadow.

Weston
Old English
Western town.

Whallea/Whallee/Whalleigh/Whalley/Whally
Old English
Meadow hall; wall in the meadow.

Wharton
Old English
Wharf town.

Wheatlea/Wheatlee/Wheatleigh/Wheatley/Wheatly
Old English
Wheat meadow.

Wheaton
Old English
Wheat town.

Whitaker
Old English
White meadow.

Whitby
Old English
Near the white place.

Whitcombe
Old English
White cottage.

Whitford
Old English
White, shallow river crossing.

Whitlea/Whitlee/Whitleigh/Whitley/Whitly
Old English
White meadow.

Wicklea/Wicklee/Wickleigh/Wickley/Wickly
Old English
Willow meadow in the village.

Wildon
Old English
Hill in the forest; wild hill.

Wilea/Wilee/Wileigh/Wiley/Wily
Old English
Meadow with willow trees.

Wilford
Old English
Shallow river crossing by the willow trees.

Wiloughby
Old English
Farm with willow trees close by.

Winchell
Old English
Windy corner.

Windell/Wyndell
Old English
Windy valley.

Windham/Wyndham
Old English
Windy village; windy farm. *'John Wyndham' was the pen-name of English science fiction writer, John Beynon Harris (1903–69). His novels include* The Day of the Triffids, *a story about an invasion by mobile carnivorous plants, which was made into a film directed by Steve Sekely in 1962.*

Windsor
Old English
Windy, river bend.

Winfield/Wynfield
Old English
Friendly meadow.

Winston/Wynston
Old English
Friendly town. *'Winston' is the middle name of Australian Prime Minister John Howard (b. 1930) and also singer/songwriter John Lennon (1940–80). Sir Winston Churchill (1874–1965) was Prime Minister of the United Kingdom during World War II.*

Winterdell
Old English
Winter valley; cold valley.

Wolcott
Old English
Cottage in the forest.

Woodburn Cottage
Old English/Scottish
Small house by the forest stream.

Woodfield
Old English
Forest meadow.

Woodford
Old English
Shallow river crossing in the woods.

Woodford Estate
Old English
Large, stately house by the forest river crossing.

Woodlands
Old English
Forest land.

Woodlea/Woodlee/Woodleigh/Woodley/Woodly
Old English
Forest meadow.

Woodrow
Old English
Forest pathway.

Woodville
Old English
Forest village.

Worchester
Old English
Army camp in the forest.

Worth
Old English
Farm; farmstead; enclosure

Worthy
Old English
Enclosure.

Worton
Old English
Farm town.

Wriston
Old English
Town with shrubs.

Wycliff
Old English
Village on the cliff.

Wyndham
Old English
Windy farm; windy village (See Windham).

Wythe
Middle English
Willow tree.

Y

Yardslea/Yardslee/Yardsleigh/Yardsley/ Yardsly
Old English
Land in the meadow.

Yates
Old English
Gates.

York
Celtic
Yew tree farm.

CHAPTER 8

GRAND OLD LADIES AND GENTLEMEN OF DISTINCTION

Older style houses, especially those of the Victorian era, may be known affectionately as 'The Grand Old Dame', or 'The Grand Old Lady', by their owners. Other houses may have a feminine air about them that would exhibit a female name well. A prominent example of this type of naming is the house 'Tara' in *Gone with the Wind.*

Just as some houses have a feminine feel about them, others may have a masculine ambience that calls for a male name. One of the best examples used in Britain, Scotland and Australia is 'Glen'. 'Glen' can be added to other masculine names to come up with further examples: 'Glenrowan', 'Glenroy' or 'Glengary'. Other names such as 'Charles' (Charleston), 'Stan' (Stanwick) or 'Ray' (Raywood), also feature strongly in masculine house names.

A

Adelaide
Teutonic
Noble. *Adelaide is the capital city of South Australia.*

Adelaide Hills
Teutonic/Old English
Noble hills.

Adorlee/Adorlea/Adorleigh/Adorley/Adorly
French/Old English
From the adorable meadow.

Airlea Cottage/Airlee Cottage/Airleigh Cottage/Airley Cottage/Airly Cottage/Airlie Cottage
Scottish/Old English
Small house in the airy meadow.

Airlea Court/Airlee Court/Airleigh Court/Airley Court/Airly Court
Old English
The airy courtyard.

Alansdale/Alandale
Irish/Gaelic/Old English
Handsome valley.

Albert Cottage
German/Old English
Small house of noble, industrious and famous one.

Alexanderville
Greek/Old English
Village of the defender of humankind.

Alexandra Cottage
Greek/Old English
Small house of the defender for humankind.

Alexandria
Greek/Old English
Defender of humankind. *Alexandria is a city in Egypt built by the Greek architect Dinocrates (332–1 BC) and named after Alexander the Great.*

Alfredton
Old English
The old counsellor's town.

Alma
Latin/Old English
Nourishing, small house.

Almeric Manor
Old German/Old English
Powerful estate house.

Alston
Old English
The noble town.

Amberton
Old French/Old English
Amber jewel town.

Amelia Court
Teutonic/Old English
The hard working one's courtyard.

Amity Gardens
Latin/Old English
Friendly gardens.

Anastasia
Greek
Resurrection; springtime. *Anastasia Romanov, born 1901, was the youngest daughter of Nicholas II. The mystery surrounding Anastasia's fate after the Russian Revolution in 1918 is one of the biggest mysteries of the twentieth century.*

Angelica
Greek
Messenger of God.

Annabella
Latin/French
Lovable and graceful.

Annabelle
Latin/French
Lovable and graceful.

Ammon Estate
Egyptian/Old English
Hidden, large and stately house.

Anguston
Scottish/Gaelic/Old English
Venerable town; town of supreme dignity or grandeur.

Anno Cottage
Celtic/Old English
Small, graceful house.

Anthony Estate
Latin/Old English
Priceless, large and stately home.

Apollo Manor
Greek/Old English
Bright estate house. *Apollo in Greek mythology is the god of prophesy, music and healing.*

April Brooke/April Brook
Old English
Small stream that appears (due to rain) in the month of April.

Archibald
Old German
Very brave; bold; valuable. *The Archibald Prize is Australia's premier portraiture award. The 2004 winner was Craig Ruddy for his portrait of Australian actor David Gulpilil titled* Two Worlds.

Arjuna House
Sanskrit/Old English
White home.

Armon
Hebrew
Castle.

Arnfinn Cottage
Old Norse/Old English
Small, white house.

Ashdale
Old English
Ash tree valley.

Ashlea Cottage/Ashlee Cottage/Ashleigh Cottage/Ashley Cottage/Ashly Cottage
Old English
Small house in the ash tree meadow.

Ashlea Court/Ashlee Court/Ashleigh Court/Ashley Court/Ashly Court
Old English
Ash trees growing in the courtyard meadow.

Ashlea Grove/Ashlee Grove/Ashleigh Grove/Ashley Grove/Ashly Grove
Old English
Small, ash tree wood in the meadow.

Atherton
Old English
Small house by the stream in the town. *The Atherton Tablelands are situated in Tropical Queensland and feature World Heritage listed rainforests, abundant wildlife and rich agricultural land.*

Atholton
Old English/Gaelic
Dweller in the hollowed area; from Ireland; small Irish house. *Maybe the people who reside in this house are Irish or have an Irish ancestry.*

Audric
Old English
Town with the wise ruler.

B

Barclay
Old English
Clay meadow where birch trees grow.

Barden Cottage
Old English
Small house in the barley hill; small, hill house owned by the poet.

Barlow
Old English
Lower barley field.

Bartley
Old English
Barley meadow.

Barton Cottage
Old English
Small house in the barley town.

Bartonvale
Old English
Barley town in the valley.

Beatrice Brae
Latin/Scottish
Bringer of happiness to the hillside. *Princess Beatrice (b. 1988) is the eldest daughter of Prince Andrew The Duke of York and Sarah Ferguson.*

Beatrix
Latin/Scottish
Bringer of joy and happiness. *Beatrix Potter (1866–1943) was the illustrator and author of* The Tale of Peter Rabbit *(1902).*

Bella Court
Italian/Old English
Beautiful courtyard.

Bella Manor
Italian/Old English
Beautiful estate house.

Belle Castle
Italian/Old English
Beautiful, fortified estate house.

Belle Manor
Italian/Old English
Beautiful estate house.

Beaumont
French
Beautiful mountain.

Bennes
Czech
Blessed.

Bentley
Old English
Meadow marshland.

Bergren
Scandinavian
Mountain stream.

Berkley
Old English/Irish
Birch tree meadow.

Berkley Cottage
Old English/Irish
Small house in the birch tree meadow.

Berkleyvale
Old English/Irish
Birch trees in the valley meadow.

Bethania
Aramaic
From the house of God's grace.

Bethany
Aramaic
From the house of God's grace.

Bonny Cottage
Scottish/Old English
Small, pretty and good house.

Bonny Hills
Scottish/Old English
Pretty hills.

Bonny Manor
Scottish/Old English
Pretty estate house.

Bonnyvale
Scottish/Old English
Pretty valley.

Bradshaw Manor
Old English
Estate house by the wide shore.

Bradwell Manor
Old English
Estate house by the wide stream or well.

Brandon Cottage
Old English/Irish
Small house of the raven.

Brontë House
Gaelic/Old English
House presented as a gift or honour. *Charlotte (1816–55), Emily (1818–48) and Anne (1820–49) Brontë are not only sisters but also famous authors. Charlotte wrote* Jane Eyre, *Emily wrote* Wuthering Heights *and Anne wrote* Agnes Grey.

Burley Manor
Old English
Castle meadow.

C

Caldwell
Old English
The old, cold stream or well.

Calliope Cottage
Greek/Old English
Small house of the muse. *Calliope in Greek mythology was the muse of epic poetry.*

Calliope Court
Greek/Old English
Courtyard of the muse.

Calypso Manor
Greek/Old English
Hidden estate house. Calypso *was the name of the ship used by Jacques Cousteau, the famous oceanographer.*

Camlo
Gypsy
Lovely.

Carlton Cottage
Old English
Small house in the courageous town.

Carmelita
Latin
Song of light.

Chandler's Cottage
Old French
Small house where the candle maker resides.

Chantelle Cottage
French/Old English
Small house owned by the singer.

Chantelle Estate
French/Old English
Large, stately house owned by the singer.

Chaplin
Old English
One in charge of the chapel. *Charlie Chaplin (1889–1977) was a famous actor in silent films. His first film,* Making a Living, *was made in 1914.*

Charleston
Old English/Old German/Old French
Strong and courageous town.

Charlotte Cottage
Latin/Old English
Small house where the courageous one resides.

Charlotte's Web Cottage
French/Old English
Small, strong house with a spider web. Charlotte's Web *is a much-loved children's book by Elwyn Brooks White. A cartoon movie of* Charlotte's Web *was made in 1973. It is about a pig named Wilbur and a spider named Charlotte who strike up a friendship and try to save Wilbur from the dinner table.*

Chatham
Old English
The warrior's farm or village.

Chatham Cottage
Old English
Small house where the warrior resides; small farm where the warrior resides; small village where the warrior resides.

Chelsea Cottage
Old English
Small house by the shipping port. *The Chelsea Flower Show is a famous garden show in England that is even attended by Queen Elizabeth, the Duke of Edinburgh and other members of the royal family.*

Chelsea Court
Old English
Courtyard by the shipping port. (See Chelsea Cottage)

Chelsea Manor
Old English
Estate house by the shipping port. (See Chelsea Cottage)

Chik
Gypsy
Earth.

Churchill
Old English
Church on the hill. *Sir Winston Churchill (1874–1965) was Prime Minister of Great Britain from 1940–5 and again from 1951–5. A memorial trust in his name established the Churchill Fellowship in Australia in 1965.*

Claire Cottage
Latin/Old English
Small, brilliant house.

Claire Court
Latin/Old English
Brilliant courtyard.

Clairedale/Clairesdale
Latin/Old English
Brilliant valley.

Claraville
Latin/Old English
Brilliant village.

Claremont
Latin/French
Brilliant mountain.

Clay Cottage
Old English
Small house made of earth.

Claybourn/Claybourne/Clayburn/Clayburne
Old English/Scottish
Clay stream.

Clifton Cottage
Old English
Small house by the cliff town.

Clydedale
Scottish/Gaelic/Old English
High and rocky valley.

Cobham
Old English
Homestead by the river bend; farm by the river bend; village by the river bend.

Cobham Cottage
Old English
Small home by the river bend; small farmhouse by the river bend; small house in the village by the river bend.

Cobham House
Old English
Home by the river bend; farm house by the river bend; small home in the village by the river bend.

Coburn
Old English/Scottish
Where the streams meet.

Coburn Cottage
Scottish/Old English
Small house where the streams meet.

Constance Cottage
Latin/Old English
Small, steadfast house.

Constance Court
Latin/Old English
Steadfast courtyard.

Coopernook
Old English
The barrel maker's small and secluded place.

Covington
Old English
Town by the bay.

Covington Cottage
Old English
Small house in the bay town.

Covington Estate
Old English
Large, stately home in the bay town.

Covington Manor
Old English
Estate house in the bay town.

Craigellach/Craigellachie/Craigelloch/Craigellochie
Scottish
Rocky meadow by the lake.

Craiglea Cottage
Scottish/Old English
Small house in the rocky meadow.

Craigston Cottage
Scottish/Old English
Small house in the rocky town.

Cromwell
Old English
Winding stream.

Cromwell Cottage
Old English
Small house by the winding stream.

Cromwell House
Old English
Home by the winding stream.

Culley
Irish
Forest.

D

Dal
Scandinavian
Valley.

Dale
Old English
Valley.

Dale Cottage
Old English
Small house in the valley.

Dalman
Australian Aboriginal
The place of plenty.

Dalston Cottage
Old English
Small house in the valley town.

Dame Manor
Old English
The estate house owned by the Dame. *Dame is a title given to a woman in the Order of the British Empire and in the Order of Australia. Dame Edna Everage is arguably the most famous Dame. Her character was invented by and played by Barry Humphries.*

Dannon
Old English
Gathering in the meadow.

Darby Cottage
Old English
Small house of freedom.

Dawn Cottage
Old English
Small house able to be seen at dawn.

Dawson Manor
Old English
Estate house owned by the son of the beloved.

Devon House
Irish/Old English
The poet's house.

Devonshire
Irish/Old English
The poet's county; people of the deep valley. *Devonshire has a long association with the breeding of dairy cattle and the production of dairy product as well as the Devon sausage. Devonshire teas traditionally consist of a pot of tea and scones with jam and cream. It is believed to have originated from the county of Devon in England and is famed throughout the United Kingdom, India, Australia and New Zealand.*

Dietrich Manor
Teutonic/Old English
Wealthy estate house. *'Marlene Dietrich' was the stage and screen name of Maria Magdalene von Losch (1904–92). Sometimes billed as 'the world's most glamorous grandmother', she enjoyed a career as a singer, actress and cabaret performer spanning almost five decades.*

Dixon Cottage
English/Old English
Small house owned by the powerful ruler's son.

Donnell Estate
Irish/Old English
Large, dark and stately house.

Dunmore Manor
Old English
Estate house by the brown fort in the marshland.

Dunstan
Old English
Small house on the hill, made from brown stones.

Dural
Australian Aboriginal
Smoke rising from the hollow.

E

Earlmont
Old English/French
The perfect mountain; the earl's mountain.

Eaton/Eton
Old English
Estate town by the river; eastern town. *'Eaton' is the name of a small town in Western Australia, situated near the mouth of the Collie River. Eton is a famous English public school, founded by Henry VI in 1440.*

Eden Croft/Edencroft
Old English
Small pasture paradise.

Edithvale
Old English
Prosperous, happy village

Edwardton
Old English
Town of the wealthy, ruling guardian.

Elwellton
Old English
Town with the old well.

Elizabeth Cottage
Hebrew/Old English
Small house that is sacred to God. *The most famous Elizabeths are Queen Elizabeth I and II; Elizabeth Taylor (b. 1932) is another. Her beautiful violet-coloured eyes brought her fame as a child and at twelve she starred in* National Velvet. *Elizabeth also made* Cat on a Hot Tin Roof, Who's Afraid of Virginia Woolf? *and in 1960 won an Oscar for Best Actress for* Butterfield 8.

Ellentree Cottage
Scottish/Gaelic/Old English
Small, bright house by the tree.

Emily House
French/German/English
Home of the flatterer. *Emily Brontë (1818–48) was one of the famed Brontë sisters and she wrote the novel* Wuthering Heights.

Erin Cottage
Celtic/Old English
Small house on the western island; small house of peace. *'Erin' is also another name for Ireland.*

Erindale
Irish//Old English
Valley of peace; valley on the western island; valley in Ireland. (See Erin Cottage)

Erinvale
Irish/Old English
Valley of peace; valley on the western island; valley in Ireland. (See Erin Cottage)

Erinville
Irish/Old English
Village of peace; village on the western island. (See Erin Cottage)

Estella Estate
Latin/Old English
Large, stately house under the stars.

Estelle Estate
Latin/Old English
Large, stately house under the stars.

Evaline
French/Hebrew
Life.

Evanslea
Welsh/Old English
Well-born meadow.

Evanth Court/Evanthe Court
Greek/Old English
Flowers in the courtyard.

Evelyn
Hebrew/Welsh
Pool of life.

F

Farrington
Old English
The blacksmith's town.

Fielding House
Old English
Home by the meadow.

Floranz
Latin
Flowering.

Florence Cottage
Latin/Old English
Small cottage of blossoming flowers.

Florent
French
Flowering.

Florentino
Spanish/Latin
Blossoming flowers

Florian
Latin
Flowering.

Florus
Latin
Flowering.

Francis Cottage
Latin/French/English
Small house by the blossoming flowers.

G

Galt
Norwegian
High ground.

Galton House
Old English
Rented house in the town.

Garryowen
Old English/Welsh
The well-born spear carrier.

George's Cottage
Old English
The farmer's small house.

Gilmore
Irish/Old English
Devoted one from the marshland. *Dame Mary Gilmore (1865–1962) was a famous Australian writer remembered as an activist for peace and social change as well as for her literary achievements.*

Ginger Cottage
Old English
Small house where ginger is grown. *Ginger Rogers (Virginia Katherine McMath, 1911–95) was a US film actor and dancer, who rose to fame for her performances in musicals, particularly dancing with Fred Astaire. Ginger Meggs was the red-headed boy hero of the popular comic strip of the same name, created by Australian cartoonist Jimmy Bancks. Bancks began the comic strip in 1922 and continued it until his death in 1952.*

Glenbank/Glennbank
Scottish/Old English
Valley by the shore.

Glenbrook/Glenbrooke/Glennbrook/ Glennbrooke
Scottish/Old English
Stream in the valley.

Gleneden/Glenneden
Scottish/Old English
Valley paradise.

Glenelm/Glennelm
Scottish/Old English
Valley of elm trees.

Glenhope/Glennhope
Scottish/Old English
Valley of hope.

Glenpark/Glennpark
Scottish/Old English
Valley recreational area.

Glenrowan
Scottish
Rowan-tree valley. *Glenrowan is a small town at the foot of the Warby Ranges in Victoria, Australia. It is infamously known as the place Ned Kelly had his last stand.*

Glenroy/Glennroy
Scottish
The king's valley.

Glennthorne/Glennthorne/Glenthorn/ Glenthorne
Scottish/Old English
Prickly valley.

Gloriavilla
Latin/Italian
Glorious, country home.

Glorien
Latin
Glorious.

Godiva
Old English
Gift of God. *The tale of Lady Godiva (1057) began when she was so distressed about the taxing of the people in Coventry that she struck up a deal with her husband. He stated that he'd change the tax if she rode through the village on her horse naked, never thinking she would do it, but she did. The villagers were asked to stay inside and not look. They did as asked, except for a boy called Tom who did peep, hence the phrase 'peeping Tom'. Her husband kept his word and abolished the heavy tax.*

Graceton
Latin
Graceful town.

Graham/Grahame
Old English
Grey-coloured house. *Scottish author Kenneth Grahame (1859–1932) was famous for his children's stories. His best-known story* The Wind in the Willows *was published in 1908. Alternatively the name 'Graham' might be chosen by an admirer of any of several famous Grahams, including US evangelist Billy Graham, Australian golfer David Graham, and US dancer and choreographer Martha Graham.*

Grantland Court
Old English
Courtyard on the grand field.

Gratiana
Hebrew
Graceful.

Griselda Manor
Teutonic
The estate house of the war heroine.

Grosvenor Manor
Old French
Estate house of the great chief hunter resides.

Guildford
Old English
Yellow flowers by the shallow river crossing.

Guinevere
Welsh
White wave. *Guinevere was King Arthur's queen.*

Gwendolyn
Welsh
White moon.

H

Hadley Manor
Old English
Estate house in the heather meadow.

Hagan House
Irish/Old English
Ruler of the house.

Hagley Manor
Old English
Estate house with a hedged meadow.

Halbrook/Halbrooke
Old English
Stream in the valley; hall by the brook.

Halen
Swedish
Hall.

Halford
Old English
Shallow, river crossing by the valley.

Halifax
Old English
Holy field. *Halifax is the capital city of Nova Scotia in Canada as well as a town in West Yorkshire in England.*

Hallward
Old English
Guardian of the hall.

Hamilton
Old English
Proud town; crooked hill.

Hamilton Manor
Old English
Estate house in the proud town.

Hamlet
Old French
Little village; little home. Hamlet *was written by William Shakespeare around 1600.*

Hamlin
Old English
Village pond or pool.

Hammond
Old English
Village.

Hammond Cottage
Old English
Small house in the village.

Hammond House
Old English
Home in the village.

Hamon
Teutonic
Home.

Hampton
Old English
Proud town. *The Hamptons is a resort-style community of villages located on New York's Long Island. It is well known for its gourmet foods, wine, beaches and art scene.*

Hanford
Old English
From the high, shallow river crossing.

Hanley
Old English
High meadow.

Harden Cottage
Old English
Small house in the hare valley.

Hardy Cottage
Teutonic/Old English
Small, bold and daring house.

Harford
Old English
Hares by the shallow river crossing.

Harley Manor
Old English
Estate house in the hare meadow.

Harpers Cottage
Old English
Small house where the harp player resides.

Harrington
Old English
The army ruler's town.

Harrison
Old English
Son of the army ruler. *Harrison Ford (b. 1942) is an American actor who had his breakthrough role of Han Solo in* Star Wars *(1977). He is also known for the movies* The Fugitive *(1993),* Raiders of the Lost Ark *(1981) and* What Lies Beneath *(2000).*

Harrysville/Harryville
Old English/Scandinavian
The army ruler's village. *Prince Harry is the youngest child of Prince (of Wales) Charles (b. 1948) and Princess Diana (1961–97). His full name is Prince Henry Charles Albert David Windsor (b. 1984).*

Harwood Estate
Old English
Large, stately house by the hare forest.

Heathcliff/Heathcliffe
Old English
Heather by the ledge. *Heathcliff is the hero of Emily Brontë's only novel,* Wuthering Heights.

Heatherdale
Old English
Heather valley.

Heaton Cottage
Old English
Small house in the high town.

Heaton House
Old English
Home in the high town.

Heinrich Cottage
German/Old English
Ruler of the small house.

Hendrix House
Dutch/German/Old English
Ruler of the small house. *Jimi Hendrix (1942–70) was a guitarist known for songs such as 'The Wind Cries Mary' and 'Purple Haze'.*

Henley House
Old English
House in the high meadow. *Don Henley (b. 1947) is the most successful solo performer of the super-group The Eagles. He has had hit songs with 'All She Wants to Do Is Dance' and 'Boys of Summer'.*

Henrick
Dutch/German
Ruler of the home.

Hester Cottage
Greek/Old English
Small house under the evening star.

Holbrook
Old English
Hollow by the small stream. *Holbrook is a town in southern New South Wales Australia. It has had many previous names including Ten Mile Creek (1838) and German Town (1876) and changed to its current name in 1914, named after Submarine Commander Norman Douglas Holbrook.*

Holcomb Cottage
Old English
Small house in the deep valley.

Holly Cottage
Old English
Small house with holly growing near by; small, holy house. *This house would generally be located by a church.*

Houghton Estate
Old English
Grey-coloured town on a steep bank.

Houston
Old English
The intelligent town.

Hughesville
Old English
The intelligent village. *Hugh Grant (b. 1960) is an English actor known for such movies as* Four Weddings and a Funeral, Bridget Jones's Diary *and* Bridget Jones: The Edge of Reason.

Huntington
Old English
The hunter's town.

Hurley Cottage
Old English
Small house in the wood clearing meadow.

Hurst House
Old English
Home on the hill with a forest.

Hyatt Cottage
Old English
Small house with a high gate.

Hyatt Manor
Old English
Estate house with a high gate.

Hyde Cottage
Old English
Small house on the acreage.

I

Ilysa
Latin
Blissful.

Ivanhoe
Hebrew
God's gracious soil tiller.

J

Jacinta Cottage
Greek/Spanish/Old English
Small house where hyacinths grow; purple-coloured house.

Jericho
Arabic
Moon city. *Jericho is an ancient city located 36 kilometres east of Jerusalem and is frequently mentioned in* The Bible.

K

Kareela
Australian Aboriginal
Southern wind.

Keighley
Irish/Old English
The pure one's meadow.

Kellyton
Irish/Gaelic/Old English
The warrior's town.

Keniworth/Kenniworth
Old Welsh
Valued relation; bright and clear water; valued farm.

Kenwood
Old English
The warrior's forest.

Kiley House
Old English
House on narrow land.

Kimberley Court
Old English
Royal meadow courtyard.

Kiraville/Kirraville
Maori/Old English
Tree bark village.

Kirton House
Old English
House in the church town.

Kyle
Irish
From the strait.

L

Langdon House
Old English
Home on the long hill.

Langley
Old English
Long meadow.

Larsondale
Swedish/Old English
Victory valley. *Garry Larson (b. 1950) is the author and cartoonist of many books, cards and calendars and the very funny 'The Far Side' cartoons.*

Laurel Cottage
Latin/Old English
Small house by the laurel tree; small house of victory.

Laurel Manor
Latin/Old English
Estate house by the laurel tree; victorious estate house.

Laurelton
Latin/Old English
Laurel tree town; victorious town.

Laurieton
Latin/Old English
Laurel tree town; victorious town.

Lawley House
Old English
House on the lower meadow.

Lawson Flats
Latin/Old English
Victorious meadows. *Henry Lawson (1867–1922) was a great Australian poet and writer known for being able to capture the spirit of Australians in his prose. Some of his poems are* While the Billy Boils, The Ballad of the Drover *and* The Glass on the Bar.

Lealee/Lealeigh/Lealey/Leelea/Leelee/Leeleigh/Leeley/Leighlea/Leighlee/Leighleigh/Leighley/Leylea/Leylee/Leyleigh/Leyley
Old English
Meadows.

Leeland
Old English
Shelter; meadows.

Lincoln
Old English
Place by the pond or pool. *Abraham Lincoln (1809–65) was the sixteenth American president.*

Lindsay Manor
Old English
Estate house on the linden tree island; estate house on the lime tree island.

Linleigh/Linlea/Linlee/Linley/Linly
Old English
Meadow pond.

Lorelei's Cottage
German/Old English
The small house of the alluring one; small house in the victorious meadow. *In Germanic legend Lorelei was a siren who lured sailors on the Rhine River to their deaths with her song.*

Lorinda
Italian
Victory.

Lynton
Old English
Spring town; pool or pond town.

M

Macharios
Greek
Blessed.

Mackenzie Manor
Irish/Old English
Estate house of the wise and handsome leader.

Maldon Manor
Old English
Estate house meeting place in the wood hollow. *Maldon is a town in Victoria established during the gold rush.*

Marcellus Manor
Latin/Old English
Estate house of the warrior.

Marshall Manor
Old French
Horse groom at the estate house.

Maxvale
Latin/Old English
The extreme valley.

Maxwell
Latin/Old English
The extreme stream.

Melbourne
Old English
Mill stream. *Melbourne (founded 1835) is the capital city of Victoria, Australia. It is well known for its arts, gourmet food and multiculturalism.*

Melbourne Cottage
Old English
Small house by the mill stream. (See Melbourne)

Melbourne Manor
Old English
Estate house by the mill stream. (See Melbourne)

Mercedes Estate
Spanish/Old English
Large, rewarding, stately house.

Merlindale
Welsh/Old English
Fort in the valley overlooking the sea. *Merlin is the wizard in the legend of King Arthur.*

Miranda Moor
Latin/Old English
Worthy of more love; one who loves the marshland. Miranda *was a movie made in 1948 about a mermaid who is caught by fishermen and rescued from them.*

Mitchellvale
Old English
Big valley.

Mona Vale/Monavale
Celtic/Irish/Old English
Gentle valley. *Mona Vale is a northern beach suburb of Sydney, NSW.*

Montez
Spanish
Mountain.

Moorak
Australian Aboriginal
Mountain.

Moreland
Old English
Marshland.

Morganville
Celtic/Old English
Village by the sea.

Murrayton
Scottish/Celtic/Old English
Sailor from the settlement town.

N

Nathanael/Nathaniel
Hebrew
Gift of God.

Nayland
Old English
From the island.

Neville Cottage
Old English
Small house in the new village.

Octavious
Latin
Eighth. *Caius Octavius was adopted by his uncle Julius Caesar and became Caius Julius Caesar Octavianus although he is better known by his imperial title Augustus. He was the first Roman Emperor.*

Old Susannah
Hebrew/Old English
Old, graceful lily.

Orlando
Italian
Famous. *Orlando Bloom (b.1977) is an English actor who starred in* The Lord of the Rings *(2001, 2002, 2003) movies as Legolas and also appeared in* Ned Kelly *(2003). Orlando is also a city in Orange County, Florida, most famous for Walt Disney World, Universal Studios and Sea World. Virginia Woolf's novel* Orlando, *published in 1928, concerned a person who changed sex during the course of a 400-year long life and explored the nature of sexual identity. Vittore Emanuele Orlando (1860–1952) was an Italian statesman.*

Orville
Old French
Golden city. *Orville (1871–1948) and Wilbur (1867–1912) Wright invented and built the first controllable airplane.*

Parker Cottage
Old English
Small house by the recreational area.

Parkglen/Parkglenn
Old English/Scottish
Recreational area in the valley.

Patrickmore
Latin/Old English
Noble marshland.

Patton
Old English
The warrior's town.

Pelham
Old English
Village with a stream.

Pembroke
Celtic/Welsh
Headland; hill stream.

Queensberry
Old English
Where the queen's berries grow; the queen's shire or castle.

Queenscliff
Old English
The cliff by the queen's residence.

Queensland
Old English
The queen's land. *Queensland is a state in Australia known as 'The Sunshine State', due to its tropical climate.*

Queenswood
Old English
The queen's forest.

Ransford
Old English
The raven's shallow river crossing.

Raydon
Old English
Rye hill; hill stream.

Rayfield
Old English
Rye meadow; stream meadow.

Rayford
Old English
Rye by the shallow river crossing.

Rayleen
French
Royal meadow.

Raywood
Old French/Old English
The king's forest; rye forest; sunshine rays filtering through the forest; stream in the forest.

Rembrandt Cottage
Old English
Small, fiery house. *Rembrandt (1606–1669) was a famous Dutch painter and engraver of landscapes, portraits and Biblical scenes.*

Rexford
Old English
The king's ford.

Rexton
Old English
The king's town.

Rhiannon
Welsh/Gaelic
Sorceress. *Rhiannon is part of Welsh legend. She was married to Pwyll and gave birth to a son who disappeared. The servants claimed Rhiannon killed him and her punishment was to carry strangers on her back as though she were a packhorse. The son Pryderi was found by a couple in the woods and raised as their own until his identity was discovered and he was returned. 'Rhiannon' is also the title of a song by Fleetwood Mac.*

Robin's Nest
Old English
The nest of the robin bird. Robin's Nest *was also the title of a popular British TV sitcom that screened during the 1970s and early 1980s.*

Rochester
Old English
Stone camp. *Rochester is a city that has the second oldest Cathedral in England.*

Romney
Welsh
Curving river.

Rosalie
Latin/Old English
From the rose meadow.

Rowan Cottage
Old Norse/Old English
Small house by the mountain ash tree.

Rowanville
Old English
Village with mountain ash trees.

Rowley
Old English
Rough forest clearing.

Roxbury
Old English
Castle fortress.

Roxbury Cottage
Old English
Small house or castle fortress.

Roystone
Old French/Old English
The king's stone.

Rudyard
Old English
Red yard.

Russell's Retreat
Old French/Old English
The fox's refuge; the red haired one's refuge.

Rutherglen
Old English/Scottish
Castle in the valley. *'Rutherglen' is a very popular name for properties, houses and towns. It is also the name of a small town in Victoria, Australia, known for its wines.*

Saraville
Hebrew/Old English
The princess's village; the barren village.

Seaton House
Old English
House in the sea town.

Shakespeare Cottage
Old English
Small house inspired by or named after William Shakespeare. *Shakespeare (1564–1616) was born in Stratford-upon-Avon. He is often claimed to be the greatest English playwright, with such plays as* The Tempest, Midsummer Night's Dream *and* Macbeth, *to name just a few.*

Shannon Cottage
Irish/Gaelic/Old English
Small house by the slow moving stream.

Shannon Manor
Irish/Gaelic/Old English
Estate house by the slow moving stream.

Shelton
Old English
Shell town.

Shipley
Old English
Sheep meadow.

Sidwell
Old English
Wide stream.

Skye Villa/Sky Villa
Old English/Italian
Country house under the sky.

Stanbury
Old English
Stone fortress.

Stanfield
Old English
Stone meadow.

Stanley Manor
Old English
Estate house in the stony meadow.

Stanmoore
Old English
Stony marshland.

Stanwick
Old English
Stony village.

Sturt Estate
Old English
Large, stately house on the hill.

T

Tara
Irish/Gaelic
Rocky hill. *'Tara' is the name of the plantation in* Gone with the Wind, *a novel by Margaret Mitchell that in 1939 was made into a movie starring Vivien Leigh and Clark Gable.*

Tara Manor
Irish/Gaelic/Old English
Estate house on the rocky hill. (See Tara)

Taraville
Irish/Gaelic
Village on the rocky hill. (See Tara)

The Baron's Manor House
Old English
The noble one's estate house.

The Grand/The Grande
French/English
The great.

The Grand Dame/The Grande Dame
French/Old English
The most eminent & experienced woman in her field; the old, respected and much loved house. *This is an affectionate name given to an old house.*

The Grand Old Lady/The Old Lady/The Olde Lady
Old English
The old, respected and much loved house. *This is an affectionate name given to an old house.*

The Imperial
Middle English/French/Latin
Royal; the royal place. *Many hotels, pubs, bars and places of accommodation are named 'The Imperial' to draw in patrons with their supposed air of royalty.*

The Old Lass
Old English/Scottish
The old girl; the old, respected and much loved house. *This is an affectionate name given to an old house.*

The Painted Lady
Old English
Prostitute; woman wearing makeup; colourful house.

The Regent
Old English
One who exercises ruling power in place of a sovereign deemed unable to rule (for example because of absence, illness or infancy).

The Victorian House
Latin/Old English
Victorious home. *The name for a Victorian-style (1837–1901) house; an affectionate name for an old house.*

The Victorian Lady
Latin/Old English/Middle English/English
The victorious lady; a lady of the Victorian era. *A name for an old Victorian-style (1837–1901) house. An affectionate name for an old house.*

The Warren
Middle English
A whole in the ground where an animal, especially a rabbit or fox resides.

Thomaston
Aramaic/Hebrew/Old English
Twin towns.

Thornton
Old English
Prickly town.

Tucker's Cottage
Old English
Small house where the cloth tucker resides.

Ulrich Manor
Teutonic
Fierce ruler of the estate house.

Ulysses
Latin/Greek
Wrathful. *In Homer's epic poem* The Odyssey *he writes about the tales of the wanderer Ulysses.*

Valentine Cottage
Italian/Old English
Small house where the sweethearts reside. *This cottage may also have been built, bought or given as a gift on St Valentine's Day, 14 February.*

Verina
Latin
Faithful.

Verity House
Latin/Old English
True home.

Victor Estate
Old English
Victorious manor house.

Victoria Cottage
Latin/Old English
Small house of victory. *Queen Alexandrina Victoria (1819–1901) or Queen Victoria as she was known, was Queen of England from 1838 until her death in 1901.*

Victoria Croft/Victoriacroft
Latin/Old English
Small, victorious pasture.

Victoria House
Latin/Old English
Victory house.

Violet Cottage
Latin/French/Old English
Small house with violets flowers; purple-coloured house.

Violeta Manor/Violetta Manor
Latin/French/Old English
Estate house with violet flowers; purple-coloured estate house. *'Violetta' is the name of the heroine in Verdi's opera* La Traviata.

Virginia
Latin
Purity. *Virginia is a state in the USA and features the Allegheny and Blue Ridge mountains and the Shenandoah Valley.*

Virginia Cottage
Latin/Old English
Small, pure house. (See Virginia)

Wentworth
Old English
The white estate.

Williamton
Old English
The wilful one's town.

Xavier
Basque
New home owner.

Xavion
Basque
New home owner.

Xion
Hebrew
The guarded land.

Yardley
Old English
From the enclosure. *Yardley London is a perfume company that started making soaps in 1770. Its trademark scent was lavender.*

York
Old English
Yew tree farm.

Zoe
Greek
Life.

Zoia
Russian
Life. Zoia *is a novel by Danielle Steele.*

Zoia Cottage
Russian/Old English
Small house of life.

Zola/Zolah
Italian
Mound or earth. *Emile Zola (1840–1902) was a famous French novelist.*

CHAPTER 9

MY COTTAGE, MY CALLING

A sign stating your employment is a wonderful means of naming your house with the extra benefit of advertising your skills. Some aged homes have a very interesting history of once being shops, schools, churches or farms and you may choose to acknowledge your home's previous life in its name. Some examples of this naming method would be 'Tailor's Cottage', 'The Cobbler's Cottage' or 'The Mariner's Cottage'. Properties which were once used for public life may also show their history by retaining the original concept: 'The Old School House', 'The Old Church' or 'The Old Post Office'.

A

Admiral's Manor
Old English
Estate house where the admiral resides.

Admiral's Rest
Old English
Where the admiral relaxes.

Ale Maker's Cottage
Old English
Small house where the beer maker resides.

Ambassador's Estate
Old English
Large, stately house where the ambassador resides.

Archbishop's Cottage
Old English
Small house where the archbishop resides.

Archery Cottage
Old English
Small house where the archer resides.

Archive House
French/Latin/Greek/Old English
The house where historical records are kept.

B

Bakersville
Old English
The bread maker's village.

Bandit Wood Cottage
Old English
Small forest house used for a hideout.

Bard Cottage
Old English
Small house where the poet resides.

Bardham
Old English
The poet's village; the poet's farm.

Bardon Cottage
Old English
The poet's small house in the valley.

Barrister's Manor
English/Old English
Estate house where the barrister resides.

Beachcomber's Haven
English/Old English
One who searches the beach for washed up articles. *This is a popular name for homes situated by the beach.*

Beelea/Beelee/Beeleigh/Beeley/Beely
Bee meadow.

Bishop's Cottage
Old English
Small house where the bishop resides.

Bishop's Court
Old English
The bishop's courtyard.

Boreham
Old English
Village that farms pigs; pig farm.

Bowen Estate
Old English
Large, stately house where the victorious one resides; the archer's friend.

Bowman's Field
Old English
The archer's meadow.

Brewer's Cottage
Old English
Small house where the ale maker resides.

Buchanan Cottage
Scottish/Gaelic/Old English
Small house where the clergyman resides.

Buchanan Estate
Scottish/Gaelic/Old English
Large, stately home where the clergyman resides.

Burlington
Old English
The wine servant's town.

Burlington Cottage
Old English
Small house in the wine servant's town.

Bushman's Retreat
Australian/Old English
The place where the bushman retires to.

Bushranger's Retreat
Australian/Old English
The bandit's hideout.

Butler's Field
Old English
The butler's meadow.

Buttonwood
Old English
Forest where the honorary servant resides; where wooden buttons are made.

Buttonwood Cottage
Old English
Small house where the page boy (honorary servant) resides in the forest; small house where buttons are made from wood.

C

Cameo Cottage
Italian/Old English
Small cottage where cameos (carved stone) are made.

Cameo Rose Cottage
Italian/Old English
Small cottage where rose cameos (carved stone) are made.

Cannons Cottage
French/Old English
Small house of cannons; small house where the cannon maker resides.

Chandler's Cottage
Old French
Small house where the candle maker resides.

Cider House
Old English
Home where cider is made.

City Hall
Old English
The community hall in a city or town.

Clerk's Cottage
Old English
Small house where the office worker resides.

Commodore's Estate
Old English
The merchant shipping line captain's large, stately home.

Cooper's Cottage
Old English
Small house where the barrel maker resides.

Cooper's House
Old English
Home of the barrel maker.

Cricketer's Rest
English/Old English
Where the cricket player relaxes.

D

Dayan
Hebrew
Judge.

Dempster House
Old English
Home of the judge.

Digger's Den
Australian/Old English
The war hero's comfortable room.

Diggory Cottage
Old English
Small house where the ditch digger resides.

E

Eastminister
Old English
The minister from the eastern side of town.

Edgar Moore
English
The successful spear thrower who resides on the marshland.

Exhibition House
Old English
Gallery or art home.

Eyar
Norse
Island warrior.

F

Farmer's Close
Old English
The cultivator lives nearby.

Farmer's Cottage
Old English
Small house where the cultivator resides.

Farrington
Old English
The blacksmith's town.

Ferry Cottage
English
Small house on a boat used to carry vehicles, people or goods; where the ferry owner resides.

Ferry View
English
Vista of the ferry on the water.

Ferryboat House
English
Small house on a boat used to carry vehicles, people or goods; where the ferry owner resides.

Fireman's Cottage
Old English
Small house where the fire fighter resides.

Fisherman's Cabin
Old English/English
Lodge where the fish catcher resides.

Fisherman's Haunt
Old English/English
Where the fisherman resides.

Fisherman's Loft
Old English/English
Upper room where the fisherman resides.

Fleece Cottage
English
The small house of wool. *The owner of this house may be a keen knitter of wool, a spinner of wool or may own a farm, ranch or station with sheep. Hopefully the name will not indicate a business where customers should expect to get fleeced!*

Foresters
Old English
Forest rangers.

Forrester's Lodge
Old English
The forest worker's cabin.

Freemasons
Old English
Members of a secret fraternity. *The Freemasons are believed to have started in the twelfth century and are also known as The Masonic Lodge and The Knights Templar.*

G

George Cottage
Old English
Small house where the farmer resides.

Georgeton
Old English
The farmer's town.

Goldsmith's Cottage
Old English
Small house where the goldsmith resides.

Good Medicine Lodge
Native American/Old English
Healing cabin. *A medicine lodge is used by some Native Americans for ceremonies and to secure assistance from the spirit world.*

Governor's Cottage
Old English
Small house where the chief ruler resides.

Governor's House
Old English
House where the chief ruler resides.

H

Harcourt
Old English
Hawker's cottage.

Harpers Cottage
Old English
Small house where the harp player resides.

Harrington
Old English
The army ruler's town.

Harrison
Old English
Son of the army ruler.

Harrysville/Harryville
Old English/Scandinavian
The army ruler's village.

Hatpin Cottage
Old English
Home where the hatpin maker resides.

Horseshoe Cottage
Old English
Small and lucky house; small house where horseshoes are made; small house where the farrier or blacksmith resides. *It is believed (even today) that horseshoes are good luck. For the luck to work, you have to find a horseshoe that has been lost by a horse and found by you with the open end facing your way. To hang, fix with seven iron nails over the front door with the open end up so the good fortune doesn't spill out. Horseshoes were originally made from iron; this was due to its ability to withstand fire and its strength. Superstitions about iron are thought to have originated in the Middle Ages when it was used as a charm to ward off evil spirits.*

Hunter's Rest
Old English/English
The hunter's retreat.

Huntsdale
Old English
The hunter's valley.

Huntingdon
Old English
The hunter's hill.

I

Iakona House
Hawaiian/old English
The healer's home.

Ifor House
Welsh/Old English
The archer's home.

Ives/Ivan/Iven
Old English
Archer.

J

Jace Cottage/Jason Cottage
Greek/Old English
Small house where the healer resides.

Jasper
Persian
Guardian of the treasure.

Jevan House
Welsh/Old English
The young warrior's home.

Justice House
Old French/Old English
The home of the judge.

K

Kabil House
Turkish/Hebrew/Old English
Spear gatherer.

Kaga Cottage
Native American/Old English
Small house where the writer resides.

Kalhana Cottage
Hindi/Old English
Small house where the poet resides.

Kateb Cottage
Arabic/Old English
Small house where the writer resides.

Kaukau Shack
Tongan/English
The surfer's crudely-built cabin.

Keeper's Cottage
Old English
Small house where the estate keeper resides.

Keiffer Cottage
German/Old English
Small house where the barrel-maker resides.

Kiln Cottage
Old English
Small house where pottery is fired.

Knightly House
Old English
Home where the knight resides.

Knight's Dale
Old English
The knight's valley.

L

Landry Cottage
Old English
Small house where the ruler of the land resides.

Leggett Estate
Old French/Old English
The manor house of the ambassador.

Lian Cottage
Irish/Old English
Small house of the protector.

Little Church
Old English
Small church.

Lorimer Estate
Old French/Old English
Manor house of the saddle-maker.

Lowranger
Old English
The lower forest guardian.

Lynch Cottage
Irish/Old English
Small house where the mariner resides.

Lyric Cottage
Old English/English
Small house where the lyric writer resides.

M

Makya House
Hopi/Old English
The home of the eagle hunter.

Mariner's Cottage
Italian/Spanish/English
Small house where the sailor resides.

Mason's Cottage
Old English
Small house where the stone carver resides.

Mato House
Native American/Old English
Home of the warrior.

Millerswood
Old English
The mill owner's forest.

Milner Cottage
Middle English/Old English
Small house of the miller.

Murtagh Cottage
Irish/Scottish/Old English
Small house of the wealthy sailor.

N

Nautical Cottage
Latin/Greek/Old English
Small house of the sailor.

Nautilus House
Latin/Greek/Old English
Home of the sailor.

Northminister
Old English
The minister from the northern side of town.

Nunnington
Old English
The town where nuns reside.

O

Oboe Cottage
Old English
Small house where the oboe is played; small house where the oboe maker resides.

Ocean Breakers
Old English/English
Breaking waves.

Orman Cottage
Teutonic/Old English
Small house of the mariner; small house of the spearman.

Owney Cottage
Irish/Old English
Small house where the elder resides.

P

Parliament House
Old English
Where the government meets. *Parliament House is situated in Canberra, Australia's capital city. 'Canberra' is also a variant of an Aboriginal word, 'Kamberra', meaning meeting place.*

Pepper's Cottage
Old English
Small house where the pepper grower or grinder resides.

Pilgrim House
House where the foreigners stay.

Pioneer Cottage
Old English
Small house where the pioneer resides.

Porcelain Cottage
French/Old English
Small house where the translucent, ceramic ware is made or collected.

Porterhouse
Old English
Place where port is sold; place where steaks were sold; the home where the luggage carrier resides. *A porterhouse steak is a cut from the back end of sirloin.*

Potter's Cottage
Old English
Small house where ceramics are made.

Potter's Field
Old English
From the meadow where pottery is made.

Potter's Manor
Old English
Estate house where the pottery is made.

Prescott
Old English
The priest's cottage.

Prince's Hall
Old English
The prince's hall.

Princess Estate
Old English
Large, stately home where the princess resides.

Priorsmeade
Old English
The owner of the religious house in the meadow. *Mead is also a very sweet alcoholic drink made from honey, water, malt and yeast.*

Quadamah Estate
Arabic/Old English
The courageous one's manor house.

Quiller's Cottage
Old English
Small house where the writer resides.

Quiver Estate
English/Old English
The arrow holder or maker's manor house.

R

Racecourse Vista
English/Italian
View of the racecourse.

Rambler's Cottage
Old English/English
Small house where the country walker resides.

Ramiro Estate
Portuguese/Spanish/Old English
The manor house of the supreme judge.

Ranger's Cottage
Old English
Small house where the forest keeper resides.

Regin Manor
Scandinavian/Old English
Estate house of the judge.

Ritter Estate
German/Old English
Manor house of the knight.

Ryder Estate
Old English
Manor house of the horse rider.

Rymer Manor
Polish/Old English
Estate house of the saddle maker.

Sailor's Cottage
Old English
Small house where the sailor resides.

Saka Estate
Swahili/Old English
The manor house of the hunter.

Sayers Cottage
Welsh/Old English
Small house where the carpenter resides.

Scafer Cottage
German/Old English
Small house where the shepherd resides.

Shepherd's Cottage
Old English
Small house where the shepherd resides.

Shepherd's Station
Old English/English
The sheep guardian's large ranch.

Sheriff Cottage
English/Old English
Small house where the law-keeper resides.

Somerled Cottage
Scottish/Old English
Small house where the sailor resides.

Sonata Cottage
Italian/Latin/Old English
Small, musical house.

Sonnet Cottage
Italian/Latin/Old English
Small house of poetry.

Sonnet Dale
Italian/Latin/Old English
Poetic valley.

Southminister
Old English
The minister from the southern side of town.

Spinning Wheel Cottage
Old English
Small house where yarn is spun; small house where the spinning wheels are made.

Stockwell Cottage
Old English
The small house of the tree stump remover; small house by the stream the farm animals drink from.

Stoker Cottage
English/Old English
Small house where the fire-tender resides.

Strahan Estate
Irish/Gaelic/Old English
Manor house of the poet.

Swain House
English/Old English
The home where the knight's attendant resides.

T

Tailor's House
Old English
Where the one who alters clothes resides.

Tanner's Cottage
Old English
Small house owned by the leather tanner.

Teacher's Rest
Old English/English
Where the teacher retreats.

The Admiral's Cottage
Old English
Small house where the admiral resides.

The Ambassador's Lodge
Middle English/French
The sovereign's cabin.

The Archbishop's House
Old English
Home where the archbishop resides.

The Archer's Field
Old English/English
Where the archer resides in the meadow.

The Bakery
Old English
Where bread is baked.

The Barn
Old English
Farm building used for storage or grain or equipment.

The Barracks
Old English
The soldiers' accommodation.

The Blacksmith's Cottage
Old English
Small house where the blacksmith resides.

The Bohemian Cottage
Old English
The small, unconventional and artistic house.

The Brewery
Old English
Where beer is made.

The Bricklayer's Cottage
Old English/English
Small house where the brick layer resides.

The Bride's House
Old English/English
Where the bride resides.

The Buccaneer's Cottage
French/Old English
Small house where the pirate resides.

The Bushman's Lodge
Old English
The cabin of the country worker.

The Butler's Cottage
Old English
Small house where the butler resides.

The Captain's Quarters
Old English/English
Where the captain of the ship resides.

The Cattleman's Cottage
Old English
Small house where the cattleman resides.

The Chancellor's Cottage
Middle English/French/Latin/Old English
Small house where the chief minister resides.

The Clansman's House
Scottish/English
The Scottish man's house.

The Cobbler's Cottage
Old English
Small house where the leather worker or shoe maker resides.

The Colonial Cottage
Old English
Small house where the colonials reside.

The Constable's Cottage
Old English/English
Small house where the policeman/woman resides.

The Cook's Cottage
Old English
Small house where the chef resides.

The Court House
Old English
The place where court was held.

The Coven House
Old English/English
Where the witches reside.

The Cutter's Lodge
Old English
Cabin where the tree feller resides.

The Dairy
Old English
Where cows graze and are milked.

The Dairy Cottage
Old English
Small house on the milking farm.

The Dairy Farm
Old English
Ranch for milking cows.

The Deanery
Old English/English
Where the dean of the school resides.

The Doctor's House
Old English/English
Where the doctor resides.

The Explorer's Cottage
Old English
Small house where the explorer resides.

The Farm House
Old English
The farmer's home.

The Farm Shed
Australian/Old English/English
The barn.

The Farmer's House
Old English
Where the cultivator resides.

The Fishing Cottage
Old English
Small house where the fisherman resides.

The Flour Mill Cottage
Old English
Small house where the flour maker resides.

The Fox Hunter's Cottage
Old English
Small house where the fox hunter resides.

The Gallery House
French/Latin/English
Exhibition home. *A wonderful name for a home where an artist lives and exhibits his or her works.*

The Gate Hangers' Hall
Old English
The gate makers' meeting place.

The Gate Keeper's Cottage
Old English
Small house where the gate keeper resides.

The Globetrotter's House
Old English/English
The traveller's house.

The Governor's Cottage
Old English
Small house where the chief ruler resides.

The Guard House
Old English
House where the guard resides.

The Guardian
Old English
The watcher.

The Headmaster's Cottage
Old English
Small house where the head of the school resides.

The Healer's Cottage
Old English
Small house where the healer resides.

The Hermitage
Old English
Where the hermit resides; a private retreat. *Grange Hermitage is an Australian red wine, famous for being very expensive.*

The Hermit's House
Old English/English
Home of the lone person who avoids company.

The Hobby House
Old English
House of recreational activities.

The Hunter's Lodge
Old English/English
The hunter's cabin.

The Hunter's Moon Lodge
Old English/English
Cabin of the hunter, under a bright moon.

The Infirmary
Old English
The hospital.

The Jolly Huntsman
Old English
Happy hunter.

The Jolly Swagman
Old English/English/Australian
Happy, travelling itinerant.

The Judge's House
Old English
Home where the judge resides.

The Judge's Manor
Old English
Estate house where the judge resides.

The Knight's Estate
Old English
Manor house where the knight resides.

The Lamplighter's Cottage
Old English
Small house where the lighter of the lamps resides. *It was the Lamplighter's job to light the wick of street lights at a time before we had powered street lights.*

The Librarian's Cottage
Old English
Small house where the book worker and knowledge keeper resides.

The Lighthouse Keeper's Cottage
Old English
The lighthouse worker's small house. *The Lighthouse Keeper had the very important job of keeping the light maintained in the lighthouse to warn ships of rocks and to prevent shipwrecks.*

The Mariner's Lodge
Italian/Spanish/English
Cabin where the sailor resides.

The Mason's Cottage
Old English
Small house where the stone carver resides.

The Merchant's House
Old English
Home where the trader resides.

The Milking House
Old English
Home where cows are milked.

The Miner's Cottage
Old English
Small house where the miner resides.

The Ministry
Old English
Religious building.

The Mission
Old English
The ministry.

The Music Room Cottage
Old English
Small house where music is taught or played in one room.

The Needles
Old English
Pine needles. *This name might also suit the home of a dressmaker or tailor.*

The Naval Cottage
Old English
Small house used by the Navy.

The New Barn
Old English
The newly built farm shed.

The Observatory
Old English/English
Where observations are made from.

The Office
English
Where one works.

The Officer's House
Old English
Home where the officer resides.

The Old Bakehouse
Old English
The old bakery.

The Old Baker's Cottage
Old English
Small house where the baker once resided.

The Old Bakery
Old English
Property that was once a bakery.

The Old Bank
Old English
Property that was once a bank.

The Old Brewery
Old English
Building where beer was once made.

The Old Bridge House
Old English
Old home by the bridge.

The Old Chapel
Old English
Building that was once a chapel.

The Old Church
Old English
Building that was once was a church.

The Old Convict House
Old English
A building that was once home to criminals; an old jail/gaol.

The Old Cornmill
Old English
Property that was once a corn mill.

The Old Court House
Old English
House that was once a court.

The Old Dairy
Old English
Where cows once grazed and milked.

The Old Dairy House
Old English
Home that once stood on a dairy.

The Old Dairy Meadow
Old English
Fields that once was a farm for milking cows.

The Old Farm House
Old English
Home that was once part of a farm.

The Old Farrier's Cottage
Old English
Small house where the blacksmith once resided.

The Old Ferryman's House
Old English
House where the ferry captain once resided.

The Old Fire Station
Old English
Building that was once a fire station.

The Old Forge
Old English
Old metal work building.

The Old Friar's Cottage
Middle English/Latin/Old French
Member of a religious order house.

The Old Gaol House/The Old Jail House
Old English
Home that was once a gaol/jail.

The Old Guide Hall
English/Old English
Hall that was once used for girl-guide meetings.

The Old Hall
Old English
Property which was once used as a hall.

The Old Kennels
Old English
Building that was once a kennel.

The Old Library
Old English/English
Building was once a library.

The Old Lighthouse
Old English
Building that was once a lighthouse used to warn ships of rocks.

The Old Magistrate's House
Old English/English
House that was once owned by the magistrate.

The Old Mason's Cottage
Old English
Small house where the stone carver once resided.

The Old Mill
Old English
Property that was once a mill.

The Old Miner's Lodge
Old English
Cabin where the aged miner resides.

The Old Orchard
Old English
Place that was once a fruit farm.

The Old Police Station
Old English
Property that was once a police station.

The Old Pool House
Old English
Property which was once a pool house.

The Old Post Office
Old English/English
Building that was once a post office.

The Old Powder Mill
Old English
A building that used to be a flour mill.

The Old Priory
Old English
This is a popular name for large homes or bed and breakfasts. Traditionally a priory was a religious building and often the name stayed with the building to reflect its history.

The Old Pub
Old English/English
Property which was once a tavern, inn or public bar.

The Old Rectory
Old English
The old parish house.

The Old Sailor's Cabin
Old English
Lodge where the aged sailor resides.

The Old Scout Hall
Old English/English
Hall where scout meetings were once held.

The Old Shoppe/The Old Shop
Old English
Building that was once a shop.

The Old Soldier's Home
Old English
Home of the aged soldier.

The Old Station
Old English
The old, large farm; the old railway station; the old police station.

The Old Stone Barn
Old English
Stone building that was once a farm shed.

The Old Stone House
Old English
Aged home made of stone; home where the stone cutter once resided.

The Old Store
Old English
Property that was once a store.

The Old Toll House
Old English/English
House that was once used to collect taxes.

The Old Town Hall
Old English
Property that was once used as a town hall.

The Old Vicarage
Old English
Aged house where the clergyman once resided.

The Old Windmill
Old English
Building that was once a windmill.

The Parson's House
Middle English/French/Latin/Old English
The clergyman's home.

The Poet's Cottage
Latin/Greek/Middle English
Small house where the poet resides.

The Pilgrim's Cottage
Middle English/Old French/Latin
Small house where the travellers stay.

The Pilgrim's Rest
Middle English/Old French/Latin/Old English
Where the traveller rests.

The Pioneer's Cottage
Old English
Small house where the pioneers reside.

The Plougher's Cottage
Old English
Small house where the plougher resides.

The Porter's House
Old English
The porter's home.

The Priest's Garden
Old English/English
The priest's garden.

The Priory
Old English
The religious house.

The Quays
English/Celtic
Pier.

The Race Course
English
Field where horses race.

The Sailor's Home
Old English
Home where the sailor resides.

The Seafarer's Lodge
Old English
The sailor's cabin.

The Shearer's Cottage
Australian/English
Small house where the sheep shearer resides.

The Shearer's Rest
Australian/English
The sheep shearer's retreat.

The Shearing Shed
Australian/English
The barn used for shearing sheep.

The Smoke House
Old English
Building where smoked meats are prepared or stored.

The Soldier's Cottage
Old English
Small house where the soldier resides.

The Soldier's House
Old English
Home of the soldier.

The Spicer's Cottage
Old English
Small house where the spice maker resides.

The Sportsman's Cottage
English/Old English
Small house where the sportsman resides.

The Stalls
Old English
The stables.

The Statesman's Cottage
English/Old English
Small house of the political man.

The Station
Australian/English
Large farm or ranch; railway or police station.

The Story House
Latin/French/Middle English
The home where the account of an incident or event is told; the house where literary work is written.

The Studio
Latin/Italian
An artist's work place.

The Summer house
Old English
Home used during summer.

The Swagman's Rest
Australian/English
The travelling itinerant's resting place.

The Tailor's Cottage
Old English
Small house where the one who alters clothes resides.

The Town Hall
Old English
The main public hall in a town.

The Trader's House
Old English
Where the merchant resides.

The Tradesman's Post
Old English/English
The tradesman's shop.

The Traveller's Cottage
Old English
Small house where travellers stay overnight.

The Treasury
Greek/French/Middle English/Old English
Hoarded wealth; where money is kept. *'The Treasury' may be an affectionate name for a very loved and cherished home.*

The Trooper's House
American/English
The policeman's house.

The Vineyard
Old English
The vineyard; where wine is made.

The Wagoner's Lodge
Old English
The wagon maker's cabin.

The Warehouse
English/Old English
Storage house.

The Watch House
Old English
House where the guard resides.

The Wayfarer's Lodge
Middle English
The traveller's cabin.

The Weaver's Cottage
Old English
Small house where the weaver resides.

The Women's Cottage
Old English
Small house of women.

The Wool Packers Lodge
English/Old English
Cabin where the wool packers reside.

The Wool Shed
Australian/Old English
Small barn that stores wool.

The Wool Station
Old English/Australian
Ranch or farm with sheep.

The Workshop
English/Old English
The shop where one works.

Toll Keeper's House
Old English
The tax collector's home.

Touchstone Cottage
Old English
Small house where the purity of gold is tested.

Trader's Cottage
Old English
Small house where the merchant resides.

Traveller's Lodge
Old English
Cabin for travellers.

Trumpeton
Old English
The trumpet player's town.

U

Ualtar
Irish
The army ruler.

Uzair
Arabic
Helper.

V

Velvet Cottage
Old English
Small house where velvet is sewn; small, soft or smooth house.

Vine Cottage
Old French/Old English
Small house where the vine-worker or wine-maker resides.

Violin Cottage
Italian/Old English
Small cottage where the violin is made or played.

W

Walnut Lodge
Old English
Foreign nut cabin; cabin where furniture is made from the wood of the walnut tree. *It is believed that the walnut was introduced to Britain by the Romans, hence it being known as the foreign nut.*

Waterman's Cottage
Old English
Small house where the water distributor resides.

Wazire House
Arabic/Old English
The minister's home.

Weaver's Cottage
Old English
Small house where the weaver resides.

Webley
English/Old English
The weaver's meadow.

Webster Cottage/Webb Cottage
English/Old English
Small house of the weaver.

Westminister
Old English
The minister from the western side of town.

White Lace Cottage
Old English
Small house with white lacework (a decorative trim, usually of a veranda, made from iron); small house where the lace worker resides.

Wisdom House
Old English
The wise house; the home where the wise one resides.

Wiseman's Cottage
Old English
Small house where the wise one resides.

Witchwood/Witch Wood
Old English
The witch's forest. *'Witchwood' may be used as a name to keep away unwanted visitors or to create an air of mystery.*

Workingham
Old English
Homestead where one works; village of workers.

Writer's Block
Old English
Where the writer lives on a small piece of land. *'Writer's block' is a temporary inability for an author to find inspiration or the organisation to write.*

Writer's Cottage
Old English
Small house where the writer resides.

X

Xander House
Greek/Old English
Home of the defender of humankind.

Xerxes House
Persian/Old English
Ruler of the home.

Y

Yates Cottage
Old English
Small house where the gate-keeper resides.

Yemon House
Japanese/Old English
Home of the guardian.

Yorick Cottage
Old English
Small house where the farmer resides.

Z

Zomeir Estate
Hebrew/Old English
Manor house of the tree-pruner.

CHAPTER 10

SUCH STUFF AS HOMES ARE MADE OF

What makes a home? What is that special something? It may be hard to say and the answer will be different for different people. Here are some ideas about sources for inspiration. The materials from which a house is built, some magical association with the property or site, colours of your environment, or the special foods lovingly prepared to share with your family and friends may give you ideas for a house name that says what is special about your special place.

A material world

The materials that a house is made of can be the source of a unique name for your house. For example, some houses in the United Kingdom have a thatched roof and therefore 'Thatched Cottage' might be a suitable name. Other buildings may have an unusual architectural design such as 'The Round House'. This section contains a selection of these types of names.

A

Arches
Old English
Curved support structures or openings.

Archway Cottage
Old English
Small house with an arched entranceway.

B

Barnwood
Old English
Farm storage shed made of wood.

Blackstone Cottage
Old English
Small house made of black stones; small house by the black stones.

Blackstone Manor
Old English
Estate house made of black stones; estate house by the black stones.

Bluestone
English
Type of stone commonly used in building.

Bluestone Cottage
Old English/English
Small house made from bluestone; small house by the blue-coloured stones.

Brick Shack
Old English/Modern English
Roughly built shelter made from bricks.

Brickwood Cottage
Old English
Small house made of bricks and wood.

Broadstone Manor
Old English
Estate house made from wide stones.

C

Capstone Cottage/Copingstone Cottage
Old English
Small house with capstones.

Cedar House
Latin/Greek/French/Middle English/Old English
Home made from cedar tree wood.

Cherrywood Cottage
Old English
Small house made of cherry wood.

Cobblestone Cottage
Old English
Small house with a paved path or road.

Cobblestones
Old English
Area with a paved path or road.

Concrete Castle
English/Old English
Fortified estate house made from concrete.

Cornerstone
Old English
A stone block that is placed in the corner or at an angle in a wall to form a base corner, laid to ceremonially mark the commencement of construction.

Cornerstone Cottage
Old English
Small house with a cornerstone.

Decoupage
French
The art of applying decorative cuttings usually of paper, and coating it with varnish. *This may apply to a house that has had many extensions or changes giving it an unusual collage effect.*

Diamante House
French/Old English
Sparkling house made of crystals.

Double Decker
English
Two storey house.

Earth Cottage
Latin/Old English
Small house made from mud bricks.

Earthtone Estate
Latin/Old English
Large, stately house made from varying shades of brown.

Fascia House
Italian/Latin/English
House with flat piece of board under the eaves.

Filigree Cottage
French/Latin/Old English
Small and delicately decorated house.

Five Gables
Old English/Old French/Old Norse
Five triangular sections near a roof.

Fullcircle
Old English
To start over again; circular house.

Goldwell
Old English
Well or stream containing gold; gold-coloured stream.

Goodstone Cottage
Old English
Small house made of good stones.

Gothic Manor
The estate house built or influenced by those built in the twelfth–sixteenth centuries. *This architecture is characterised by vaulting and pointed arches and large windows. Many churches are designed in this style.*

Greystone Cottage
Old English
Small house made from grey-coloured stones.

Havenstone Manor
Old English
Estate house of stone that provides refuge.

Hay Cottage
Old English
Small house made from hay mud bricks; small house by the haystacks. *Hay is also a town in NSW, Australia.*

Heartstone
Old English
Heart shaped stone; the centre of the stone was used to build this structure; stone of compassion.

Heartstone Cottage
Old English
Small house made from a heart shaped stone; centre of a stone used to build the small house; small house of compassion.

Highwall House
Old English
Home with a high wall or fence.

I

Icehouse
Old English
A building where ice is made or housed. *'Icehouse' is the name of an ARIA (Australian Recording Industry Association) award-winning band most well known for the song 'Great Southern Land'. Iva Davies, the singer of Icehouse, also composed the music for the movie* Master and Commander *(2003), starring Russell Crowe.*

Iron House
Old English
Home made out of iron; home featuring an iron fence, gate, door, roof or bars.

Jet House
Latin/French/Middle English/Old English
Home made of jet stone, a hard, black stone usually used in jewellery.

Kaleidoscope
Greek
Small, beautiful and ever-changing.
A kaleidoscope is a tubular instrument with coloured glass between plates and displays a variety of changing symmetrical patterns.

Keystone
Old English
Wedge-shaped stone placed at a high point in an arch that locks the other pieces together.

L

Lattice Cottage
Middle English/Old English
Small house with lattice. *'Lattice' is a light wood crossed frame usually used in gardens or for light structures such as pergolas.*

Lightwood Manor
Old English
Estate house made from light-coloured wood.

Limestone Cottage
Old English
Small house made out of limestone.

Limestone Estate
Old English
Large, stately house made of limestone.

Limestone Manor
Old English
Estate house made of limestone.

Little Gables
Old English
Small triangular sections near the roof.

Little Rock Cottage
Old English
Small house made from small stones; small house surrounded by small stones.

Lonestone Cottage
Old English
Small house with one stone. *This is usually a monument stone situated in the garden or by the entrance to the property or home. It is usually in remembrance of a loved one, to give a history of the original builder of the home or to mark an important event.*

Mahogany House
Old English
House made of mahogany timber.

Mahogany Manor
Old English
Estate house made from mahogany wood or a red coloured wood.

Marble Cottage
Old English
Small house with a marble structure; small house made of marble or polished stone.

Mudbrick Cottage
Old English
Home made of mud bricks.

Natural House
Latin/French/Middle English/Old English
Home produced by nature. *In a more ecologically aware world, the environment has become an important element in the building of a home. The winter sun, summer breezes, water and renewable energies are important factors for saving the environment and money.*

Neon House
Greek/Old English
Fluorescent home; bright home. *Neon is used mainly for signs.*

Oak House/Oake House
Old English
Home made from the wood of an oak tree.

Oakwood Manor
Old English/English
Estate house made of oak wood.

Pebble House
Old English
Home with small stones in the garden or on the path.

Pebble Mansion
Old English
Estate house with small stones in the garden or on the path.

Pebble Stone Cottage
Old English
Small house with small stones in the garden or on the path.

Pebblestone Estate
Old English
Large, stately house with small stones in the garden or on the path.

Pine Lodge
Old English
Cabin made from pinewood.

Pinewood
Old English
Wood from the pine tree.

Quarters
Latin/French/Middle English
Dwellings.

Quarter House
Latin/French/Middle English/Old English
Four room house.

Red Brick House
English/Old English
Home made of red bricks.

Red Hill Estate
Old English
Large, stately house on the red hill.

River Stone Cottage/Riverstone Cottage
Old English
Small house made of river stones; small house by the river stones.

Rock Villa/Rockvilla
Old English/Italian
The rocky country house; country house made from rocks.

Rockwall Estate
Old English
Large, stately house with a wall made of rock.

Sandstone Cottage
Old English
Small house made of sandstone.

Sandstone Estate
Old English
Large, stately house made of sandstone.

Slate Cottage
Old English
Small house made of slate.

Stepping Stone Cottage
Old English
Small house with stepping-stones.

Stepping Stone Estate
Old English
Large, stately house with stepping-stones.

Stone Cottage
Old English
Small house of stone.

Stone Grange
Old English/Middle English/Latin
Large, stone house with smaller houses surrounding it.

Stone Hill Manor
Old English
Estate house made of stone.

Stone Villa
Old English/Italian
Country house made of stone.

Stone Wall Manor
Old English
Estate house with a stonewall.

Strawbale Manor
Old English
Estate house with straw bales.

Terracott/Terracotta/Terracotte
Latin/English
Small, orange/brown-coloured house; small tiled house. *A play on the words 'terracotta' (Latin meaning baked earth) and the 'cott' representing 'cottage'. A perfect name for a cottage-style house with terracotta roof tiles.*

Terracottage
Latin/English
Small, orange/brown-coloured house. *A play on the words 'terracotta' (Latin meaning baked earth) and 'cottage'. A perfect name for a cottage-style house with terracotta roof tiles.*

The Archway
Old English
Arched entranceway.

The Attic House
Old English
Home with an attic.

The Bath House
Old English
Place where a bath/pool was used for bathing; home with a pool. *The Romans built many public baths in Britain.*

The Brick Cottage
Old English
Small house made of bricks.

The Brick House
Old English
Home made of bricks.

The Circular House
Old English
The round house.

The Cobbles
Old English
A place with cobblestones or a paved path.

The Cobblestones
Old English
A place with cobblestones or a paved path.

The Colonial Estate
Old English
Large, stately house where the colonials reside.

The Eaves
Old English
An over hanging border for the roof.

The Entrance
Old English
Entry to a building, property or town.

The Gaits/The Gates
Old English
The entrance.

The Gaitway/The Gateway
Old English
The entrance through a structure.

The Georgian House
Old English
A house built or inspired by the architecture in the Georgian era (1714–1830).

The Glass House
English/Old English
A home made of glass; a home with many windows; a green house; home where the glass blower resides. 'Glasshouse' is also another name for a greenhouse. The Glass House *is a movie released in 2001 about two orphaned children who are taken by family friends who aren't what they appear to be. It stars Diane Lane and Leelee Sobieski.*

The Gravel House
English/Celtic/French
Home with a path or driveway made of loose stones.

The Hay House
Old English
House made from hay.

The Lace Work Cottage
Old English
Small house with decorative wrought iron.

The Log House
Old English
Cabin; home made of logs.

The Moat
Old English
House with a deep trench of water around it. *In medieval times, a moat was used as a security measure so attackers could not gain entry to the fortified building.*

The Old Stone House
Old English
Aged estate house made from stone; old estate house with an old stonewall.

The Painted House
Old English
Home that has been painted. A Painted House *is a novel inspired by John Grisham's own childhood on a cotton farm in Arkansas.*

The Pillars
Latin/English
Structured shafts used to decorate a building.

The Pine House
Old English/English
House made of pinewood.

The Queenslander
Australian/Old English/English
Home built for the Australian heat with distinctive architecture.

The Rock House
Old English
House made of rocks; house by the rocks; house on the rocks. *This name might also suit the home of people who play or enjoy rock music.*

The Round House/The Roundhouse
Old English
The circular house. *A name for an unusually circular shaped home. 'Roundhouse' is also a nautical term, denoting variously the captain's accommodation on the quarterdeck of Indiaman ships, the apprentices'*

accommodation on the afterdecks of some later sailing ships, and the toilets on the top deck of Royal Navy ships. Therefore the name might also be chosen for a beach house or a houseboat.

The Shingles
Old English
House with shingles on the roof.

The Slate House
Old English
House made of slate. *Possibly a name for a house featuring slate paving or a slate roof.*

The Stone Cottage
Old English
Small house made of stone.

The Stone House
Old English
Home made of stone.

The Stony House/The Stoney House
Old English
House made of stone.

The Storey House
Old English/English
Home with two or more floors.

The Thatched Cottage
Old English
Small house (especially the roof) made of twigs. *Thatched roofs still remain popular in some parts of Britain and give a beautiful charm to country houses.*

The Thatched House
Old English
Straw or reeds used instead of tiles or iron on the roof.

The Timber House
Old English/English
Home made of wood.

The Woodplank House
Old English
House made from wood planks.

Tiletop
Old English
Tiles on the top. *This usually refers to the tiles on the roof of a building.*

Timberslab Cottage
English/Old English
Small house with a timber floor.

Timbertree Cottage
Old English
Small house by the trees that are used for their wood.

Twin Gables
English/Old French/Old Norse
Two of the same triangular sections near a roof.

U

Umber House
Latin/French/Old English
Home made with umber pigments. *Umber is a green-brown coloured substance rich in manganese and oxides that goes a dark-brown colour when burnt. It is also used to give colour in paints.*

V

Veneer House
German/French/Old English
A home with an ornamental facing, made from plastic, wood etc, to hide cheaper materials underneath. *Brick veneer was a popular building material for Australians in the 1970s and 1980s until its lack of energy efficiency became an issue.*

Warmstone Cottage
Old English
Small house made of warm stones; small house made from sandstone-like stones.

Weatherboard Cottage
Old English/English
Small house made of wood.

White Lace Cottage
Old English
Small house with white lace work, (a decorative trim usually to a veranda, made from iron); small house where the lace worker resides.

Wood House
Old English
Home in the forest; home made of wood; place for storing wood.

Woodbridge Estate
Old English
Large, stately house by the wooden bridge.

Wooden Cottage
Old English
Small house made of wood.

Woodside
Old English
Forest on the flowing hills.

A magic touch

For centuries people with superstitions have been using horseshoes over their doors for good luck. Others have placed jade plants, also known as money trees, beside the entrances to their homes to welcome good fortune. Crystals, star-signs, fate, fortune and mythical creatures all can be used to add originality to your house name and give a magical and mysterious ambience to a house.

A

All Saints
Old English
A house name in honour of all the saints; a home that is watched over by all the saints.

Ambience Cottage
French/Old English
Small house with atmosphere.

Ambience Falls
French/Old English
The atmospheric waterfalls.

Amethyst
Greek
Beneficial; purple gem. *Amethyst is the birthstone for February.*

Amethyst Cottage
Old English
Small house of the beneficial; small house with the purple gem. *A good name for a house that is purple-coloured.* (See Amethyst)

Angel Cottage
Old English
Small house watched over by an angel.

Angel Manor
Old English
Estate house watched over by an angel.

Angelic Cottage
Old English
Small house where the angel resides; small and angelic house.

Angel's Cottage
Old English
Small house of the angel.

Angel's Hideaway
Old English
Secluded area where the angels hide.

Aphrodite
Greek
Goddess of love and beauty.

Aquarius
Latin
Water carrier. *The sign for those born 30 January–18 February.*

Aries Haven
Latin/Old English
Refuge for the ram. *The sign of Aries is for those who were born 21 March–19 April.*

Aurora
Latin
Golden beauty of the dawn. *An aurora is caused by electrically charged particles that accelerate along the magnetic fields into the upper atmosphere. Here they collide with gas atoms that give off light. Also called the 'Northern Lights'.*

Aurora Australis
Latin
Coloured lights in the southern sky. *The Aurora Australis, also known as the 'Southern Lights', is a dazzling display of lights that appear in the Antarctic skies in winter. An aurora is caused by electrically charged particles that accelerate along the magnetic fields into the upper atmosphere. Here they collide with gas atoms and give off light.*

Aurora Borealis
Latin
Coloured lights in the northern sky. *The Aurora Borealis, also known as the 'Northern Lights', is a dazzling display of lights that appear in the Arctic skies. An aurora is caused by electrically charged particles that accelerate along the magnetic fields into the upper atmosphere. Here they collide with gas atoms and give off light.*

Avalon
Latin
Island. The small house on the island. *Avalon is a place believed to be near Glastonbury in Britain. It is thought to be a magical and a spiritually enlightening place since the time of the pagans.*

Avalon Cottage
Latin/Old English
Small house on the island. (See Avalon)

Avalon House
Latin/Old English
Home on the island. (See Avalon)

Avalonia
Latin/Old English
House on the island. (See Avalon)

Avlon House
Latin/Old English
House on the island. (See Avalon)

Aztec Lodge
Spanish
The Aztec peoples' cabin. *Aztecs are an ancient race and are believed to have founded the Mexican Empire.*

Azure Cottage
Middle English/French/Arabic
Small, deep blue-coloured house. *Azure is a semiprecious stone that is blue in colour.*

Azurite
French
Blue, semi-precious stone.

B

Babylon
Akhadian via Greek
Gate of the god Il. *An ancient city of Mesopotamia that was famed for its sensual living. It was destroyed (c. 689 BC) by the Assyrians, but subsequently restored and regarded as a great city in 339 BC when Alexander the Great visited.*

Bewitched
Old English
Enchanting. Bewitched *was much loved television show that aired 1964–72 and starred Elizabeth Montgomery. It was about a good-hearted witch named Samantha Stevens, who was married to a mortal, Darrin Stevens. Samantha's mother Endora (Agnes Moorehead) disapproved of their marriage and sought to break it up.*

Black Opal
Old English/Latin/Sanskrit
Black opal. *The black opal is held by many to be the most precious of all opals. The only place in the world the black opal is found is in Lightning Ridge, New South Wales, Australia.*

Blessings
Old English
God's favour.

C

Cancerian
Latin
The crab. *In astrology, Cancer is the star sign for those born 19 June–22 July.*

Capricorn Cottage
Latin/Old English
Small house where the owner raises goats. *Capricorn in astrology is the star sign for people born 22 December–19 January.*

Centre of Balance
English
Area of health and wellbeing.

Chance Cottage
Old English
Small house of fortune.

Charmed Cottage
Old English
Small and lucky house.

Charmed Estate
Old English
Large and lucky stately home.

Charmed House
Old English
Lucky home.

Charmed Manor
Old English
Lucky estate house.

Conway Village
Welsh/Old English
Holy water village.

Crystal Cottage
Old English
Small house of crystal; clear house. *This name may be given to a house with lots of glass windows or perhaps next to a clear stream, lake or pool. Quartz crystal is one of the most abundant minerals in the world.*

Crystal Creek
Old English
Clear, small stream; crystals in the stream. (See Crystal Cottage)

Crystal House
Old English
Clear home; home of crystals. (See Crystal Cottage)

Crystal Lake
Old English
Clear lake; crystals in the lake. (See Crystal Cottage)

Cupid Cottage
Roman/Old English
Small house of the god of love; desired home. *'Cupid' is the Roman name for Eros and is depicted in Greek art as beautiful and child-like.*

Cupid's Cottage
Roman/Greek/Old English
Small house of the god of love; desired home. (See Cupid Cottage)

Cupid's Crest
Old English/Latin
Desired summit; the god of love's summit. (See Cupid Cottage)

D

Daydream Den
English/Old English
Comfortable room where one can daydream.

Destiny
Latin
Fate.

Destiny Cottage
Latin/Old English
Small house of fate.

Destiny House
Latin/Old English
Home of fate.

Dionysus
Greek
God of wine.

Dragonwood
Old English/Greek
The dragon's forest. *A dragon is a mythical creature with a reptile body, wings and breathe fire.*

Dreamcatcher
Native American/English
Dream sifter. *The dreamcatcher is from a Native American legend that varies from tribe to tribe, including the Navajo, Sioux, Zuni and in Canada the Cree. The Chippewa/Ojibwa legend is of Nokomis (grandmother) who had been watching a spider spin its web for days. Her grandson wanted to kill the spider but Nokomis stopped him. As a reward for saving the life of the spider, it spun a 'dreamcatcher' web that would catch any bad dreams and sift the good dreams through the small hole in the middle to save Nokomis from nightmares.*

E

Eden
Latin/Greek/Hebrew/Old English
Paradise. *The Garden of Eden was the original home of Adam and Eve, according to the Book of Genesis in* The Bible.

Elf Farm
Old English
Farm inhabited by fairies.

Elfdale
Old English
Elf valley.

Elfwood
Old English
Elf forest.

Elixer
Latin/English
Prolong life; turned into gold.

Emerald Beach
Old English
Green beach waters. *Emerald is the birthstone for May.*

Emerald Palace
Old English
Castle with emerald jewels. *Emerald is the birthstone for May.*

Emerald Pines
Old English
Green pines; emerald-coloured pine trees. (See Emerald Palace)

Enchantaville/Enchantedville
Old English
Bewitching village.

Enchantress Cottage
Old English
Bewitching woman of the small house.

Eros Estate
Roman/Old English
Large, stately house of the god of love. *'Eros' is the Greek name for Cupid.*

Eternal Jewel
Old English
Precious gem that lasts forever.

F

Faerie Manor/Fairy Manor
Old English
Estate house where the fairies live. *'Faerie' or 'Faery' are old alternative spellings of 'fairy'.*

Faerie Haven/Faery Haven/ Fairie Haven/Fairy Haven
Old English
Refuge for the fairies.

Fairielea/Fairielee/Fairieleigh/Fairieley/ Fairiely
Old English
Fairy meadow.

Fairy Meadow
Old English
Fairy field.

Felicitas
Greek
Goddess of fortune.

G

Garnet House
Old English
Red-coloured jewel home; red house. *Garnet is the birthstone of January.*

Gem Cottage
Old English
Small house of jewels.

Gemini House
Latin/Old English
Home of the twins. *Gemini is the star sign of those born 21 May–20 June.*

Ghost Town Cottage
Old English
Small house in the haunted town.

Glimmering
English
Shining.

Gothica
Old English
Influenced by buildings in the gothic style (twelfth–sixteenth centuries). *This architecture is characterised by vaulting and pointed arches and large windows. Many churches are designed in this style.*

Gothica Manor
Old English
Estate house built in the gothic style (twelfth–sixteenth centuries). (See Gothica)

Granite Creek
Latin/Old English
Quartz-like rock found in the small stream.

H

Half Moon Cottage/Halfmoon Cottage
Old English
Small house under the half moon; half-moon-shaped house.

Haunted Woods
Old English
Ghosts in the forest. *This name gives a feeling of foreboding and as a result, may keep people away; this may be the idea behind the name.*

Heaven
Old English
Paradise.

Heavenly Haven
Old English
Refuge paradise.

Horseshoe Cottage
Old English
Small and lucky house; small house where horseshoes are made; small house where the farrier or blacksmith resides. *It is believed (even today) that horseshoes are good luck. For the luck to work, you have to find a horseshoe that has been lost by a horse and found by you with the open end facing your way. To hang, fix with seven iron nails over the front door with the open end up so the good fortune doesn't spill out. Horseshoes were originally made from iron; this was due to its ability to withstand fire and its strength. Superstitions about iron are thought to have originated in the Middle Ages when it was used as a charm to ward off evil spirits.*

I

Imperial Manor
Latin/Middle English
Royal estate house where the emperor and empress reside.

Irondale
Old English
Valley where iron can be found; strong valley. *Iron in the Middle Ages was believed to ward off evil spirits. For those who are superstitious, naming a property or home anything to do with iron is supposed to give protection to those who reside there.*

Ironwood Estate
Old English
Large, stately home in the forest where iron can be found; large, stately home in the strong forest. *Iron in the Middle Ages was believed to ward off evil spirits. For those who are superstitious, naming a property or home anything to do with iron is supposed to give protection to those who reside there.*

J

Jade house
Old English
Green jewel home; green home.

Jade Valley
Spanish/French/Old English
Green gemstone found in the valley; green valley. *Jade is a gemstone.*

Juju Cottage
West African/Old English
Small house of magical powers. *A juju is a fetish or charm with magic powers.*

K

Karma Cottage
Sanskrit/Old English
Small house of action. *Karma is believed to be a force generated by one's actions and to influence their fate.*

Kismet
Turkish
Fate. *The popular musical* Kismet *(George Forrest and Robert Wright, also drawing on music of Alexander Borodin) enjoyed long seasons on Broadway and London in the 1950s and was subsequently made into a film by MGM.*

L

Leo
Latin/Old English
The lion. *This is the star sign for those born 23 July–22 August.*

Leprechaun
Irish/Gaelic
Mischievous elf. *According to popular belief, a leprechaun possesses a pot of gold and a human may obtain it if he or she succeeds in capturing the leprechaun, a very difficult task.*

Libra
Latin/Old English
The scales. *This is the star sign for those born 23 September–22 November.*

Luna Cottage
Latin/Old English
Small house under the moon.

Magnetic Hill
Latin/Old English
Hill with magnetic properties; one may be drawn to this hill.

Marble Lodge
Latin/Greek/Middle English/English
Cabin of marble.

Mermaid Cottage
Old English
Small house where the mermaid resides. *This would be a good name for a home where the owner has a passion for the mythical tales of the mermaids.*

Minerva's Cottage
Roman/Greek/Old English
Small house of Minerva, Roman goddess of wisdom, the arts and war.

Minerva's Garden
Roman/Greek/Old English
Garden of the goddess of wisdom, the arts and war. (See Minerva's Cottage)

Mistletoe Manor
Celtic/Old English
The estate house of healing; estate house where the mistletoe grows. *There are many beliefs surrounding mistletoe. The ancient Celts believed it possessed healing powers and that it held the soul of the host tree. In Victorian times, kissing under the mistletoe at Christmas was a ritual hoped to lead to romance or marriage. Today, mistletoe is used as a Christmas decoration.*

Moonglow Manor
Old English
Estate house under the glow of the moon.

Moonlight Cottage
Old English
Small house under the moonlight.

Moonlight Hideaway
Old English
The moonlit and secluded place.

Moonstone
Old English
Milky-white gemstone.

Morning Star
Old English
The first star seen in the morning sky.

Mystery Bay
Old English
Mysterious inlet.

Mystery Manor
Old English
Estate house that conveys an air of mystery.

Mystical Cottage
Old English
Small house of magic.

Natural Magic Cottage
Old English
Small house where one assumes power over the natural world in order to produce spells (for good or evil). *Lucianus speaks of 'natural magic' in Shakespeare's* Hamlet, *'Thy natural magic and dire property', as he addresses his drug just before pouring it into the king's ear.*

New Moon Cottage
Old English
Small house under the phase of the dark moon.

Oberon Cottage
French/Old English
Small house of the obedient one. *Oberon is the king of the fairies in Shakespeare's* A Midsummer Night's Dream, *written in 1594–95 and first printed in 1600.*

Opal Cove
Latin/Sanskrit/Old English
The bay where opals are found. *Opal is the birthstone for October.*

Opal Fields
Latin/Sanskrit/Old English
Opal gem meadows. (See Opal Cove)

Oracle Cottage
Latin/French/Middle English/Old English
Small house that is the divine answer.

Oriental Oasis
Latin/French/Old English
A paradise made of Oriental flora in an arid area. *This would be a perfect name for a home in an arid area with a section of lush green Oriental style gardens.*

Pandora
Greek
In Greek mythology, Pandora was the first woman on earth created by Zeus who endowed her with charm, curiosity and deceit. Zeus gave her a box that he forbade her to open. She opened the box and let out all the evils that have since afflicted humans; only hope remained inside the box.

Paradise
Old English
Heaven.

Patchwork Cottage
Old English
Small house made of miscellaneous materials; small house where the patchwork quilter resides.

Pegasus
Greek/Mythological
Winged horse. *Pegasus, according to Greek mythology, was born from the blood of Medusa. Pegasus was fond of drinking from the spring of Peirene and it was there that Bellerophon saw Pegasus and being in need of a mount to attack the Chimaera, he caught the winged horse and tamed it by using a golden bridle that Athena had given him.*

Phoenix
Greek
Resurrection; immortality; purple.
The phoenix is a mythical bird, sacred in ancient Egypt and Greece. It is a solitary male bird with gold and red feathers and is said to have a long life. It is famed for building a nest from cinnamon twigs that it then ignites and from its ashes arises a new phoenix.

Pisces
Latin
The fish. *Pisces is the star sign of those born 19 February–20 March.*

Quartz Cottage
German/Slavic/Old English
Small house made from hard stone. *'Quartz' crystal is used in watches to assist in oscillation.*

Quetzalcoatl
Aztec
Feathered serpent deity of the Aztec and Toltec people.

Rainbow Cottage
Old English
Small house under the rainbow; small house of many colours. *Rainbows are traditional signs of good luck and a promise of better days. This belief comes from the Biblical story of Noah and the flood.*

Rainbow Falls Cottage
Old English
Small house by the colourful waterfalls. (See Rainbow Cottage)

Rainbow Wood
Old English
Colourful forest. (See Rainbow Cottage)

Rainbow's End
Old English
Pot of gold at the end of the rainbow. *There is a popular myth that at the end of the rainbow there is a pot of gold.* (See Rainbow Cottage)

Red Earth Cottage
Old English
Small house built on the red earth; small house built from red earth

Sagittarius
Latin
The archer. *Sagittarius is the star sign of those born 22 November–21 December.*

Sapphire Bay
Old English
Blue inlet. *A sapphire is a blue-coloured, precious gem. 'Sapphire' is a word often used to describe the blue colour of water.*

Sapphire Manor
Old English
Blue, precious stone found in the estate house. (See Sapphire Bay)

Scorpio
Latin
The scorpion. *Scorpio is the star sign of those born 23 October–21 November.*

Serendipity
Sri Lankan
To find something pleasing by chance. *'Serendip' is a former name of Sri Lanka. Horace Walpole (1717–92) coined the term 'serendipity' from a Persian fairytale,* The Three Princes of Serendip.

Serpent's Lodge
Old English
Serpent's cabin.

Seven Stars Estate
Old English
Large, stately house under the seven stars.

Shalom
Hebrew
Peace; greetings.

Shaman Lodge
Old English
A spiritual leader who performs healings and religious ceremonies to protect his people from supernatural forces or to communicate with spirits. *The most famous of shamans are perhaps the Native American medicine men and women, although shamans are found all over the world.*

Skyfire
Old English/American
Red, orange and yellow-coloured sky.

Sorcery Cottage
Latin/French/Middle English
Small, magical house.

Spirit Cottage
English/Old English
Small house of spirits.

Spirit Mountain
English/Old English
The spirit of the mountain.

Sprite Cottage
Middle English
Small house where elves or fairies reside.

Star Dust
Old English
Dust from a star.

Starfield
Old English
Starry meadow.

Starry Meadow
Old English
Star field.

Stonehenge
Old English
Prehistoric monument made of a circular structure. *Stonehenge is a famous and mysterious stone structure near Salisbury England. It is believed to have been built about 3100 BC.*

Suncatcher
American/English
One who catches the sun. *A decorative item, usually made of glass and used to reflect light.*

T

Taurus
Latin
The bull. *Taurus is the star-sign for those born 20 April–20 May.*

The Black Cat Cottage
Old English
Small house with a black cat. *Black cats are associated throughout the world with magic or as companions for witches. They are also associated with bad luck.*

The Castle
Old English
Fortified estate house of royalty; the home. The Castle *was a 1997 movie about a Melbourne family being forced to move out of its home by the government and the family's fight to keep the house.*

The Cauldron
Middle English/French/Latin
Cooking pot. *Cauldrons are usually associated with magical incantations and witches.*

The Dancing Dragon
English/Greek
Happy serpent. *A dragon is a mythical creature with a reptile body, wings and breathes fire.*

The Dragon
English/Greek
The dragon. (See The Dancing Dragon)

The Dragon Tower
Middle English/Greek
Serpent tower. (See The Dancing Dragon)

The Dragon's Lair
Greek/Old English
The den of the dragon. (See The Dancing Dragon)

The Dreamtime
Australian Aboriginal/English
The Dreamtime is the Australian Aboriginal understanding of the creation of the world. *Ancestor beings emerged from the earth at the time of the creation and were half human and half animal or plant. They*

moved across the barren earth and as they travelled and hunted, they created the landscape, mountains, rivers, trees, waterholes, plains, sun and stars. It is believed that the people today are descendants of the Dreamtime ancestors.

The Echoes
Latin/Old English
Repeated sound.

The Enchanted Cottage
Old English
Small, bewitching house. The Enchanted Cottage *was a movie made in 1945 about a homely woman and a scarred ex-army soldier who meet at the cottage and eventually agree to marry (out of loneliness). However, the romantic cottage weaves a spell and soon they begin to look beautiful to each other, but no-one else can see it.*

The Enchanted Vista
Old English/Italian
The bewitching view.

The Enchanted Wood
Old English
The bewitching forest.

The Enchanting Cottage
Old English
Small, bewitching house. (See The Enchanted Cottage)

The Enchantress
Old English
Bewitching woman.

The Falling Star Estate
Old English
Large, stately house under the falling stars.

The Four-Leaf Clover
Old English
Luck. The shamrock is the national emblem of Ireland. *The superstition of the four-leaf clover is believed to have originated with the Druids, who believed that the shamrock helped them to see evil spirits giving them time to hide. It is also used to protect both humans and animals from evil spells and bad luck.*

The Four Pillars
Old English
Four structured shafts used to decorate a building.

The Galaxy
Latin/Greek
A system of stars.

The Glamour House
English/Old English
Alluring home. *'Glamour' derives from 'glammar', an archaic word meaning magic, enchantment or witchery.*

The Haunted Woods
Old English
Ghostly forest.

The Haven
Old English
The refuge.

The Jewel
Old English
A precious gem. *This would make a good house name for those who truly value their home.*

The Magic Cottage
Old English
Small, magical house. The Magic Cottage *is a novel by James Herbert about a cottage that at first seemed peaceful and helped the occupants with their creativity and their love for each other but later revealed a terrifying side.*

The Magic Garden
Old English
Magical garden.

The Medicine Lodge
Old English/Native American
Place of healing. *The Native Americans use 'Medicine Lodges' for healing not only bodily ills but also spiritual ills.*

The Milky Way
Old English
The white path. *The Milky Way is a galaxy that may be seen as a band of light running across the heavens, containing two hundred billion stars as well as other objects.*

The Northern Star
Old English
The brightest star seen from the northern skies. *Also known as the 'Pole Star', it is a constellation of Ursa Minor and lies near the northern celestial pole.*

The Old Witch Cottage
Old English
Small house where the witch resides. *Witches have traditionally conjured up images of ugly women riding broomsticks and practising magic. 'Wicca' was the name of a magic craft first practiced by the ancient Celts. A 'witch' may also refer to an alluring woman. 'The Old Witch Cottage' may be used as a name to keep away unwanted visitors or to create an air of mystery.*

The Pearl House
Old English
Home with a pearl jewel; white and precious home.

The Secret Garden
Old English
The garden of hidden knowledge. The Secret Garden *is a novel by Frances Hodgson Burnett (1849–1924) and has had many movies based on it, the first in 1919 and others in 1949, 1952, 1960, 1975, 1976, 1988, 1993. It is about a spoiled English girl called Mary, who is orphaned and sent to live with her uncle and invalid cousin in a gloomy mansion full of secrets. Mary brings laughter and joy back to the house.*

The Ruins
Old English
Old remains of a building.

The Treasure Chest
Greek/French/Middle English/Old English
Hoarded wealth; cherished. *'The Treasure Chest' may be an affectionate name for a very loved and cherished home.*

The Treasure Trove
Greek/French/Middle English/Old English
Wealthy discovery.

The Wheel of Fortune
Old English
Fate. *In the Tarot deck, the Wheel of Fortune is a card of fortune and good destiny.*

The Witching Hour
Old English
The witching hour is the hour of midnight on a full moon. *It is believed to be the time when witches cast their spells and when their powers are at their most powerful. Its history may be traced to ancient times of goddess worship also associated with fertility and the moon.* The Witching Hour *is also the name of a novel by Anne Rice about a family of witches known as the 'Mayfairs'.*

Thunderbird
Old English/Native American
Bird of thunder. *There is a Native American legend about a killer whale that was eating all the salmon and threatened the people with starvation. He was asked to leave but refused. A congress of chiefs asked for help from the spirits and a spirit bird of lightning and thunder appeared and asked what it would get in return for solving the problem. The chiefs agreed to make the Thunderbird's image famous. The Thunderbird agreed, swooped down, lifted the killer whale from the water and placed it on land. It later became a mountain.*

Treasure Cottage
Greek/French/Middle English/Old English
Small house with a hoard of wealth; cherished. *'The Treasure' may be an affectionate name for a very loved and cherished home.*

Turquoise Stone
French/Turkish/Old English
Semi-precious, blue-coloured gemstone. *Turquoise is a stone that is believed to ward off evil when set in silver.*

U

Unicorn
Middle English/French/Latin
Mythological horned horse. *The Unicorn has many legends about it, including if one drinks from its horn, one will be protected from poison.*

V

Virgo
Latin
Virgin. *Virgo is the star sign for those born 23 August–22 September.*

W

Witch Cottage
Old English
Small house where the witch resides. *Witches have traditionally conjured up images of ugly women riding broomsticks and practising magic. 'Wicca' was first practiced by the ancient Celts. The name 'witch' may also refer to an alluring woman. 'Witch Cottage' may be used as a name to keep away unwanted visitors or to create an air of mystery.*

Witchblade
Old English
Witches knife; witch's narrow leaf. (See Witch Cottage)

Witches' Abode
Old English
Where witches reside. (See Witch Cottage)

X

Xanadu
Literary
Imaginary place of beauty. *'Xanadu' was used in the poem 'Kubla Khan' by S. T. Coleridge (1772–1834). Olivia Newton John*

starred in the movie Xanadu *(1980) about a muse from Olympus who comes to earth to inspire an artist.*

Yeti Cottage
Tibetan/Old English
Small house where the Big Foot creature was sighted. *A Yeti is also known as the 'Abominable Snowman' or 'Big Foot'. It is a creature half man, half animal, believed to be living in the Himalayas.*
(See also Yowie Point)

Yowie Point
Australian Aboriginal/Old English
Mythical yeti-like creature by the headland. *The yowie is also known as 'Doolagahl' which means 'great hairy man'. The yowies are similar to their overseas cousins, 'The Abominable Snowman', 'Bigfoot' and the 'Yeti'. They are all described similarly as being large, hairy and man-like.*

Zen Cottage
Mahayana (Buddhist)/Old English
Small house of enlightenment and meditation. *Zen affirms that enlightenment occurs through meditation and intuition rather than faith*

Colour my world

Consider a house with a vibrant colour an asset to be used to advantage by incorporating it into the house name. Coloured doors, walls, roofs and even the surrounding flora can aid you in the search for a colourful house name.

Alabaster Cottage
Middle English/Latin/Greek/Old English
Small, white house; house made from white, translucent stone. *The alabaster stone is usually used to carve ornaments.*

Amberlea/Amberlee/Amberleigh/ Amberley/Amberyly
Old French/Old English
The golden/brown-coloured meadow.

Apricot Cottage
Latin/French/Old English
Apricot trees by the small house. Apricot-coloured house.

Apricot House
Latin/French/Old English
Apricot-coloured house; house with apricot trees.

Azure Cottage
Middle English/Old English/French
Small, blue-coloured house.

Bianca
Italian
White.

Black Heath/Blackheath
Old English
Black heather. *Blackheath is in the Blue Mountains in New South Wales and is well known for its Rhododendron Festival held annually in November.*

Blackhills
Old English
Burnt hills; black hills.

Blackstone Cottage
Old English
Small house made of black stones; small house by the black stones.

Blackstone Manor
Old English
Estate house made of black stones; estate house by the black stones.

Blackthorn/Blackthorne
Old English
Dark or black prickles.

Blakely
Old English
Black meadow.

Blandford
Old English
Light-coloured river crossing.

Blue Dior
Old English/French
Christian Dior (1905–57) was a famous couturier and founder of the fashion house that bears his name and still survives today.

Blue Door
Old English
Blue-coloured door.

Blue Gable
Old English
House with a blue-coloured, triangular section by the roof.

Blue Haven
Old English
Blue-coloured refuge.

Blue Hill
Old English
Blue-coloured hill.

Blue Holme
Old English
Blue-coloured house; blue-coloured hamlet or village; blue-coloured inshore island; blue-coloured floodplain. *'Holm/holme' is also a form of 'hamlet'. Contemporarily used as alternative spelling of 'home'.*

Blue Horse Cottage
Old English
Small house by the blue-coloured horse.

Blue Mountains
Old English
Blue-coloured mountains. *The Blue Mountains west of Sydney Australia, is a World Heritage area covering one million hectares. It is famous for its beautiful views, bushwalking tracks and a rock formation known as the Three Sisters.*

Blue Skies
Old English
Blue-coloured skies.

Blue Sky Cottage
Old English
Small house under the blue-coloured sky.

Blue Spring Manor
Old English
Estate house by the blue-coloured stream.

Blue Velvet Garter
English/French/Celtic
A blue velvet band; a blue-coloured badge. *The Order of the Garter is the oldest and most senior British Order of Chivalry. It was founded by Edward III in 1348. The Order consisted of the King and 25 knights. It was the highest reward for military bravery or loyalty.*

Bluestone
English
Type of stone commonly used in building.

Bluestone Cottage
English
Small house made from bluestone; small house by the blue-coloured stones.

Blunden
Old French/ Old English
White valley.

Brassy Hills
Old English
Yellow-coloured hills.

Bright House
Old English
Happy house of sunshine; bright-coloured house; the intelligent house owner.

Bronzeton
Old English
Bronze-coloured town.

Brownhill
Old English
Brown-coloured hills.

Brownescombe
Old English
Brown-coloured valley.

Brownstone
Old English
Brown-coloured stones.

Brownstone Cottage
Old English
Small house made with brown-coloured stones.

Brownstone House
Old English
House made of brown-coloured stones; house by the brown-coloured stones.

Burgundy Manor
French/Old English
Deep, red-coloured estate house; estate house where wine is made.

Butterblonde Cottage
Old English
Small, yellow-coloured house.

C

Canola Cottage
Latin/Old English
Small house near the canola plants; the yellow coloured house.

Canola Fields
Latin/Old English
Meadow where the canola grows; yellow-coloured meadow.

Charcoal Cottage
Old English
Small, black-coloured house; small house where coal is sold.

Chequers
English
Black and white; a game. *A house featuring a black and white colour scheme would be perfect for this name.*

Classic Ruby Cottage
English/Old English
Small, classical-styled, red house; small house where the ruby jewel is kept.

Clear Blue Skies
Old English
Blue and cloudless skies.

Cobalt Blue Cottage
German/Old English
Small, blue-coloured cottage.

Copper Cottage
Old English
Reddish/gold-coloured small house.
A copper was a large, metal vessel used to boil and wash laundry in before washing machines were invented.

Copperfields
Old English
Copper-coloured meadows. *David Copperfield is a famous literary character invented by Charles Dickens and hero of the novel* David Copperfield.

Cranberry Cottage
Old English
Small house where cranberries grow; red/pink-coloured house.

Cream Cottage
Old English
Small, white/yellow-coloured house; small house where cream is made. *A good name for a house on a dairy farm.*

Crimson Cottage
Old English
Small, red coloured-house.

E

Earthtone Estate
Latin/Old English
Large, stately house made from varying shades of brown.

Ebony Cottage
Greek/Egyptian/Old English
Black wood estate house; black coloured estate house.

Ebony House
Old English
Blackwood house; the black coloured house.

Ebony Manor
Old English
Black wood estate house; black-coloured estate house.

Emerald Fields
Old English
Green meadows. *The emerald is a precious, deep green jewel.*

Emerald Pines
Old English
Green-coloured pine trees. (See Emerald Fields).

F

Fair Cottage/Fayre Cottage
Old English
Light-coloured, small house; good and small house.

Fair Estate/Fayre Estate
Old English
Good, large and stately home; light-coloured stately home.

Fairmont/Fayremont
Old English /French
Light-coloured mountain; the good mountain.

Flambeau House
French/Old English
Beautiful and bright home.

Flamboyant House
Old French/Old English
The ostentatious home. *A name for a home that stands out from the crowd due to architecture or colour.*

G

Gold Hill
Old English
Gold-coloured hill.

Gold Strike
Old English
To find gold.

Golden Amber Cottage
Old English
Small house where the golden amber tree grows near by; small gold-coloured amber stone house.

Golden Cottage
Old English
Small, gold-coloured house.

Golden Pond
Old English
Gold-coloured pond. *This name conjures up images of golden sunsets over a pond. Playwright Ernest Thompson wrote a screen version of his stage play* On Golden Pond *for the 1981 film directed by Mark Rydell and starring Henry Fonda and Katharine Hepburn. The film is about a retired professor and his wife and their relationship with their daughter who marries and brings a step-grandson into her parents' lives.*

Golden River Cottage
Old English
Small house by the gold-coloured river.

Goldsborough
Old English
Gold-coloured municipality; golden grass.

Graham/Grahame
Old English
Grey-coloured house. *Scottish author Kenneth Grahame (1859–1932) was famous for his children's stories. His best-known story* The Wind in the Willows *was published in 1908. Alternatively, the name 'Graham' might be chosen by an admirer of any of several famous Grahams, including US evangelist Billy Graham, Australian golfer David Graham, and US dancer and choreographer Martha Graham.*

Grape Cottage
Old English
Small, dark purple-coloured house; house where grapes grow.

Grey Mountains
Old English
Grey-coloured mountains.

Grey Manor
Old English
Grey-coloured estate house.

Greycott
Old English
Grey-coloured cottage.

Greycourt
Old English
Grey-coloured courtyard.

Greycrest
Old English
Grey-coloured summit.

Greycrest Cottage
Old English
Small house on the grey-coloured summit.

Greystanes
Old English
Grey-coloured stones.

Greystanes House
Old English
Home made from grey-coloured stones.

Greystone Cottage
Old English
Small house made of grey-coloured stones.

Greystones
Old English
The grey-coloured stones.

Greylake Cottage
Old English
Small house by the grey lake; small grey house by the lake.

Greylands
Old English
Grey-coloured fields.

Greystanes
Old English
Grey-coloured stones.

Greystoke
Old English
Grey-coloured stones around a campfire. *'Greystoke' is the name of the estate house in the movie* Greystoke: The Legend of Tarzan, Lord of the Apes *(1984).*

Greystone
Old English
Grey-coloured stones.

Greeley
Old English
Grey-coloured meadow.

Green Dior
English/French
Green, named for Christian Dior.

Green Door
Old English
Green-coloured door.

Green Lawn/Greenlawn
Old English/English
House with green grass.

Green Mountains
Old English
Green-coloured mountains; grassy mountains.

Green Oasis
Old English/Latin
Green fertile area in a desert or dry area. *This would be a perfect name for a home in an arid area with a section of lush green gardens or a pool.*

Green Trees Estate/Greentrees Estate
Old English
Large, stately house where the green trees grow.

Green View
Old English
Vista of the green-coloured grass or forest.

Greenacres
Old English/English
Green-coloured fields; land measurement. Greenacres *was a television series starring Eva Gabor, about a city socialite who married a farmer and had to adjust to farm life instead of New York.*

Greenfield/Greenfields
Old English
Green-coloured meadow; grassy meadow.

Greenhead
Old English
Green-coloured headland; grassy headland.

Greenhorn
Old English/North American
Inexperienced; green-coloured horn.

Greenland Cottage
Old English
Small house in the green-coloured field; grassy fields.

Greenlands/Greenland
Old English
Green-coloured fields.

Greenlawn Manor
Contemporary/Old English
Estate house with the green lawn.

Greenmont
Old English/French
Green mountain.

Greenmount
Old English
Green mountain.

Greenshutters Cottage
Old English
Small house with green-coloured shutters.

Greentree
Old English
Green and leafy tree.

Greenville
Old English
Green-coloured village; grassy village.

Greenway
Old English
Green path. *Francis Greenway (1777–1837) is known as Australia's first architect. He was originally sent to Australia as punishment for forgery in 1812. Governor Macquarie recognised Greenway's talent and put him to work designing buildings. Greenway's first job was to design Macquarie Lighthouse at South Head. It is believed that there are still 49 buildings in Sydney attributed to his designs.*

Greenwich Cottage
Old English
Small, green-coloured house; grassy cottage. *'Greenwich' England has been the home to Greenwich Mean Time (also known as Greenwich Meridian Time) since 1884. All the world's time is measured from the Greenwich Meridian Line at the Royal Observatory (0° longitude). All maps and Global Positioning Systems (GPS) devices use longitude and latitude for referencing).*

Greenwich Village
Old English
Green-coloured village; grassy village.

Greenwood
Old English
Green forest.

Greenwood Cottage
Old English
Small house in the green forest.

Greenwood Estate
Old English
Large, stately home in the green forest.

Greenwood House
Old English
Home in the green forest.

Greston
Old English
Grey town.

Grice
German
Grey.

Grimshaw
Old English
Dark woods.

Guildford
Old English
Yellow flowers by the shallow river crossing.

Guinevere
Welsh
White wave. *Guinevere was King Arthur's queen.*

Gwendolyn
Welsh
White moon.

H

Houghton
Old English
Grey-coloured town on the steep bank.

Houghton Estate
Old English
Grey-coloured town on a steep bank.

I

Indigo Cottage
English/Latin
Small, purple/blue-coloured house.

Ivory House
Old English
White home; home where animal bones are collected. *Ivory trade is outlawed in many countries as it has lead to the depletion of animal species such as elephants.*

Ivory Manor
Old English
White estate house; estate house where animal bones are collected.

Jacinta House/Jacinda House
Spanish/Greek/Old English
Purple home; hyacinth. *Also a girl's name.*

Jenilee Cottage
Welsh/Old English
White wave on the meadow.

Kaleidoscope Cottage
Greek/Old English
Small, beautiful and ever-changing house. *A 'kaleidoscope' is a tubular instrument with coloured glass between plates and displays a variety of changing symmetrical patterns.*

Keir
Gaelic
Dark.

Kilduff
Old English
Black forest.

Kirralee/Kirrilea/Kirrileigh/Kirriley/Kirrily
Irish
Dark.

L

Lake Topaz Estate
Large, stately house by the blue lake.

Lavender Blue Cottage
Old English
Small, pale purple/blue-coloured house; small house where the lavender grows.

Lavender Cottage
Old English
Small, pale purple-coloured house; small house where the lavender grows. *'Lavender Cottage' is a very popular name throughout Britain and Australia due to the popularity, beauty and perfume of this shrub.*

Lilac Cottage
Arabic/Persian/Sanskrit/Old English
Light purple-coloured small house.

Lilac Mountains
Arabic/Persian/Sanskrit/Old English
Light purple-coloured mountains.

Lily White/Lilywhite/Lily Whyte/Lilywhyte/
Old English
White lilies.

Lime Cottage
Spanish/French/Old English
Small house where lime trees grow; lime-coloured, small house.

Mauve Cottage
Old English
Small, pale purple-coloured house.

Mauve Manor
Old English
Light purple-coloured estate house.

Midnight Blue Cottage
Old English
Small, dark blue-coloured house.

Mountain Ebony House
Old English
Home where the mountain ebony tree grows; home on the black mountain.

Neel
Hindi
Blue.

Neva
Spanish
White.

O

Old Yeller/Old Yellow
Old English
Old yellow. *'Old Yeller' was the name of the dog from a novel by the same name written by Fred Gipson; in 1957 it became a Disney movie.*

Olive Dale
Old English
Dark green-coloured valley; olive tree valley.

Olive Manor House
Old English
Dark green-coloured estate house; house with olive trees growing nearby.

Orange Wood
Old English
Orange-coloured forest; oranges growing in the forest.

Periwinkle
Old English
Small, blue-coloured house; small house where the aromatic herb (mint) is grown; myrtle tree.

Periwinkle Cottage
Old English
Small, blue-coloured house; small house where the aromatic herb (mint) is grown; small house with a myrtle tree.

R

Radburn
Old English
Red stream.

Radcliff/Radcliffe
Old English
Red cliff.

Radley/Radlea/Radlee/Radleigh/Radly
Old English
Red meadow.

Radnore
Old English
Red shore.

Ransford
Old English
The raven's shallow river crossing.

Raspberry Cottage
Old English
Small, red-coloured house; small house where raspberries grow.

Red Clover Cottage
Red Clover Cottage
Small house by the red clover field.

Red Dior
English/French
Red-coloured, named after Christian Dior.

Red Door
Old English
Red-coloured door. *Also the name of a famous perfume by Elizabeth Arden.*

Red Fields
Old English
Red-coloured meadows; meadows flowering with red flowers.

Red Hill Estate
Old English
Large, stately house on the red hill.

Red Holme/Red Home
Old English
Red-coloured house; red-coloured hamlet or village; red-coloured inshore island; red-coloured floodplain. *'Holm/holme' is also a form of 'hamlet'. Today the name is sometimes used as an alternative spelling of 'home'.*

Red House
Old English
Red-coloured house.

Red Leaf Cottage
Old English
Small house with red-coloured leaves on the tree.

Red Willow Cottage
Old English
Small, red-coloured house by the willow tree.

Redcliffs/Redcliff
Old English
Red-coloured ledges.

Reddell
Old English
Red valley; reedy valley.

Redding
Old English
Red. *Otis Redding Jr (1941–67) was an American singer famous for the song '(Sittin' on) the Dock of the Bay' for which he won Grammies including Best Rhythm & Blues Song and Best R & B Vocal Performance—Male.*

Redford
Old English
The red, shallow, river crossing; reedy, shallow, river crossing. *Robert Redford is an American actor/director (b. 1937), known for many films including his film* Butch Cassidy and the Sundance Kid *(1969),* The Way We Were *(1973),* The Horse Whisperer *(1998) and many others. He also won an Academy Award, Best Director, for* Ordinary People *(1981).*

Redlands
Old English
Red-coloured fields; fields with red-coloured flowers.

Redlea/Redlee/Redleigh/Redley/Redly
Old English
Red meadow; reedy meadow.

Ridesdale
Old English
Reedy valley; red valley.

Royal Blue Gate
Old English
The blue-coloured entrance gate to the royal estate; the dark blue-coloured entranceway.

Royal Blue Manor
Old English
Blue-coloured estate house where royalty reside; dark blue-coloured estate house.

Rudstone
Old English
Red stone.

Rudstone Cottage
Old English
Small house made of red stones.

Ruford
Old English
Red, shallow, river crossing.

Rumour House
Latin/Old English
Home of furphies.

Rutlea/Rutlee/Rutleigh/Rutley/Rutly
Old English
Red meadow.

Sable Cottage
Middle English/French/Old English
Small, black house; small house where the sable mammal is kept or where its pelts are made into coats.

Sandstone Mansion
Old English /French
Stately home made out of sandstone; yellow-coloured stately home.

Scarlet Cottage
Old English
Small, red-coloured house. (See Scarlett)

Scarlet House
Old English
Red-coloured home. (See Scarlett)

Scarlet Ribbons Cottage
Old English
Small house with red ribbons. (See Scarlett)

Scarlett
Old English
Red. *Scarlett O'Hara is the main character in Margaret Mitchell's 1935 novel,* Gone with the Wind. *It was made into a movie of the same name in 1939 which starred Vivien Leigh and Clark Gable.*

Silver Birch
Old English
Silver barked birch tree.

Silverfern
Old English
Fern with a silver-coloured leaf, also the emblem of New Zealand.

Silver Estate
Old English
Large, stately, silver house.

Silver Holme
Old English
Silver-coloured home; silver-coloured hamlet or village; silver-coloured inshore island; silver-coloured floodplain. *'Holm/holme' is also a form of 'hamlet'. Today the name is sometimes used as an alternative spelling of 'home'.*

Silver Oak/Silver Oake/Silver Oakes/ Silver Oaks
Old English
Silver-coloured oak tree.

Silvermead/Silvermeade
Old English
Silver-coloured meadow. *Mead is also a very sweet alcoholic drink made from honey, water, malt and yeast.*

Silvermere
Old English
Silver lake.

Silverton
Old English
Silver town.

T

Tangerine Cottage
English/Old English
Small, orange-coloured house; small house where tangerines are grown nearby.

Terracotta House/Terracott House
Latin/Old English
Small, orange/brown-coloured house; small tiled house. *A play on the words 'terracotta' (Latin meaning baked earth) and the 'cott' representing 'cottage'. A perfect name for a cottage-style house with terracotta roof tiles.*

The Beige House
French/Old English
Yellow/grey-coloured house.

The Blue Cottage
Old English
Small, blue-coloured house.

The Blue House
Old English
Blue-coloured house.

The Blue Lagoon
Old English/Latin/French/Italian
A body of water separated by a sand bank from a larger body of water. The Blue Lagoon *was a 1980 movie starring Brooke Shields, about two children who were marooned on an island and grew up there.*

The Brown House
Old English
Brown-coloured house.

The Chocolate House
Spanish/Old English
Brown-coloured house; house where chocolate is made.

The Clay House
Old English
Earth coloured house, brown house.

The Ginger House
Old English
Yellow/orange-coloured house; house where ginger grows.

The Golden Age
Old English
Time of great prosperity and happiness.

The Gilded Pines
Old English
Gold-coloured pine trees.

The Green Cottage
Old English
Small green-coloured house.

The Green Dragon
Old English
Large, green mythical creature. *A dragon is a mythical creature with a reptile body, wings and breathes fire.*

The Green House/The Greenhouse
Old English
Green-coloured house; glasshouse.

The Jade House
French/Old English
Green-coloured home; house with jade stone.

The Lavender House
Old English
Pale purple-coloured house; home where lavender grows. (See Lavender Cottage)

The Little Blue Cottage
Old English
Small, blue-coloured house.

The Little Green Cottage
Old English
Small, green-coloured house.

The Little Grey Cottage
Old English
Small grey-coloured house.

The Little Red Cottage
Old English
Small, red-coloured house.

The Little White Cottage
Old English
Small, white house.

The Little Yellow Cottage
Old English
Small, yellow-coloured house.

The Mustard House
Old English
House where mustard is made; yellow-coloured home.

The Peach House
Old English
Pink/yellow-coloured house; home where peaches are grown.

The Pink House
Old English
Pink-coloured home.

The Purple Cottage
Old English
Small, purple-coloured house.

The Purple House
Old English
Purple-coloured home.

The Red Cottage
Old English
Small, red house.

The Red Garter
English/French/Celtic
Red-coloured band.

The Red House
Old English
Red-coloured home.

The Teal House
English/Old English
Green/blue-coloured house.

The White Cottage
Old English
Small, white house.

The White House
Old English
White home.

The Yellow Cottage
Old English
Small, yellow-coloured house.

The Yellow House
Old English
Yellow-coloured home.

V

Varde
Old French
Green hills.

Violet Cottage
Old English
Small, purple-coloured house.

Violet Mountains
Old English
Purple-coloured mountains; mountains where the violet flower grows.

W

Wakefield
Old English
White meadow.

Waklea/Waklee/Wakleigh/Wakeley/Wakly
Old English
White meadow.

Wentworth
Old English
The white estate.

Whitaker
Old English
White meadow.

Whitby
Old English
Near the white place.

Whitcombe
Old English
White cottage.

White Cross
Old English
Shallow, white river crossing; white church cross.

Whitehall
Old English
White hall. *Whitehall can refer to the British government, after Whitehall Palace, situated near the British Houses of Parliament.*

White Manor/Whyte Manor
Old English
White estate house. *'Whyte' is an alternative spelling for 'white'. Scots-born James Whyte was Premier of Tasmania 1863–6.*

White Mountains
Old English
White mountains.

White Mountains Estate
Old English
Large, stately house on the snowy mountains.

White Orchard Cottage
Old English
Small house with white fruit trees.

White Picket Fence
Old English
White fence made up of slates of wood with a small space between each picket. *The White Picket Fence is the romantic 'ideal' or 'dream house'.*

White Picket House
Old English
House with a white fence. (See White Picket Fence)

Whitefield
Old English
White meadow.

Whitehart Cottage
Old English
Small, centred, white house.

Whitestone Manor
Old English
Estate house made of white stone.

Whitford
Old English
White, shallow river crossing.

Whitlea/Whitlee/Whitleigh/Whitley/Whitly
Old English
White meadow.

Wintergreen Cottage/Wyntergreen Cottage
Old English
Small house with green winter flora.

Y

Yellow Dior
English/French
Yellow-coloured, named for Christian Dior.

Yellow Door
Old English
Yellow-coloured door.

Yellow Holme
Old English
The yellow house.

Yellow Mountains
Old English
Yellow mountains.

Yellowbrae
Old English/Scottish
Yellow hill.

Yellowhue House
Old English
Yellow coloured house.

Yellowin
Old English
Small, yellow inn or tavern; yellow friend.

Yellowstone
Old English
Yellow-coloured stone.

Z

Zehava
Hebrew
Golden.

Food for thought

It was once tradition to give a house a name that reflected the food produced on the surrounding property. Culinary skills may be called upon to produce a sweet or tasty name that reflects one's abilities in the kitchen. A favourite dish may be an good choice for a house name.

Alfalfa Farm
English/Old English
Ranch where alfalfa is grown.

Apple Croft Cottage
Old English
Small house by the small apple orchard.

Apple Garth
English/Scandinavian
Apple tree enclosure.

Apple Lodge
Old English
Cabin situated close to the apple tree.

Apple Orchard
Old English
Apple tree fruit farm.

Apple Tree Cottage
Old English
Small house by an apple tree.

Applewood
Old English
Apple tree fruit farm.

Applewood Cottage
Old English
Small house in the apple orchard.

Apricot Cottage
Old English
Small house by the apricot trees; small and light-orange-coloured house.

Barley Cottage
Old English
Small home where barley is grown.

Barley House
Old English
Home where barley is grown.

Barleyton
Old English
Barley town.

Berry House
Old English
Home where berries grow.

Berrymeade/Berrymead
Old English
Berry meadow. *Mead is also a very sweet alcoholic drink made from honey, water, malt and yeast.*

Birnbaum
German
One who resides by the pear tree.

Butterfield
Old English
The butter maker's meadow. Butterfield 8, *directed by Daniel Mann and based on the novel by John O'Hara, won Elizabeth Taylor her first Oscar for best actress for her portrayal of Gloria Wondrous in 1969.*

Cappuccino Cottage
Italian/Old English
Small house where cappuccino is made; tan-coloured house; brown and cream-coloured house. *This name is for the coffee lover.*

Caramel Cottage
Old English
Small house where caramel is made; golden/tan-coloured house.

Caramel House
Old English
Home where caramel is made; golden/tan-coloured home.

Cherry Valley
Old English
Cherry trees in the dale.

Cherryburn
Old English/Scottish
Stream by the cherry trees.

Cherrywood
Old English
Cherry forest.

Chestnut Cabin
Old English
Lodge where chestnut trees grow near by; a deep reddish/brown-coloured lodge.

Chestnut Cottage
Old English
Small house by the chestnut tree; a deep reddish/brown-coloured, small house.

Chillies/Chilies
Spanish
Place where chillies grow.

Chocolate Cottage
Old English
Small house where chocolate is made; brown-coloured house. *A name for chocoholics.*

Chutney Cottage
Old English
Small home where relish is made. *Chutney is similar to relish.*

Chutney House
Old English
Home where relish is made. (See Chutney Cottage)

Corncob Cottage
Old English
Small house where corn is grown near by.

Cranberry Cottage
English/Old English
Cranberries growing by the small house; reddish/pink-coloured, small house.

Cranberry Park
English/Old English
Cranberries growing in the recreational area; reddish/pink-coloured recreational area.

Cream Cottage
Old English
Small house where cream is made; yellow/white-coloured house. *A good name for a small house on a dairy farm.*

Cressbrooke/Cressbrook
Old English
Small stream where the cress grows.

D

Devonshire
Irish/Old English
The poet's county; people of the deep valley. *Devonshire has a long association with the breeding of dairy cattle and the production of dairy products as well as the Devon sausage. Devonshire teas traditionally consist of a pot of tea and scones with jam and cream. It is believed to have originated from the county of Devon in England and is famed throughout United Kingdom, India, Australia and New Zealand.*

G

Gingerbread House
Old English
Home made of gingerbread; brown/golden-coloured home. *The Gingerbread House featured in the fairytale* Hansel and Gretel *by the Brothers Grimm. Hansel and Gretel get lost in the woods and stumble upon a Gingerbread House owned by a witch who built the delicious house to entice children to her so that she may fatten them up and eat them.*

Gingerbread Manor
Old English
Estate house where gingerbread is made; brown/golden-coloured estate house. (See Gingerbread House)

Grapefruit Cottage
Old English
Small house where the grapefruit trees grow.

Grapeview
Old English
Vista of the grape vines.

H

Honey House
Old English
Home where honey is collected; home where bees are kept for their honey.

Honeycombe Cottage/Honeycomb Cottage
Old English
Small house where honeycomb is collected.

Honeygrove
Old English
Small wood where honey is collected.

Honeymede/Honeymeade
Old English
Honey meadow. *Mead is also a very sweet alcoholic drink made from honey, water, malt and yeast.*

Honeywell
Old English
Honey by the well or stream; honeybees by the stream or well.

L

Lemon Court
Arabic/Persian/Old French/Middle English/Old English
Lemons growing in the courtyard.

Lime Cottage
Spanish/French/Old English
Small house where lime trees grow; lime-coloured, small house.

Lime Court
Spanish/French/Old English
Lime trees growing in the courtyard.

M

Macadamia Cottage
Latin/ Old English
Small house near to where the macadamia trees grow.

Macadamia Meadows
Latin/Old English
Macadamia tree field.

Maplewood Manor
Old English
Estate house in the maple tree forest.

N

Nectarine Meadows
Latin/Greek/Old English
Nectarine fields. *Nectarines are similar to peaches but they have smooth skin.*

Nutmeg House
Middle English/Old French/Latin/Old English
Home where the aromatic seed is used as spice.

P

Passionfruit Cottage
Old English
Small house where the passionfruit grows.

Pavlova
Russian
Graceful. *Anna Pavlova was one of the world's best-known ballerinas. She was most famous for performing the 'Dying Swan' (1907) and it became her signature piece for the rest of her life. Pavlova is also an Australian dessert made of soft meringue and topped with cream and some further garnish, typically fruit, such as strawberries, kiwi fruit or passionfruit.*

Plum Tree Cottage
Old English
Small house near to where the plum trees grow.

Poppy Seed Cottage
Old English
Small house where the poppy seeds are sewn. *Poppy seeds come from the poppy flower and are used to decorate cakes, breads and pastries. The opium poppy is a variety of flower that is infamous for producing the illegal drug opium. The red poppy is also a symbol used on Remembrance Day in Australia, New Zealand, Canada and Britain, commemorating those who died in World Wars I and II.*

Q

Quennel/Quenelle
German/French
One who resides by the oak tree. *Quenelles are meatballs or fishballs.*

Quince Cottage
Old English
Small house where quinces are grown.

R

Raspberry House
Old English
Home where raspberries are grown; reddish/pink-coloured house.

S

Strawberry Cottage
Old English
Small house where strawberries are grown; reddish/pink-coloured house.

Strawberry Fields
Old English
Strawberries growing in the meadows; reddish/pink-coloured (flowering) meadows. *'Strawberry Fields Forever' is a well-known song by The Beatles.*

Strawberry Hill
Old English
Strawberries growing on the hillside; reddish/pink-coloured (flowering) hill.

Sugar Hill
Old English
Sweet hill; hill where sugar is made.

Sugarton
Old English
Sugar town; sweet town.

T

The Apple Orchard
Old English
Pasture of fruit trees.

The Barley Meadows
Old English
Meadows where barley is grown.

The Berry Patch
Old English
Small area where berries grow.

The Brambles
Old English
Secluded place; blueberry shrub.

The Cabbage Patch
Old English
Small area where cabbages grow. *'The Cabbage Patch' is also where parents*

once told their children babies came from, to avoid having to approach the subject of sex.

The Coffee Cottage
Italian/Old English
Small home where coffee is made; brown-coloured house. *A name for coffee lovers.*

The Coffee House
Italian/English
Home where coffee is made; brown-coloured house. *A name for coffee lovers*

The Corn Fields
Old English
Corn growing in the meadows.

The Grape Leaf
Old English/Middle English
The leaf of the grape vine.

The Pea Farm
Old English
The ranch where peas are grown.

The Pumpkin Patch
Old English
Small area where pumpkins grow.

The Strawberry Farm
Old English
Ranch where strawberries are grown.

The Strawberry Patch
Old English
Small area where strawberries grow.

The Wheatfield/The Wheatfields
Old English
Wheat meadows.

Vanilla Cottage
Spanish/Old English
Sweetly scented house; a sweet flavouring; small, beige-coloured house.

Vanilla Fields
Spanish/Old English
Sweetly scented meadows; a sweet flavouring; beige-coloured meadow.

Watercress Cottage
Old English
Small house by the watercress.

Watermelon Dell
Old English
Secluded valley where watermelons grow.

Whiskey Cottage/Whisky Cottage
Gaelic
Small house where whisky is made. *In the liquor industry, the spelling 'whisky' is reserved for Scotch whisky; the spelling 'whiskey' is used for Irish, American and other whiskeys.*

CHAPTER 11

IF I COULD TALK TO THE ANIMALS

Animals, both in the country and city, play an important role in the home. They also provide a wealth of inspiration to the homeowner in selecting a house name. In the city, one may be limited by a choice of animals but those who live in rural areas have a vast amount of farm animals, domestic pets and wild fauna to draw from in choosing a name for their house.

B

Badger's Hall
Old English
Where the badger resides by the hall.

Badger's Rest
Old English
Where the badger resides.

Barking Dog Cottage
Old English
Small house where the barking dog resides.

Bear Creek Cabin
Old English
Lodge by the bear fishing in the stream.

Bear Creek Lodge
Old English
Cabin by the bear fishing in the stream.

Bear Paw Lodge
Old English
Cabin with a bear-paw marking on it. *Bears have been known to seek out food from cabins in times when food is not as bountiful as it may have once been. A bear may even leave scratches on a wooden surface to mark its territory.*

Bear Wood
Old English
Bear in the forest.

Big Dog Cottage
Old English
Small house with a large dog.

Black Bear Cabin
Old English
The lodge where the black bear resides near by.

Black Cat Cottage
Old English
Small house with a black cat. *Black cats are associated throughout the world with magic or as companions for witches. They are also associated with bad luck.*

Black Dog Cottage
Old English
Small house with the black dog.

Black Horse Estate
Old English
Large, stately house with the black horse.

Black Horse Manor
Old English
Estate house with the black horse.

Boreham
Old English
Village that farms pigs; pig farm.

Brumby Station
Australian/Old English
Large ranch where the wild horses roam. *Brumbies were originally stock horses from the Snowy River region in Australia. There are many theories about the brumby's heritage including one about a prospector named Brumby who let his horses out free*

in his remote mountain property. Another theory is that a Lieutenant Brumby released his horses into the Blue Mountains west of Sydney and they found their way to the mountains of the Snowy River. The brumby is still a romantic figure today with many Australians growing up with tales of The Man From Snowy River *and* Clancy of the Overflow *and other bush poems and stories by A.B. 'Banjo' Patterson.*

Buffalo Cottage
American/Old English
Small house near to where the buffalo roam. *Buffalo was a source of life and spiritual beliefs for the Native Americans residing on the plains. All of the buffalo was used by the people for food, clothes, warmth, shelter and tools. The Native American word for buffalo is 'tatanka'.*

Buffalo Plains
American/English
Fields where buffalo roam. *An estimated sixty-million buffalo once roamed America in the mid-1800s. Between 1840 and 1880 a mass extermination program began against the buffalo, driving them to near extinction by 1883. The railroaders wanted the buffalo removed as they were a threat to their trains, settlers wanted their hides for trade and the buffaloes' tongues were considered a delicacy. The end of the buffalo meant the end of the Native American way of life on the plains. The Native Americans had relied heavily on the buffalo for food, shelter, clothing and tools and they were forced into submission or to life on reservations.* (See also Buffalo Cottage and White Buffalo Lodge).

C

Canine Court
Old English
Dog in the courtyard.

Caribou Cottage
Algonquian/Old English
Small house by the large elk.

Cat Call Cottage
Old English
Small house where the cat can be heard to call out or 'meow'.

Cat Cottage
Old English
Small house with a cat.

Cat Court
Old English
Cat in the courtyard.

Catbrooke/Catbrook
Old English
The cat's small stream.

Catnap Cottage
Old English
Small house of siestas; small house where the cat sleeps.

Cawton
Old English
Cow town.

Cheshire Cat Cottage
Old English
Small house in Cheshire England with a cat. *The Cheshire Cat is a character in Lewis Carroll's* Alice in Wonderland *1865. It was noted for its habit of disappearing, leaving only its smile hanging in the air.*

Cockington
Old English
Town of the king's rooster.

Coniber
Old English
Rabbit grove.

Cougar Ranch
Latin/French
The puma farm.

Coyote Lodge
Mexican/Spanish/English
Cabin of the wild dog.

Crazy Bear Lodge
Old English
Cabin where the crazy bear resides.

D

Darlea/Darlee/Darleigh/Darley/Darly
Old English
Deer meadow.

Deer Cottage
Old English
Small house near to where the deer reside.

Deer Crossing
Old English
The place where the deer cross.

Deer Hill
Old English
Deer on the hill.

Deer Park
Old English
The recreational area where deer reside.

Deer Pine Lodge
Old English
Cabin in the pine forest near to where the deer reside.

Deerhurst
Old English/Middle English
Deer in the hill forest.

Doe Meadow
Old English
Field where the female deer resides.

Doe's Peak
Old English
The female deer's summit.

Dog Cottage
Old English
Small house with a dog.

Dog Fence House
Old English
House near the fence that keeps out dogs. *'The dog fence' stretches 5400km from the Great Australian Bight through most of Queensland and is the longest man-made structure in the world. It was built to protect livestock from wild dogs or dingoes (an Australian native dog).*

Dog Paddle Cabin
Old English
Lodge close to where the dog swims.

Dogleg Ranch
Old English
Farm with a sharp bend in it; farm shaped like a dog's leg.

Dogmar
Old English
Dog on the marshland

Dogstar
English/Old English
Sirius, the brightest star in the sky.

Dogwood
Old English
Dog in the forest; the dogwood tree.

Dolphin Cottage
Latin/Old English
Small house that overlooks the place where the dolphins swim.

Dolphin Cove
Latin/Old English
Dolphins in the bay.

Dolphin House
Latin/Old English
The home overlooking the place where dolphins swim.

Donkey Field
English/Old English
Donkey in the meadow. *Eddie Murphy is the voice of 'Donkey', a character in the movies* Shrek *(2001) and* Shrek 2 *(2004).*

E

Elk River Lodge
Old English
Cabin near where the elk dwell by the river.

Elkhorne/Elkhorn
Old English
Deer horn.

Elkhorne Cottage/Elkhorn Cottage
Old English
Small house by the elk horn.

Emu Plains
Old English
Emus on the meadows. *Emus are the second largest bird on the planet after the ostrich. They are found in Australia and like the ostrich, emus do not fly; however, they can run at a speed of 50km per hour.*

Ewe Farm
Old English
The female sheep ranch.

F

Fox Grove /Foxgrove
Old English
Small, secluded woods where the foxglove plant grows; small, secluded wood where the fox resides.

Fox Hill
Old English
Fox on the hill.

Fox Hill Manor
Old English
Estate house where foxes can be seen on the hill.

Fox Hollow
Old English
Fox in the small valley.

Fox Inn
Old English
The fox hotel or bar.

Fox Wood/Foxwood
Old English
Fox forest.

Foxdale
Old English
Fox in the valley.

Foxden
Old English
Fox lair.

Foxdown Estate
Old English
Large, stately house where foxes roam on the flowing hills.

Foxfield
Old English
Fox meadow,

Foxfoot Estate
Old English
Large, stately house where foxes wander about.

Foxgrove Cottage
Old English
Small cottage in the secluded fox wood.

Foxholme/Foxholm
Old English
Fox house; the hamlet or village with foxes; the fox on the inshore island; fox on the floodplain. *'Holm/holme' is also a form of 'hamlet'. Today the name is sometimes used as an alternative spelling of 'home'.*

Foxton
Old English
Fox town.

Foxwood Estate
Old English
Large, stately house with foxes in the forest.

Foxwood Manor
Old English
Estate house in the fox forest.

G

Giraffe Fields
Italian/Arabic/English
Giraffe in the meadow; tall meadows.

Goat House
Middle English/Old English
Home of the goat. *The star sign Capricorn is symbolised by the goat.*

Greyhound Cottage
Old English
Small house where the greyhound resides. *This would be a good name for a greyhound trainer's house or for anyone who has a greyhound as a pet.*

Guinea Pig Cottage
West African/Old English
Small house where the guinea pigs are kept.

H

Hare Meadow
Old English
Hares in the field.

Hareton
Old English
Hare town.

Hargreaves
Old English
Grove of hares.

Harlea/Harlee/Harleigh/Harley/Harly
Old English
Wooded hare meadow.

Harmsworth
Old English
Farm with hares.

Hartford
Old English
The deer's shallow river crossing.

Hartlea/Hartlee/Hartleigh/Hartley/Hartly
Old English
The deer's meadow.

Hartop
Old English
Hares on the hill summit.

Hartwell
Old English
Deer stream.

Hartwood
Old English
Deer forest.

Hedgehog Cottage
Old English
Small house where hedgehogs reside near by.

Hog Haven
Middle English
Hog refuge.

Hog Heaven
Middle English
Hog bliss.

Horse Cottage
Old English
Small house with a horse.

Horse Farm
Old English
Horse ranch.

Horselea Cottage/Horselee Cottage/Horseleigh Cottage/Horseley Cottage Horsely Cottage
Old English
Small house with a horse in the meadow.

Horseshoes
Old English
Horse shoes; lucky. *It is believed (even today) that horseshoes are good luck. For the luck to work you have to find a horseshoe that has been lost by a horse and found by you with the open end facing your way. To hang it, fix with seven iron nails*

over the front door with the open end up so the good fortune doesn't spill out. Horseshoes were originally made from iron. This was due to its strength and ability to withstand fire. Superstitions about iron are thought to have originated in the Middle Ages when it was used as a charm to ward off evil spirits.

Hound's Tooth Cottage
Old English
Small house made of light and dark materials; small house where the dog's tooth was found. *Hounds-tooth is a distinctive pattern of jagged checks, usually in strongly contrasting colours used in textile weaving.*

I

Ibex Cottage
Latin/Old English
Small house where the wild goat reside near by.

Impala Fields
Zulu/Old English
Meadows where the impala (African antelope) reside.

J

Jackal House
Turkish/Sanskrit/Old English
Home of the wild dog. *Jackals are pack animals from Africa, Asia and Europe. They are smaller than their relative the wolf.*

Jaguar House
Spanish/Portuguese/Old English
Home of the wild cat. *A jaguar is a member of the cat family and is found in Central and South America.*

K

Kangaroo Cottage
Australian Aboriginal/Old English
Small house where the kangaroos reside near by.

Kangaroo Court
Australian Aboriginal/Old English
Courtyard where the kangaroo is kept. *An unofficial court where justice is disregarded. The word 'kangaroo' comes from the Gungu Yimidhirr language of the Northern Queensland Aboriginals.*

Kitten's Corner/Kitten's Korner
Old English
The young cat's corner.

Kittywell
Old English
Cat by the well or spring.

Kyloe
Old English
Meadow of cows.

L

Lamb Cottage
Old English
Small house where the lamb resides near by.

Little Fox Cottage
Old English
Small house where the small fox resides near by.

M

Merino Manor
Latin/Old English
Estate house with merino sheep.

Moose Manor
English/Old English
Estate house where the moose resides near by.

Mustang Ranch
American/Old English
Wild horse farm.

N

Newfoundland Lodge
Old English/English
Cabin where the newfoundlands reside. *A 'newfoundland' is a large, intelligent breed of dog that is believed to have originated from Newfoundland, an island near the Canadian coast.*

Numbat Cottage
Australian Aboriginal (Nyungar)/Old English
Small house where the numbat resides. *A 'numbat' is a small marsupial that feeds mainly on termites.*

O

Opossum Cottage
Old English
Small house visited by the opossum.

Oxbrow
Old English
Where oxen are kept on the hill.

Oxford
Old English
Shallow river crossing used by oxen. *The University of Oxford is the oldest English-speaking university in the world and lays claim to at least nine centuries of teaching. It developed rapidly after 1167, when Henry II banned English students from attending the University of Paris.*

Oxenham
Old English
The ox village or farm.

Oxlea/Oxlee/Oxleigh/Oxley/Oxly
Old English
Meadow of oxen.

Oxton
Old English
Ox town.

P

Possum Gully
Old English
Possums in the valley.

Possums Hideaway
Old English
Refuge for the possum.

Pussy Cat Manor
English/Old English
Estate house with a cat.

Q

Quagga Creek
African (Bantu)/Old English
Small stream where the quagga may be found. *'Quagga' or 'kwagga' is a breed of zebra that is near extinction.*

R

Rabbits Rest
Old English
Rabbit burrow.

Ramsden
Old English
The ram's valley.

Rats Rest
Old English
The place where the rats reside. *Possibly not the ideal name if you're renovating with a view to selling soon.*

Rawdon
Old English
Rough hill; roe-deer hill.

Rawlea/Rawlee/Rawleigh/Rawley/Rawly
Old English
Rough meadow; roe-deer in the meadow.

Rayburn
Old English
Roe-deer stream.

Raydon
Old English
Rye hill; roe-deer on the hill; river hill.

Rayfield
Old English
Rye meadow; stream in the meadow; roe-deer meadow.

Rayford
Old English
Shallow river crossing; rye by the shallow river crossing; roe-deer by the shallow river crossing.

Rocking Horse Cottage
Old English
Small house where wooden play horses are made.

Rodden
Old English
Roe-deer valley.

Roebuck
Old English
A male deer.

Roebuck Cabin
Old English
Male deer lodge.

Rowell
Old English
Roe-deer spring or well.

Rowland
Old English
Roe-deer field.

S

Sable Cottage
Middle English/French/Old English
Small, black house; small house where the sable mammal is kept or where its pelts are made into coats.

Shelpy
Old English
Sheep meadow.

Sheplea/Sheplee/Shepleigh/Shepley/Sheply
Old English
Sheep meadow.

Squirrel View
English/Old English
High vista from where the squirrel resides.

Swindel
Old English
Pigs in the valley. *Possibly not the ideal name if you're renovating with a view to selling soon.*

Swinford
Old English
Shallow river where the pigs cross over.

T

The Bear's Den
Old English
The bear's lair.

The Bear's Lair
Old English
The bear's den.

The Black Bull
Old English
Black bull.

The Black Horse Farm
Old English
Ranch with a black horse.

The Blue Boar Cottage
Old English
Small house with the blue, wild pig.

The Cat's Cottage
Old English
Small house where the cat resides.

The Cat's Meow
English
A good place.

The Crazy Cat Cottage
English/Old English
Small house where the odd cat resides.

The Dog House
Old English/Colloquial
Home where the dog resides. *The saying 'in the dog house' refers to someone who is in trouble, usually with his wife.*

The Feline Retreat
Latin/Old English
Refuge for cats.

The Flying Fox
Old English
An Australian fruit-eating bat.

The Fox and Hound
Old English
The fox and the hound dog. *This refers to the so called 'sport' of hunting foxes in England. Hunting hounds are let loose to follow the fox's scent trail and are followed by people on horseback until the fox is killed. Today, this 'sport' is unpopular due to its cruelty to animals.*

The Golden Lion
Old English
Gold-coloured lion. *The lion is symbolic of regal strength and power.*

The Hare And The Tortoise
Old English
This name would be chosen by a fan of the old Aesop fable of the same name. This is where the famous saying 'slow and steady wins the race' is derived from.

The Horse Pond
Old English
Small lake in the horse enclosure.

The Hound and the Hare
Old English
The dog and the hare. *This name comes from an Aesop fable about a hunter who laughed at a hound who was chasing a hare and did not catch it. The hound explained that the man had failed to see the difference between himself and the hare: the hound was running for his dinner while the hare was running for its life.*

The Moose House
Old English
Home where the moose reside near by; home with a moose head mounted on the wall.

The Mouse House
Old English
Home where the mice reside.

The Paint Horse/The Painted Horse
Old English
The horse of different colours. *In 1519 Hernando Cortez was recorded as the first person to bring the paint horse to the American West. These horses had great stamina and the Native Americans loved them for their beauty and grace and the cowboys loved them for their agility and speed.*

The Pony House
Old English
Home with a small horse.

The Pony Place
Old English
The place where the pony resides.

The Rabbit Burrow
Old English
The hole rabbits burrow into.

The Red Horse
Old English
Red-coloured horse.

The Sassy Moose
American/English
The cheeky moose.

The Squirrels
Latin/Greek/French/Middle English
The place where the squirrels play.

The Warren
Middle English
A hole in the ground where an animal, especially a rabbit or fox resides. *This may*

also be used to describe a home with many corridors or rooms.

The White Horse Estate
Old English
Manor house with white horses.

The White Horse Farm
Old English
Ranch with a white horse.

The White Lion Estate
Old English
Manor house with a white lion guardian statue. *The 'lion' is symbolic of regal strength and power.*

The White Rabbit
Old English
The place where the white rabbit resides.

Three Stallion Ranch
English/Old English
The farm or stud with three stallion horses.

Two Dog Ranch
Old English
The place where two dogs live on a farm.

Unicorn Cottage
Middle English/French/Latin
Mythological horned horse. *The unicorn has many legends about it, including if one drinks from its horn, one will be protected from poison.*

Velvet Paws
Old English
Cats paws; soft paws; the house where the cat resides.

White Buffalo Lodge
American/English
Cabin near the sacred buffalo. *Some Native Americans (Lakota, Sioux, Plains, Cree and many more) believe that the rare white buffalo is a sign of change for the better. In 1994 a white buffalo calf was born in Janesville, Wisconsin, USA. She is believed to be the first white calf born in that century. As a result, many Native Americans have made a pilgrimage to visit the sacred white buffalo aptly named Miracle.*

White Horse Cottage
Old English
Small house with a white horse.

White Wolf Cottage
Old English
Small house where the white wolf resides.

Wild Bear Cabin
Old English
Lodge near to where the wild bear resides.

Wildboar Ranch/Wild Boar Ranch
Old English
Farm with a wild pig.

Wolf Manor
Old English
Wolf by the estate house.

Wolfeborough
Old English
The municipality of the wolf.

Wolfen Manor
Old English
Estate house of the wolf.

Wolfton Manor
Old English
Estate house in the wolf town.

Wombat Cottage
Australian English/Old English
Small house where the wombat resides. *A wombat is an Australian plant-eating marsupial mammal.*

Wombat Woods
Australian English/Old English
Wombat forest. (See Wombat Cottage)

Ye Old Dog Cottage/ Ye Olde Dog Cottage
Old English
Small house with an old dog.

Zebra Cottage
Old English/African
Small black and white house; small home near the zebra enclosure; small home by the zebra crossing.

A hive of activity

Insects, arachnids and the like are everywhere and some are more beautiful than others. A butterfly or a ladybeetle can make for a wonderful name for a cottage. For those a little less squeamish, there are plenty of spiders and other creepy-crawlies lurking around to draw inspiration from.

B

Bee Cottage
Old English
Small cottage by the beehive.

Beecroft
Old English
Bees in the small pasture.

Beelea/Beelee/Beeleigh/ Beeley/Beely
Bee meadow.

Blue Beetle Cottage
Old English
Small house by the blue beetle.

Bumble Bee Cottage/Bumblebee Cottage
Old English
Small house where the bumblebee resides; small house by the beehive; the beekeeper's small house.

Bumble Bee Hall
Old English
Hall by the beehive; the beekeeper's hall.

Butterfly Cottage
Old English
Small house with butterflies.

Butterfly House
Old English
Home by the butterflies.

C

Christmas Beetle Cottage
Old English
Small house with Christmas beetles.

Cicada Cottage
Old English/Latin
Small house by the cicadas.

Cicadavale
Old English/Latin
Cicadas in the valley.

Cobweb Cottage
Old English
Small house with spider webs in the eaves.

Cricket Cottage
Old English
Small house with the crickets. *This may also refer to the game of cricket for sports lovers.*

D

Damselfly Cottage
Old English
Small house with a damselfly.

Dragonfly Sanctuary
Greek/Latin/English
Refuge for the dragonfly.

F

Firefly Cottage
Old English
Small house with the fireflies.

Flutterby Cottage
Old English
Small house with butterflies. *'Flutterby' is an anagram of 'butterfly'.*

G

Grasshopper Manor
Old English
Estate house with grasshoppers.

Green Beetle Cottage
Old English
Small house with a green beetle.

H

Honey Grove
Old English
Honey found in the small wood; the bee-keeper's small wood.

Honey House
Old English
The house by the honey beehive; the home where the bee-keeper resides.

Honeysett Cottage
Old English
Small house in the settlement where the beehives may be found.

L

Lady Beetle Cottage
Old English
Small house where the lady beetle resides.

Ladybird Cottage
Old English
Small house where the ladybird resides.

Ladybug Cottage
Old English
Small house where the lady beetle resides.

M

Monarch Butterfly House
Old English
Home visited by the monarch butterfly.

Mosquito Manor
Old English
Estate house with mosquitoes.

Moth House
Old English
Home with moths.

R

Red Beetle Cottage
Old English
Small house with a red beetle.

T

The Ant Hill
Old English
Ants on the hill; ant home.

The Bee Hive
Old English
Where bees live and honey is made. *This house may be a very busy place.*

The Painted Lady
Old English
Woman wearing makeup; prostitute; colourful house. *This is an affectionate name given to an old house, especially in the Victorian style (1837–1901). It is also the common name of a brightly coloured butterfly found in Europe and North Africa.*

Wasp Cottage
Old English
Small house with wasps.

The nesting instinct

Birds are a wonderful and colourful part of life in our gardens. Naming a house after our feathered friends is a wonderful way to show your love for nature. You may be fortunate to have a variety of birds that visit your garden to assist you in finding a house name that reflects the bird life in your garden.

Albatross Manor
Old English
The estate house close to where the albatross roosts.

Barn Owl Cottage
Old English
Small house where the barn owl roosts.

Bellbird Cottage
Old English
Small house where bellbirds roost.

Bird Of Paradise House
Old English/English
Home where the bird of paradise plant grows or where the bird of paradise lives.

Birdsville/Bridville
Old English
Village of birds.

Birdwood/Birdswood
Old English
Forest of birds.

Blackbird Cottage
Old English
Small house where the blackbird roosts.

Blue Heron
Old English
Blue heron bird.

Bluefeather
Old English
Blue feather.

Bowerbird Nest
English/Old English
The hoarder; nest of the bowerbird.

Bransgrove
Old English
Raven grove.

Budgie Cottage
Australian Aboriginal/Old English
Small house where the budgerigar roosts. *A 'budgie' is the short form of 'budgerigar', an Australian small blue, yellow, grey or green bird renowned for its talking ability.*

Budgiebourne/Budgieburn
Australian Aboriginal/Old English/Scottish
Budgerigar by the stream. (See Budgie Cottage)

Budgiewood
Australian Aboriginal/Old English
Budgerigar forest. (See Budgie Cottage)

Buzzards Ranch
Middle English/French
Buzzard farm. *A buzzard is an American bird of prey; in Britain the name is given to certain genera of slower, less heavily built hawks.*

Cockatiel Cottage
Dutch/Malay/Old English
Small house where cockatiels roost. *A cockatiel is a small, Australian grey parrot with a yellow crest on its head.*

Cockatoo Close
Malay/Dutch/Old English
The cockatoo is nearby. *A cockatoo is a crested parrot of any of the sub-family*

Kakatoeinae, found in Southeast Asia and Australia. One of the best known is the sulphur crested cockatoo, which is white with a yellow crest on its head, renowned for being able to talk.

Cockatoo Cottage
Malay/Dutch/Old English
Small house where the cockatoo roosts. (See Cockatoo Close)

Cockatoo Court
Malay/Dutch/Old English
Cockatoo in the courtyard. (See Cockatoo Close)

Cocky's Court
Malay/Dutch/Old English
Cockatoo in the courtyard. *'Cocky' is the short form of 'cockatoo'. It is also a nickname for a struggling farmer.* (See Cockatoo Close)

Cocky's Crest
Malay/Dutch/Old English
Cockatoo's crest. (See Cockatoo Close)

Cracknell
Old English
Crow by the well or stream. *Australian actor Ruth Cracknell (1925–2002) starred as Maggie Beare in the Australian television series* Mother and Son. *Ruth also worked on stage and appeared in many movies including* The Chant of Jimmy Blacksmith *(1978).*

Crane Cottage
Old English
Small house where the cranes roost nearby.

Cranebrook
Old English
Cranes by the small stream.

Cranston
Old English
The town with cranes.

Craven
Old English/Gaelic
Crow or raven; garlic.

Crawford
Old English
Crow by the shallow river crossing.

Crow Cottage
Old English
Small house where the crow roosts near by.

Crow Manor
Old English
Estate house where the crow roosts near by.

D

Dove Cliff
Old English
Dove on the ledge.

Dove Cottage
Old English
Small house where doves roost; house of peace. *The dove, in Christianity represents the Holy Spirit. The dove is also a symbol of peace.*

Dove Estate
Old English
Large, stately house with doves; house of peace. (See Dove Cottage)

Dove Manor
Old English
Estate house with doves; estate house of peace. (See Dove Cottage)

Dove Tree Cottage
Old English
Small house where the dove tree grows; small house where the doves nest in the tree.

Dovedale
Old English
Doves in the valley; peaceful valley. (See Dove Cottage)

Dove's Rest
Old English
The dove nest. (See Dove Cottage)

Drake Cottage
Middle English/German/Old English
Small house where the drake roosts. *A drake is a male duck.*

Drakemoore
Middle English/German/Old English
Male duck in the marshland.

Duck Cottage
Old English
Small house where the ducks roost nearby.

Duckton
Old English
Duck town.

Duckvale
Old English
Duck valley.

E

Eagle Farm
Old English
Eagles' ranch. *The eagle is also a symbol for America.*

Eagle Heights
Old English
Eagles on a high ridge or cliff. (See Eagle Farm)

Eagle House
Old English
Home where eagles roost nearby. (See Eagle Farm)

Eagle Rock
Old English
Eagle by the rock; eagle-shaped rock. (See Eagle Farm)

Eagle View
Old English
High vista; good vista; view of the eagle. (See Eagle Farm)

Eaglehurst
Old English/Middle English
Eagle in the forest on the hill. (See Eagle Farm)

Eagle's Field
Old English
Meadow where the eagle roosts. (See Eagle Farm)

Eagles Glide/Eagles Glyde
Old English
The place where eagles soar through the air. (See Eagle Farm)

Eagles Nest
Old English
The place where eagles roost. (See Eagle Farm)

Eagle's Rest
Old English
The place where the eagle nests. (See Eagle Farm)

Emu Station
Australian Aboriginal/English
The emu ranch. (See Emus Run)

Emus Run
Australian Aboriginal/Old English
The place where the emus are free to roam. *Emus are the second largest bird on the planet after the ostrich. They are found in Australia and, like the ostrich, emus do not fly; however, they can run at a speed of about 50km per hour.*

F

Falcon Cottage
Old English
Small house where the falcon roosts.

Falcon Court
Old English
Falcons in the courtyard.

Falcon Crest/Falconcrest
Old English
The crest or chest of the falcon; falcon on the summit. Falconcrest *was a television soap 1981–1990, starring Jane Wyman and Robert Foxworth as conflicting head members of a Californian wine-producing family.*

Falcon Heights
Old English
Falcon summit.

Falcon Manor
Old English
Estate house where the falcons are trained or where they roost near by.

Falcon Rest
Old English
The place where the falcon nests.

Falconridge
Old English
Falcon on the cliff.

Falconton
Old English
Falcon town.

Falconview
Old English
Vista of the falcon; high view.

Feather Cottage
Old English
Small house where the bird keeper resides; small house where the bird plucker resides; small house where the pillow-stuffer resides.

Featherbed Cottage
Old English
Small house with a mattress made of feathers.

Featherdale
Old English
Valley of feathers.

Featherstone
Old English
Feather-shaped stone.

Feathery Fields
Old English
Feathered meadow.

Finch Cottage
Old English
Small house where finches reside or breed.

Finch Farmstead
Old English
Homestead where finches are bred.

Finches
Old English
Finch birds.

Flying Crow Manor
Old English
Crow flying over the estate house.

Flying Eagle Cottage
Old English
Eagle flying over the small house.

Fowlford
Old English
Chickens by the shallow river crossing.

G

Gander Cottage
Old English
Small house where the gander roosts.
A gander is an adult male goose.

Gleneagles/Glenneagles
Scottish/Old English
Valley of eagles.

Goose Cottage
Old English
Small house where the goose roosts.

Goosebay
Old English
Goose by the inlet.

H

Hawk House
Old English
Hawks by the house.

Hawksdale
Old English
Hawks in the valley.

Hawksrest
Old English
The place where hawks nest.

Hawksridge
Old English
Hawks on the cliff.

Hawkwell
Old English
Hawk by the well or stream.

Hen Haven
Old English
The chicken refuge.

Henwood
Old English
Hen forest.

Heron Cottage
Old English
Small house where the herons roost nearby.

Heron House
Old English
The house where the herons roost nearby.

Heronswood
Old English
Heron forest.

Hummingbird Cottage
Old English
Small house where the hummingbird roosts.

Hummingbird House
Old English
Home where the humming bird roosts nearby.

I

Inglenook
Scottish/Old English
Small secluded place; small secluded place where the eagle may be found.

Inglewood
Scottish/English
Eagle forest.

K

Kookaburra Cottage
Australian Aboriginal
Small house where the kookaburra roosts near. *A kookaburra is an Australian bird, kingfisher, famed for its call that resembles laughter.*

L

Lonesome Dove
Old English
The lone dove. Lonesome Dove *(1989) was a television series that was based on the novel by Larry McMurtry. It was about two former Texas rangers who ran the Hat Creek Cattle Company situated near the town of Lonesome Dove.*

Lorikeet Cottage
Malay/Italian/Old English
The small house where the lorikeet roosts near by. *The lorikeet is an Australian bird with brightly coloured plumage.*

Lyrebird Cottage
Old English
Small house where the lyrebird roosts nearby.

Lyrebird Manor
Old English
Estate house where the lyrebird roosts nearby.

Magpie Cottage
Old English
Small house by the magpie's nest.

Magpie Manor
Old English
Estate house where the magpie roosts nearby.

Magpie's Nest
Old English
Place where the magpie roosts.

Morning Dove
Old English
Dove of the morning.

Nightingale Cottage
Old English
Small house where the nightingale bird roosts nearby.

Ostrich Estate
Latin/Greek/Middle English/Old English
Large, stately house where ostriches roost nearby.

Owles
Old English
Owl; one who loves the night.

Owl's Moor
Old English
The owl that lives in the marshland.

Owl's Nest
Old English
The place where the owl roosts.

Parrot Haven
Old English
The refuge for the parrot.

Peacock Cottage
Old English
Small house where peacocks roost nearby. *A peacock feather is believed to be bad luck as it has an evil eye at the end. This superstition comes from a Greek legend about a hundred-eyed monster that was turned into a peacock with all its eyes in its tail.*

Peacock Place
Old English
The place where peacocks roost nearby. (See Peacock Cottage)

Pelican Cottage
Latin/Greek/Old English
Small house where the pelican roosts nearby.

Pelican Landing
Latin/Greek/Old English
The place where pelicans land.

Pelican Ridge
Latin/Greek/Old English
Cliff where the pelicans sit.

Pelican Waters
Latin/Greek/Old English
The lake, river or sea where the pelicans roost.

Penguin Point
English/Old English
Penguins at the headland.

Penguin Retreat
Old English
The penguin refuge.

Peregrine
Middle English
Estate house of the fast flying falcon.

Pigeon Point
Old English
Pigeons by the headland.

Ransford
Old English
The raven's shallow, river crossing.

Ransleigh/Ranslea/Ranslee/Ransley/Ransly
Old English
The raven's meadow.

Raven Cottage
Old English
Small house where the raven roosts. *Some native cultures regard the raven as a messenger of death. The raven is also believed to be, by some Native American cultures, the creator of the world, the bringer of daylight, and has been portrayed as a trickster. In Cornish legend, King Arthur became a raven after his death. Edgar Allen Poe wrote his famous poem* The Raven *in 1845.*

Raven Hill
Old English
Raven on the hill. (See Raven Cottage)

Raven House
Old English
Home where the raven roosts nearby. (See Raven Cottage)

Ravenbourne
Old English/Scottish
Raven stream. (See Raven Cottage)

Ravenscourt
Old English
Raven in the courtyard. (See Raven Cottage)

Ravenshine
Old English
The shiny raven. (See Raven Cottage)

Ravensmead/Ravensmeade
Old English
The raven's meadow. *Mead is also a very sweet alcoholic drink made from honey, water, malt and yeast.* (See Raven Cottage)

Ravenstone
Old English
The raven by the stone; raven-shaped stone. (See Raven Cottage)

Ravenswood
Old English
Raven forest. (See Raven Cottage)

Ravensworth
Old English
The farm or village with ravens; valuable ravens. (See Raven Cottage)

Red Robin Ranch
Old English
Farm where the red robins roost.

Remington
French/English
The raven's town.

Renfrew
Old English
Still river; the raven's river.

Renshaw
Old English
Raven's forest.

Renton
Old English
Raven's town.

Robin's Nest
Old English
Where the robin bird roosts.

Robin's Roost
Old English
The robin's nest.

Rookery Nook
Old English/Middle English
Secluded nesting area. *Ben Traver's popular farce,* Rookery Nook *(1960), is set in Chumpton-on-Sea, Somerset.*

Snowbird Cottage
Old English
Small house where the snowbird resides nearby.

Sparrow Cottage
Old English
Small house where the sparrows roost.

Sparrowville
Old English
Village of sparrows.

Spread-eagle
English/Old English
To stretch out. *A name for a large property.*

Swallow Barn
Old English
The farm shed where swallows roost.

Swallows Cottage
Old English
Small house where swallow birds roost nearby.

Swallow's Eaves
Old English
Swallows reside in the eaves of the house.

Swallow's Nest
Old English
Where the swallow roosts.

Swan Lake
Old English
Swans on or by the lake. Swan Lake *is a famous ballet about a prince who falls in love with the swan queen, a woman transformed into a bird by an evil sorcerer and destined to remain a swan until rescued by a man's undying love.*

Swanhurst
Old English/Middle English
Swans in the hill forest.

Swanmoore
Old English
Swans by the marshland.

Swansea
Old English
Swans by the sea.

Swanston
Old English
Town of the swans.

Swanwater
Old English
Swans on the water.

T

Tawny Frogmouth Haven
English/Old English
Refuge for the tawny frogmouth owl.

The Bird Cage
Old English
Enclosure for birds.

The Bird Cottage
Old English
Small house where the birds roost in or near by.

The Bird Pond
Old English
Small lake with birds.

The Black Duck
Old English
Black duck.

The Black Swan
Old English
Black swan.

The Country Goose
Old English
Rural area with a goose.

The Cranes
Old English
The place with cranes.

The Eagle's Nest
Old English
The place where eagles roost.

The Falcon
Old English
The falcon bird.

The Feathered Nest
Old English
The nest with feathers. *A name for a house with soft and comfortable furnishings.*

The Golden Pheasant
Old English
Gold-coloured pheasant.

The Goose And Gander
Old English
The place where the goose and gander roosts.

The Goose Farm
Old English
Ranch where the goose roosts.

The Hawk Nest
Old English
The place where the hawk roosts.

The Herons
Old English
The heron birds.

The Honeyeater
Old English
The nectar or honey eating bird.

The Lyre Bird Cottage
Old English
Small house where the lyre bird roosts.

The Muddy Duck
Old English
The duck from the muddy place.

The Pelican
Latin/Greek/Old English
The pelican bird.

The Raven Haven
Old English
Refuge for the raven.

The Raven's Nest
Old English
The place where the raven roosts.

The Raven's Retreat
Old English
The raven's refuge.

The Rookery
Old English
Nesting area; where the penguins or seals breed; a maze of dwellings. *Ben Travers' popular farce,* Rookery Nook *(1926) is set in Chumpton-on-Sea, Somerset.*

The Sparrowhawk
Old English
The sparrow hawk.

The Sparrows
Old English
The place where the sparrows roost.

The Swan
Old English
The swan.

The White Bird
Old English
White bird.

The White Swan Cottage
Old English
Small house with white swans nearby.

The Wise Owl Cottage
Old English
Small house where the owl roosts.

The Wren's Nest
Old English
The place where the wren roosts.

W

Where Eagles Dare
Old English
Eagles flying in a dangerous area. Where Eagles Dare *(1968) was a movie starring Richard Burton and Clint Eastwood.*

White Ibis Estate
Old English
Large, stately house where the white ibis roosts.

White Raven Cottage
Old English
Small house where the white raven roosts.

Wild Duck Cottage
Old English
Small house where the wild ducks roost.

Willy-wagtail Cottage
Old English
Small house where the willy-wagtail resides.

Wrenhaven
Old English
Refuge for the wren.

Snakes alive!

Some people have a fascination with lizards, alligators, frogs, and snakes, and may choose a reptilian or amphibian name for their home. Fish are a further source of inspiration. Geckos, blue tongue lizards and frogs are interesting subjects for a house name that will certainly make your house name stand out from the crowd.

A

Alligator's Cabin
Spanish/Latin/English
Small house near with an alligator.

B

Blue Tongue Lizard Hollow
Old English
Blue tongue lizard in the valley. *A blue tongue lizard is an Australian species of lizard with a blue-coloured tongue.*

Bullfrog
Old English
Bull frog.

F

Fishborne/Fishburn/Fishburne
Old English/Scottish
Fishing stream.

Fishlock
Old English
Fishing lake.

Frog Hollow
Old English
Frog valley.

Frogs Hole
Old English
Frog hole.

Frogton
Old English
Frog town.

Frogwell
Old English
Frogs by the well or stream.

G

Goannaville
Arawak/Spanish/Old English
Goannas in the village; lots of goannas. *A goanna is a large Australian lizard.*

J

Jerrawa
Australian Aboriginal
Goanna. (See Goannaville)

S

Serpentine Gully
Middle English/Latin/Old French/Old English
Snake valley; winding valley.

Snake Gully
Middle English/Latin/Old French/Old English
Snake valley.

Snake Valley
Latin/English
Snake dale.

T

Tadpole Manor
Old English
Estate house where baby frogs reside.

The Alligator Hole
Spanish/Latin/English
Watering hole where the alligator resides.

The Crocodile House
Latin/Greek/French/Middle English/Old English
Home where the crocodile resides.

The Dragon's Den
Old English
Lair of the dragon. *A dragon is a mythical creature with a reptilian body, wings and breathes fire.*

The Dragon's Lair
Greek/Old English
The den of the dragon. (See The Dragon's Den)

The Earthy Frog
Old English
Brown-coloured frog.

The Frog Marsh
Old English
Frog marshland.

The Frog Pond
Old English
Small lagoon where the frog resides.

The Gecko Garden
Malay/Old English
The gecko (small, silver lizard) garden.

The Green Frog
Old English
Green-coloured frog.

The Green Tree Frog
Old English
The green tree frog.

The Sleeping Lizard
Old English
Lizard sleeping.

The Snake Farm
Old English
Snake ranch.

The Snake House
Old English
Home with snakes.

Toad Hall
Old English
Hall where the toad resides. *'Toad Hall' featured in the book* The Wind in the Willows *by Kenneth Grahame, published in 1908. It is one of the most beloved children's books of all time. It is set in the English countryside and tells about the adventures of Rat, Mole, Badger and Mr Toad.*

CHAPTER 12

UNUSUAL HOUSE NAMES

Traditional house names are most commonly used for name plaques; however, unusual house names can give a feeling of fun and can leave an impression on visitors. A name may be funny, playful or ironic. It may be made up of local colloquialisms to add personality or amusement to your house name. Bear in mind that diplomacy is needed in finding a name. You don't want to upset your neighbours, visitors or even your local council by using inappropriate words, as this may offend.

A

A Step Up
English
A better place than the last. *This name would be used to describe a better dwelling than the one the owner/s previously lived in.*

A.1.
English/American
Perfect; good condition.

A.O.K.
English/American
All is okay.

A.W.O.L.
American Military term
Absent without leave. *An amusing name for a house where the owner/s have left the city for the country.*

Acropolis
Greek
The upper city. *A good name for a building with Greek inspired architecture or pillars. It may also be used to proudly show the owner's country of origin.*

Ageing Gracefully
Old English
Growing old with dignity. *This may refer to the house or, more cheekily, its occupants.*

Airs & Graces
Old English
Someone who acts more upper class than they are.

Alcatraz
Spanish/American
An island in San Francisco Bay, California, USA, and formerly the site of a famous prison of the same name. *The name may be used as a tongue-in-cheek name for a home with high fencing and good security. Alcatraz is also known as 'The Rock' and was home, from the 1930s until the 1960s, to America's premier maximum-security prisoners. It is one of San Francisco's most prominent landmarks and tourist attractions. It even inspired a movie starring Clint Eastwood, titled* Escape from Alcatraz *(1970).*

All Smiles
Old English
A happy place.

All's Well
Old English
All is well.

Aloha
Hawaiian
Greetings/farewell.

Always Inn
Old English
Always home. *Also a play on the word 'in' meaning 'inside' and 'inn', the word referring to a pub that may provide accommodation.*

Anniversary Cottage
Old English
Small house built or bought to celebrate an anniversary.

As the Crow Flies
Old English/English Colloquial
To travel in a straight line.

At the Cross Roads
Old English
At crossing roads; a need to make a decision.

Avarest
English Colloquial
Have a rest. *It is also a play on the name 'Everest' in the Himalayas, the highest elevation in the world.*

B

Bachelordom
Middle English/Old French/English Colloquial
Where the bachelor resides.

Bachelor's Pad
Middle English/French/English Colloquial
Where the bachelor resides.

Baching
Old English/English Colloquial
Bachelor; living alone.

Back Blocks
Old English/English Colloquial
To live in a remote area.

Back of Beyond
Old English/English Colloquial
A very remote area.

Back of Bourke
Australian English
A very remote area.

Back to Nature
Old English/English Colloquial
Leaving the city for the country life; to get back to the natural life.

Back Woods
Old English/English Colloquial
An unsophisticated place; a remote area.

Backwater
Old English/English Colloquial
An unsophisticated place.

Battler's Cottage
Old English/English Colloquial
Small house where the owner has had his or her struggles in life.

BBQ Heaven
English/Old English
A place where a barbeque is enjoyed. *A fun name for those who are renowned for their BBQ techniques.*

Beauty/Bewdy/Bewdy Bottla
Middle English/Australian Colloquial English
Beautiful.

Bed of Roses
Old English
Living in good circumstances; house situated near a rose bed.

Beehive
Old English
A busy place.

Best of Both Worlds
English
The owner of this property has the best of everything.

Big Bourne
Old English/Scottish
Large stream.

Big Lake
Old English
Large lake.

Big Lake Cottage
Old English
Small house by the big lake.

Birdseye View
Old English
Good vista; a view from a great height.

Bittersweet House
English/Old English
House of happiness and sadness.

Bless This Mess
Old English/English
God is to give favour to the owner's disorder. *'Bless this mess' is a well-known saying, often taking the written form and hung on the wall of a house where the owner/s may not be very neat or tidy.*

Bless This Nest
Old English
God is to give favour to the owner's place of residence.

Blessed
Old English
Holy; given God's favour.

Bliss Cottage
Old English
Small house of pure happiness.

Bliss House
Old English
House of pure happiness.

Blissland
English/Old English
Land of pure happiness.

Blockhouse
Old English
House on a block of land. *The blockhouse was a building that was used as an observation place or fort. May be used as a house name for a tall and heavy-looking home.*

Bluegrass House
Old English/English/American
Home of the dark, green/blue-coloured grass; home of the country music fan.

Bookworm Cottage
Old English
Small house where the book reader resides.

Boots 'n' Saddles
English
Boots and saddles. *This name would be perfect for a cowboy's place of residence or where a leather worker may reside.*

Bricks 'n' Morta
English
Bricks and mortar, representing the home.

Bringacanatoo
Australian Colloquial English
Bring a can or two, referring to beer.

Broke
English
To have no money. *An amusing name for a very expensive house that has left the house owners a little strapped for cash.*

Brumby Farm
Australian/Old English
Wild horse ranch. *Brumbies were originally stock horses from the Snowy River region in Australia. There are many theories about the brumby including one about a prospector named Brumby who let his horses out free in his remote mountain property. Another theory is that a Lieutenant Brumby released his horses into the Blue Mountains west of Sydney and they found their way to the mountains of the Snowy River. The brumby is still a romantic figure today with many Australians growing up with tales of* The Man From Snowy River *and* Clancy of the Overflow *and other bush poems and stories by A.B. 'Banjo' Patterson.*

Bugger Off
English/Australian Colloquial
No trespassers; go away. *Not a very friendly name but it may be used in a tongue-in-cheek manner, as long as your visitors don't take it to heart.*

Bygone Cottage
Old English
Small house from a past era.

C

Caddy Shack
American English/English
The cabin of the assistant to the golfer. Caddyshack *(1980) starred Chevy Chase and Bill Murray.*

Calamity
French/Latin
Disaster. *Marthy Cannary Burk wrote her autobiography under the pseudonym 'Calamity Jane' about her exploits in the American Wild West. Doris Day (b. 1924) starred with Howard Keel (1919–2004) in a movie inspired by the book in 1953.*

Calamity Cottage
French/Old English
Small house of disaster. (See Calamity)

Callbackinn
Old English
Call back in. *A request for the visitor to revisit the place again another time. A play on the word 'inn' referring to a pub with accommodation.*

Callinn
Old English
Call in; come in. *A play on the word 'inn' referring to a pub with accommodation*

Cartoon Cottage
English/Old English
Small, animated house.

Cashmore House
American/Old English
Need more cash. *An amusing name for a very expensive house that may have left the owners a little strapped for cash.*

Castles in the Air
Old English
Day dreams. *A castle-like house on high ground.*

Celestial Cottage
Small and heavenly house.

Celestial Estate
Large and heavenly stately home.

Celestial Manor
Heavenly estate house.

Chalet Romantica
French/English
Small house of romance.

Charmhaven
Old English
Delightful refuge.

Charmville
Old English
Delightful village.

Chateau Relaxo
French/English Colloquial
Castle of relaxation.

Cheerio
English
Goodbye.

Chipp Inn
English Colloquial
To give assistance. *Also a play on the word 'Inn', referring to a pub with accommodation.*

Clamberinn
English/Old English
Come in. *Also a play on the word 'inn', referring to a pub with accommodation.*

Clear Blue Skies
Old English
Blue and cloudless skies.

Cloud Hill
Old English
Hill covered in cloud; high hill.

Cloudform Cottage
Old English
Clouds forming over the small house.

Cloudmont
Old English/French
Misty mountain.

Cloudsend/Clouds End
Old English
Where the clouds come to an end; clear skies. *A happy omen.*

Coo-ee
Australian
Greetings; a call to get attention.

Coolluck
English
Cool luck.

Costalot
English
Costs a lot; expensive. *A tongue-in-cheek name for an expensive house that may have left the owners a little strapped for cash.*

Cosynook
English/Old English
Cosy, small, secluded place.

Crankie's
English
Person who is easily angered.

Cubby House
Australian/English
Child's playhouse. *May be used as a tongue-in-cheek name for a small cottage, or the home of an over-enthusiastic renovator.*

Cuddlepie
Australian English/Old English
Sweet as pie and inspires affection. *'Cuddlepie' is the name of a character in Australian writer and illustrator May Gibbs's* Gumnut Babies *(1916) and* Snugglepot and Cuddlepie *(1918). The 'Gumnut' characters have been much loved by generations of Australian children and were further popularised through Gibbs's long-running comic strips.*

D

Dead End
Old English
The end. *A name for a house at the end of a street.*

Déjà View/Déjà Views
French/Old English
Having experienced the same view before. A play on the words 'Déjà vu'.

Déjà vu
French
Already seen.

Didyabringyagrogalong
English/Australian Colloquial
Did you bring your grog (alcohol) along?

Dinkum
Australian Colloquial
True; real.

Dinky-Di
English/Australian Colloquial
True; real.

Dinky-Di House
English/Australian Colloquial/Old English
True or real home.

Dog Box
Old English/Australian Colloquial
A small house.

Dog House
Old English/English Colloquial
The saying 'in the dog house' refers to someone who is in trouble, usually with his wife.

Don't Mess With The Nest
English
A request to leave the house how you found it.

Doodropinn
English/Australian
Do drop in; do come in. *Also a play on the word 'inn', referring to a pub with accommodation.*

Doo-Duckinn
English/Australian
Do duck in; do call in. *Also a play on the word 'inn', referring to a pub with accommodation.*

Doolittle
Old English
Do little. *This house may need very little repairs, or perhaps its owners have a very relaxed approach to life. The name may also be inspired by the movie* Doctor Doolittle *(1967) starring Rex Harrison, about a veterinarian who speaks a wide array of animal languages and helps solve their woes.*

Doomore
Old English
Do more. *More may need to be done in terms of repairs for this house.*

Double Decker
English Colloquial
Two stories. *May be used as a name for a house with two levels.*

Dozingville
English/Old English
Sleeping village; a place to sleep.

Dreamworld
Old English
The perfect place.

Dropinnmore
English
Drop in more; a request to visit more often.

Dunit
Australian/English Colloquial
Done it. *This could refer to having bought one's home.*

Dunlookin'
English/Australian Colloquial
Done looking. *A name for those who have found their perfect home and don't need to keep looking.*

Dunnmovin'/Dunmovin'
English/Australian Colloquial
Done moving house. *A name for those who do not wish to move house anymore.*

Dunroamin'
English/Australian Colloquial
Done roaming. *The perfect name for those who wish to settle down or get married.*

Dunworkin'
English/Australian Colloquial
Done working. *A name for the perfect retirement house.*

Duzus
English
It does us. *A house that meets all the needs of its owner(s).*

E

Elbow Room
English
A house with plenty of room. *A fun name for a large house.*

Epiphany Cottage
Greek/Old English
Small house of sudden perception.

Emoh Ruo
Australian English
Our home (reversed).

Eureka
Greek
Found. *For the owners who have just found the perfect house. It is believed that 'Eureka' (heureka) was first uttered by Archimedes (a mathematician and an inventor) when he found a method that determined the purity of gold.*

Evergreen
Old English
Always popular. Always green in colour. *A place with green trees.*

Evergreen Estate
Old English
Large, stately house with green trees.

Extraordinary Estate
Old English
Exceptionally large, stately home.

Extravagance Estate/ Extravagant Estate
Old English
Large, stately and exorbitant house.

Extravagant Cottage
Old English
Small but exorbitant house.

Every Penny
English
Expensive property. *This would be tongue-in-cheek for a very costly property or house.*

F

Fancy Free
English
No problems.

Fantasia
Latin
Fantasy. *A great name for a dream-like home. This name may also be inspired by* Fantasia *(1940), an animated movie made by Walt Disney.*

Fantasmagorical
English Colloquial
Fantastic.

Far and Wide
Old English
Over a long distance. *This name would suit a property whose owners had to search 'far and wide' to find it. It may also refer to the size of the property.*

Favourite Haunt
English/English Colloquial
A favourite place to live or hang out.

Finalé House
French/English
Last, final house. *This would be a suitable house name for owners who do not plan to move into another house.*

Fluke
English
Chance. *A home that was found by luck.* Fluke *(1995) is a movie starring Samuel L. Jackson about a man who is killed in a car accident and comes back to life as a dog. It is based on the novel of the same name by James Herbert (b. 1943).*

Fogworth
Old English
Misty farm.

Folly Cottage
Old English
Small house of foolish actions. *This name could also be suitable for a home having a large decorative sculpture or a mock ancient ruin in the garden.*

Folly House
Old English
Home of foolish actions. (See Folly Cottage)

Footloose
English
To be free; footloose and fancy free.
Fans of the 1984 movie Footloose *starring Kevin Bacon may also choose this name.*

Fortune Cottage
Old English
Small, lucky home.

Fortune Estate
Old English
Lucky, large and stately home.

Fortune House
Old English
Lucky home.

Forty Winks
Old English
Sleep. *A serene name for a home where one can take a nap without being disturbed.*

Fossil Cottage
Old English
Small, old house; small house by the place where fossils may be found.

Fossilfield
Old English
Meadow where fossils maybe found; old meadow.

Fossilton
Old English
Town where fossils maybe found; old town.

Freedom Cottage
Old English
Small house of liberty.

Freedom House
Old English
Liberated house.

Freedom Manor
Old English
Liberated estate house.

Full House
English/Old English
Home that has many people living in it; a poker hand consisting of three cards of one number kind and two of another, for example, three Jacks and two fives; a capacity audience. *This name might be chosen as a good omen for a card player, an actor or a musician.*

Fullcircle
Old English
To start over again; circular house.

Fullmoon Cottage
Old English
Small house under the full moon.

Fullup
English
A home that has many people living in it.

G

Gadabout
English
An active person; traveller.

Gallopinn
English
Ride on in; come in. *Also a play on the word 'inn', referring to a pub with accommodation.*

Garden of Eden/The Garden of Eden
Old English
Paradise. *'The Garden of Eden' was the original home of Adam and Eve, according to the Book of Genesis,* The Bible.

Gem Cottage
Old English
Small, jewelled house; small, valuable house.

Gem House
Old English
Jewelled home; small, valuable house.

Gemstone Cottage
Old English
Small, jewelled house; small, valuable house.

Getalong
English
To cope; to move on.

Glimmer House
Old English
Glowing home.

Golden Pond
Old English
Small, gold-coloured lake. On Golden Pond *(1981) was a movie starring Katharine Hepburn (1907–2003) and Henry Fonda (1905–82).*

Golf View
Vista of the golf course; vista of the gulf (large bay).

Gone Fishin'
English
The owner of this house has gone fishing; absent. *This is a fun name for the home of a keen fisherman and need not be taking literally.*

Gone Troppo
Australian/American/English
To go crazy; to go tropical.

Gonna/Gunner
English/American Colloquial English
Going to (do). (See Gunadoo)

Graceland/Gracelands
Old English
The graceful land. *In 1957, Elvis Presley (1935–77) bought a stately colonial mansion on 14 acres on the outskirts of Memphis. He named it 'Graceland' and today it is a popular tourist attraction in Memphis where Elvis fans pay homage to 'The King'.*

Gramp's Cottage
Contemporary/Old English
Grandfather's small house.

Gran's Cottage
Contemporary/Old English
Grandmother's small house.

Grandpa's Cottage
Old English
Grandfather's small house.

Granny's Cottage
Contemporary/Old English
Grandmother's small house.

Grassroots
Old English
Basic needs have been met; back to basics. *A perfect name for a country house, especially one that is self-sufficient.*

Green Thumb
Old English
Good gardener. *The owner of this house would have a beautiful garden.*

Gunadoo
Australian Colloquial English
Going to do. *If you have a house that needs a lot of work done but you never seem to get around to it, 'Gunadoo' is a good name to consider.*

Halfmoon Cottage
Old English
Small house under the half-moon.

Hallowed Ground
Middle English
Sacred area.

Hanging Rock
English/Old English
Rock overhanging a ledge or a cliff. Picnic at Hanging Rock *is an Australian movie made in 1975, based on Joan Lindsay's 1967 novel of the same title. The movie is about three students and a schoolteacher from Appleyard Cottage who disappear on an excursion to Hanging Rock. The movie is fictional although it is widely thought to be based on a true story. Hanging Rock is an actual place near Mount Macedon in Victoria, Australia.*

Hanging Rock Chalet
English/Old English/French
Small house near to the rock that overhangs a ledge or a cliff. (See Hanging Rock)

Happy Days
Old English
A place of good times. *Fans of the sitcom* Happy Days *(1980) may choose to name their house this. So may fans of Irish playwright Samuel Beckett (1906–89), although his play of the same name is somewhat bleaker.*

Happy Hideaway
Old English
Happy place of refuge.

Happy Ours
Old English
A play on the words 'happy hours'.

Happy Valley
Old English
Joyous dale. *'Happy Valley' is a popular place name in Britain, USA and Canada. Australia and New Zealand also have their own Happy Valleys near Adelaide and Wellington respectively. Hong Kong has a famous race course called Happy Valley.*

Hazy Hills
Old English
Misty hills.

Hazy Meadows
Old English
Misty fields.

Head Of The River
Old English
Mouth of the river.

Heart 'n' Soul
English
Devoted. *This name is also the title of a well-known popular song, often arranged as an easy piano duet.*

Heaven
Old English
Paradise.

Heaven Sent/Heavensent
Old English
Sent from heaven.

Heaven Mountain
Old English
Paradise mountain; high mountain.

Heavenly Cottage
Old English
Small house of paradise.

Heyday
English/Old English
The prime of life. *This house may have been the pride of the street in its heyday.*

Hicksville
American Colloquial/Old English/French
Unsophisticated village.

Hidden Springs
Old English
Secluded streams.

Hidden Valley
Old English
Secluded dale.

Hidey Hole
English/Old English
Secret place.

High And Windy
Old English
A high and windblown area.

High Hopes
Old English
High expectations.

High 'n' Dry
Old English/English
Abandoned; left alone. *A high place away from water.*

High 'n' Windy
Old English
A high and windy area.

High Roller
Old English/American
Gambler of large amounts of money.

High Society
Old English/English
Upper class. High Society *(1956) starred Bing Crosby, Frank Sinatra and Grace Kelly.*

Hill Breeze Cottage
Old English
Small, breezy house on the hill.

Hillbilly Heaven
American Colloquial /English
Paradise for an unsophisticated person or place.

His 'n' Hers
Old English
His and hers. *A name for the property shared equally between a man and a woman.*

Hocus Pocus
English
Trickery; magic.

Hodgepodge Cottage
Middle English
A cottage made of different materials; a jumble. *A possible name for a house made up of different building materials such as brick and weatherboard, corrugated iron and tile.*

Ho-Hum
English
Boring.

Holiday House
Old English
Holiday home. *A home used only at vacation times.*

Hollywood
Old English
Holy forest; holly forest. *A name for a very glamorous home. Hollywood in the USA is famed throughout the world for its movie making.*

Home Away from Home
Old English
A homely or comfortable place.

Home Farm
Old English
House attached to a farm.

Home Truth
Old English
Fact.

Homebird
Old English
Homebody.

Homebound
Old English
Confined to the home; moving toward the house.

Homegrown
Old English/English
Grown at home or in the countryside.

Homely
Old English
Comfortable; plain. *This name might be chosen for a house that is messy or looks a little shabby.*

Homeward
Old English
Towards the home; guardian of the home.

Homeward Bound
Old English
To head home.

Homey
English/Old English
Home-like; comfortable.

Honey Pot/Hunny Pot
Old English
A great place; a sweet place.

Honeymoon Cottage
Old English
Small house where the newlyweds reside.

Hooray
English
A call used to denote happiness.

Hooroo
Australian Colloquial English
Goodbye. *'Hooroo' was the last word spoken by Don Burke on his lifestyle television program* Burke's Backyard *in each episode (1987–2004). This program is believed to have launched the television life-style genre throughout the world.*

Hoot Hall
Old English
Fun hall.

Hope Ranch
Old English/American English
Farm of faith, wishes or desires.

Hopeful Cottage
Old English
Small house of faith, wishes or desires.

Hopeville
Old English/French
Village of faith, wishes or desires.

Horizon
Latin/Greek/Middle English
Where the earth and sky meet.

Hot Springs
Old English
Hot water spring, often containing minerals. *'Hot Springs' became a National Park in Arkansas in 1832 and is the oldest National Park in the USA.*

Hotchpotch
Middle English
Made of different materials; a jumble. *A house made up of different building materials such as brick and weatherboard, corrugated iron and tile.*

How-De-Doo
Old English
How do you do? A greeting.

Howyagoin'
English/Colloquial Australian English
How are you going; how are you?

Humdinger
English Colloquial
A good thing. May be used for a house that is excellent.

Humdrum
English
Boring.

Hurryback
English
Return quickly.

Inchview
English/Old English
Small view. *This would be a good name for a city apartment that may have a view of the ocean largely obstructed by another building.*

It'lldoo
English
It will do. *For a house that was settled for by its owners.*

Jamaroo
Australian Colloquial
May be used for a house that is full to capacity.

Jamboree
English
A large scout meeting camp.

Jampacked
English
A house that is full of people.

Jolly Cottage
Small and happy house.

Jolly House
Happy home.

Justanuff
English Colloquial
Just enough.

K

Knock-Down Cottage
Old English
A small house in need of some TLC (tender, loving care).

Kooky House
American Colloquial/Old English
Eccentric house.

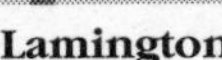

Lamington
Old English/Australian
Lamb town; a cube of sponge cake covered in chocolate icing and desiccated coconut, originating in Queensland and named after Lord Lamington, who was Governor of Queensland, 1895–1901. *A fun name for a house that is black and white or chocolate and white in colour. As a confection, the lamington is a tribute to the resourcefulness of Australian cooks, in this case in rendering stale sponge cake palatable. The invention of this concoction is humorously celebrated in a dedicated segment of Nigel Butterley and Barry Humphries' music and verse entertainment 'First Day Covers'.*

Lakeside Escape
Old English
Lake hillside.

Lazy Cloud Cottage
Old English
Small house under the slowly moving clouds.

Lazy Meadows
Old English
Idle fields.

Lazy River Estate
Old English
Large, stately house by the idle stream. *'Up a Lazy River' is a popular song written in 1931 by Hoagy Carmichael to lyrics by Sid Arodin. It has been recorded by many musicians, including Louis Armstrong and Frank Sinatra.*

Lazyville
French/Old English
Idle village.

Liberty
Latin/French/Middle English
Freedom.

Liberty Cottage
Latin/French/Middle English/Old English
Small house of freedom.

Liberty House
Latin/French/Middle English/Old English
Home of freedom.

Liberty Rose Cottage
Latin/French/Middle English/Old English
Small house of freedom and roses.

Lightning Ridge
Old English
Lightning on the ridge. *Lightning Ridge, Australia yields some of the rarest and most beautiful fossils and opals in the world including the black opal.*

Little Beaut!
English/Australian Colloquial English
Little, beautiful; very good.

Little Heaven
Old English
Small paradise.

Looneyville
American Colloquial/Old English/French
Crazy place; crazy village.

Lonely Cottage
Old English
Small house by itself.

Lonesome Cottage
Old English
Small house by itself.

Lonestar
Old English
One star. *Texas in the USA is known as 'The Lone Star State'. This comes from the star on the 1836 republican flag, consisting of a single golden star on a blue background. It symbolised Texas as an independent republic.*

Lonestar Manor
Old English
Estate house under the one star. (See Lonestar).

Luvmedoo
English
Love me, do. *This phrase can also be attributed to a Beatles song 'Love Me Do'.*

M

Made It
English
An expression of success.

Makedoo
English
Make do; to get by with limited resources. *A name for a very basic house.*

Makin' Memories
English
A home where one can live life with many memories.

Midway House
Old English
Halfway house.

Mine
English
My home. *The Italian version of this would be 'Mia'.*

Moondance Cottage
English/Old English
Small house where one dances under the moonlight.

Moonlight Sonata
Old English/Italian/Latin
Music playing under the moonlight. *Ludwig van Beethoven (1770–1827) wrote the famous 'Moonlight Sonata'.*

Moonshine
Old English
Moon shining down. *Making 'moonshine' in home distilleries has been part of American life since the first colonists arrived. Prohibition and the Great Depression spurred a boom in production that was combated first by the Treasury Department and then the Bureau of Alcohol Tobacco and Firearms (known infamously as 'The Revenuers').*

Moonstruck
Old English/English
To be struck by the moon's unusual pull resulting in a temporary insane state of mind. Also to be in a romantic, yet foolish state of mind. Moonstruck *(1987) is a movie starring Cher and Nicholas Cage.*

Muchado/Muchadoo
Middle English
Much ado; bustling with a fussy excitement. *This name may be attributed to William Shakespeare's play* Much Ado About Nothing.

My Cuppa Tea
English Colloquial
My cup of tea. *This refers to a home that meets its owner's satisfaction and personal taste.*

Myown
English
My own.

N

Nanna's House
Grandmother's home.

Nestin'
Old English
To nest; to make a house a home in preparation for a family; a cosy retreat.

Nestledown
Old English
Snuggle down; a cosy retreat.

Nestleinn
English
Snuggle in; a cosy retreat.

Neverland
English
Imaginary land. *The short form of the imaginary place featured in J.M. Barrie's* Peter Pan.

Never Never
English/Australian
The outback; a home that is in a remote area. We of the Never Never *was a movie made in 1982, after Jeannie Gunn's book of the same title, published in 1908, about a woman overcoming sexist and racial prejudice in outback Australia. Although published as a novel, Gunn's book was based on her own experience in the outback and recorded actual events.*

Never Neverland
English
Imaginary land. *The imaginary place featured in J.M. Barrie's,* Peter Pan.

Newinton/Newintown
English
New in town. *For the house owner who has just moved into a new area.*

Nirvana
Hindi/Buddhist
Bliss. *This house name may be used by fans of the grunge rock band of the same name, led by the late Kurt Cobain (1967–94).*

No Frills
Australian/English
A basic house. *A name for a house with nothing fancy done to it.*

No Worries
English/Australian Colloquial
No problems. *An easy-going or relaxed attitude to this house is reflected in this name.*

Nugget's Gully
English
Gold in the valley.

Numero Uno
Italian
Number one.

Oddfellows
English
Unconventional men.

Odds 'n' Ends
English
Bits and pieces. *For the house that may appear to be made out of miscellaneous items.*

Old Faithful
Trustworthy. *'Old Faithful' is a name given to an active geyser in the Yellowstone National Park, situated in the northwest corner of Wyoming USA.*

O'Socosy
English
Oh so cosy. A very comfortable house.

O'Soeasy
English
Oh so easy.

Our Lily Pad
English
Our home. *This in general refers to water lily leaves in a pond, a place where frogs may sit; however, it may be used tongue-in-cheek to describe a home.*

Ourton/Ourtown
English
Our town.

Over the Hill
English
Aged past its best; a house that is situated over a hill. *This may refer to the house or, if its owners had a sense of humour, may refer to them.*

Overlander
One who travels over the land. *In Australia, an overlander drives stock long distances.*

Oz
English
Unreal or magical land. *This name may come from L. Frank Baum's novel* The Wizard of Oz. *'Oz' is also a colloquial name for Australia, and was the name of a satirical magazine published in Sydney, NSW, 1963–73. In 1971 its editors, Richard Neville, Richard Walsh and Martin Sharp, were charged with obscenity offences and the magazine ceased publication in 1973.*

Palais
French/English
Public dance hall.

Palm Springs
Palm trees growing by the streams. *Palm Springs is a town in California.*

Panorama
Wide vista.

Panoramic
Having a wide vista.

Paradise Found
Old English
Heaven has been found. *May be used to name a property or a house where the owner has found a heaven on earth. The name may be inspired by John Milton's epic poems* Paradise Lost *(1667–74) and* Paradise Regained *(1671) and by John Mortimer's novel and its TV adaptation* Paradise Postponed *(1986).*

Parkyararse
English Colloquial
Park your arse; a cheeky name for a place to sit down!

Peekaboo
English
To have a quick look. *Also a game played with babies. 'Pekaboo' is Native American for shining waters.*

Pittsville
American/English/French
Horrible or boring village.

Playfair
Old English
Playful celebrations.

Playground
English
A name for a house that is a fun place to live or visit. *Also a house with playground equipment.*

Ploughinn
Old English
Come in; to plough the ground by the inn. *A play on the word 'inn', a pub or bar with accommodation.*

Polygon Wood
Greek/Latin/Old English
Forest with at least three straight sides. *Polygon Wood (a German stronghold) was fought over in 1917 and eventually captured by the Australians. Today, there stands a memorial to the Fifth Australian Division and the New Zealand soldiers who fought and died there.*

Pop's House
Old English/English
Grandfather's home. *This house name is probably given by the owner's grandchildren.*

Powwow
Native American
A place were ceremonies and feasting occur. In informal terms it also means a meeting place.

Pretty Penny
English
A name for a very expensive property.

R

Rainforest Cottage
Old English
Small house in the tropical woodland. *Rainforests are sometimes called 'The Earth's Lungs', as they help provide us with oxygen. They also contain a huge biodiversity and are home to over half the Earth's plant and animal species, even though they are only six percent of the Earth's ground surface and are diminishing rapidly.*

Ranch Grove
Old English/American English
Farm in the small woods.

Rancho
American English/Spanish
Another name for a ranch.

Rest Point
English
Relaxing headland.

Restabit
English
A place where one can rest awhile.

Restawhile
English
A place where one can rest for a period of time.

Resteasy
English
A place where one can relax.

Retired
English
Retired from working.

Risk 'n' All
English
Risking all; a gamble.

Riskinall
English
Risking all; a gamble.

Rivers Run
Old English
The river is passing through or near the property. All the Rivers Run *is a mini-series made in 1984 set in the Australia in the early 1900s. It is about a young English woman who marries a paddleboat skipper and stars Sigrid Thornton & John Waters.*

San Quentin/San Quintin
Spanish/American
Saint Quentin; also referring to a prison. *'San Quentin' is California's oldest correctional institution and has the state's only gas chamber and death row. This name may be used for a home that has high security.*

Seldom Inn
English
Rarely in. *A name for a busy person's house, although beware that this may also be seen as an invitation for burglars.*

Seldomere
English
Seldom here. *A house name for someone who is rarely at home.* (See Seldom Inn)

Serenade Cottage
French/Italian/Latin/Old English
Small house where one sings to one's love.

Serenade Estate
French/Italian/Latin/Old English
Large, stately home where one sings to one's love.

Serenade Manor
French/Italian/Latin/Old English
Estate house where one sings to one's love.

Serenade Valley
French/Italian/Latin/Old English
The valley where one sings to one's love.

Serendipity
Sri Lankan/English
Finding something pleasing by chance. *'Serendip' is a former name of Sri Lanka. Horace Walpole (1717–97) coined the term 'serendipity' from a Persian fairytale,* The Three Princes of Serendip, *in which the heroes do this.*

Serendipity House
Sri Lankan/English/Old English
Small, pleasing house found by chance.

Shamrock
Irish/Gaelic
Clover, a plant with three leaves, the national emblem of Ireland. *A home may be named 'Shamrock' to reflect the owner's original or Irish heritage.*

Shangri-la
English
Hidden paradise; paradise on earth. *Originally found in the novel* Lost Horizon *by James Hilton. Stevie Nicks had an album called* Trouble in Shangri-La *in 2001, as did Mark Knopfler in 2004.*

Shenanigans
Origin unknown
A place of mischief or trickery.

Sherwood Forest
Old English
One who resides in the bright woods. *Sherwood Forest is famed as the home of the legendary Robin Hood. Sherwood Forest can be found in Nottinghamshire, England.*

She's Apples
English/Australian Colloquial English
All is OK.

Siesta Cottage
Spanish/Old English
Small house used for resting.

Siesta Lake Cottage
Spanish/Old English
Small house of rest by the lake.

Sittin' Pretty
English Colloquial
Comfortable in life.

Sketchworth
Old English
A beautiful place worth drawing.

Sketchworthy
Old English
A beautiful place worth drawing.

Sleepy Hollow
Old English
Sleeping place; quiet hole. *Named after a place featured in Washington Irving's book,* The Legend of Sleepy Hollow.

Smoky Mountain
Old English
Smouldering mountain. *The Great Smoky Mountains can be found in North Carolina and are one of the largest protected areas in the United States. They are world renowned for their beauty, diversity of plant and animal life and were once a part of the Cherokee homeland.*

Smoky Mountain Cottage
Old English
Small house on the smouldering mountain. (See Smokey Mountain/Smoky Mountain)

Snow Angel Cabin
Old English
A snow angel is made by lying down and flapping your arms and legs in the snow. When you stand up, a marking is left in the snow in the shape of an angel.

Snowy Mountain
Old English
Snow on the mountain. *The Snowy Mountains are called 'the rooftop of Australia' or 'the High Country' due to being the highest point in Australia's Great Dividing Range. The region is popular for tourism, skiing and bushwalks and was the setting for the Australian film,* The Man from Snowy River *(1982), starring Tom Burlinson.*

Snugglepot Cottage
Australian English/Old English
Cosy little house. *The name of a character in Australian writer and illustrator May Gibbs's* Gumnut Babies *(1916) and* Snugglepot and Cuddlepie *(1918).*

Sometimes Cottage
English/Old English
Small house used occasionally.

Somewhere
English
Some place.

Southern Cross
Latin/Old English
Crossing in the south. *The 'Southern Cross' is also a star constellation most famous in southern skies and features on the Australian and New Zealand flags.*

Southern Cross Cottage
Latin/Old English
Small, southern; small house under the southern star constellation. (See Southern Cross)

Sovereign Hill
Middle English/Old French/Old English
The hill where the monarch resides. *Sovereign Hill near Ballarat was a site for a major gold rush (1851) in Victoria, Australia.*

Sportsview Field
Old English
Vista of the sports field.

Springfield
Old English
Stream meadow. *Springfield is the town where the cartoon family, the Simpsons, reside. In* The Simpsons, *Springfield was founded by Jebediah Springfield and located near Shelbyville. The series is created by Matt Groening.*

Stagger Inn
English/Old English
Come in. It also may boldly refer to staggering home drunk.

Starlight Manor
Old English
Estate house under the light of the stars.

Stayput
English
To stay. *A name for a house where the owner is determined to remain where he or she is.*

Stones Throw
Old English
A short distance away.

Summerlease
Old English/English
Leased summerhouse. *This house would generally be used in the warmer months.*

Swanky
American Colloquial
Fancy. *A name for a decorated house.*

T

Takealoadoff
English
Take a load off; a place where one can relax.

Tally-ho
English
A call given by hunters to alert their dogs to a sighting of a fox. *This may be used as a house name to reflect an owner with an English origin or a love of fox hunting; also a farewell. 'Tally-Ho' was the name of the dog featured in Louis de Bernières novel,* Red Dog. *While travelling through Karratha, Western Australia, de Bernières discovered a statue of a dog. Intrigued, he inquired about it and was swamped by locals with tales of this charismatic dog.*

Telegraph Hill
French/Old English
Hill of communication; hill where the telegraph poles are situated.

Temple of the Winds
Old English
Temple in a windy area; high house of worship.

Terra Firma/Terrafirma
Latin
Solid ground.

The Abyss
English/Latin/Greek
Deep chasm. *May be used as a house name to describe a large home in which a visitor may get lost.* The Abyss *(1989) is a movie about a diving retrieval team that encounter an alien aquatic species. It stars Ed Harris.*

The Animal Farm
Old English/English
Animal ranch; wild place. *A house where the wild people reside.* Animal Farm *(1945) is a satirical novel by George Orwell.*

The Apartment House
English/Old English
The building with separate flats or living quarters inside.

The Apex
Latin
The summit.

The Bachelor Pad
Middle English/Latin/Old French
House or apartment where a single man resides.

The Bachelorette Pad
Middle English/Latin/Old French
House or apartment where a single woman resides.

The Barracks
English
Soldiers' accommodation; the place where soldiers reside.

The Bat Cave
English
Where the bat resides in the cave. *The 'Bat Cave' may be used as a house name by a fan of television's* Batman. *It may also be the perfect name for a house with bats in its eaves.*

The Big Top
English/American English
A circus. *A name for a house that has a lot of rowdy behaviour or the home of someone who is very entertaining.*

The Black Stump
English/Australian/New Zealand
A marker showing the spot farthest away from civilisation. A very remote area.

The Block
English
A small area of land. The Block *is a television life-style program that follows the lives of couples as they renovate a block of units. It is hosted by Jamie Durie.*

The Brewery
English
The place where beer is made. *This may be used as a cheeky house name for those who bottle their own beer or drink a lot of it.*

The Bunk House
English/American English
A building that provides sleeping quarters for workers. *May be used as a name for a house that has bunk beds inside it.*

The Burrow
Middle English
A hole in the ground where an animal, especially a rabbit or fox resides.

The Caboodle/The Kit And Caboodle
English/American English
The whole lot; everything.

The Camp
English
Camping area.

The Carousel
French/Italian
The merry-go-round.

The Casino
Latin/Italian
A place of gambling. *A bold name for a house where the owners engage in gambling.*

The Castle
Old English
Fortified estate house of royalty; the home. *The name may also refer to the old saying, 'A man's house is his castle'.* The Castle *was a 1997 movie about a Melbourne family being forced to move out of its home by the government and the family's fight to keep the house.*

The Cave
Latin/French/Middle English
A small cavern. *An informal word for a house; a cave-like home. The Greek philosopher Plato used the image of a cave on the walls of which shadows of the passing traffic outside were cast in order to pose interesting questions about the nature of reality and perception.*

The Cavern
Latin/French/Middle English
Large, underground chamber. *'Cavern' may also be used in reference to an abode.*

The Centennial
Latin/Old English
One hundred year old house. *A name that celebrates the age of the house.*

The Centurion
Latin/Old English
One-hundred-year-old house. One who scores a century (especially in cricket). *A name that celebrates the age of the house. In ancient Rome, a centurion was a solder who commanded 100 men.*

The Century House
Old English
One-hundred-year-old house. *A name that celebrates the age of the house.*

The Chosen One
Old English/English
Home which was picked out of many others.

The Circuit
Latin/Middle English
A home built on a circular road.

The Club House
Old English
A members' only house.

The Cocoon
French
A protective shell. Cocoon *(1985) is a film about some trespassing seniors who are rejuvenated after swimming in a pool with alien cocoons. It starred Brian Dennehy (b. 1938) and Don Ameche (1908–93).*

The Continental House
Old English
Home of people from many different continents; home built in a distinctive style found in (some part of) Europe, but unusual in Britain.

The Cot
English Informal
A place to sleep; a bed.

The Creche
Old French/Old German
A place where children are looked after. *This may be used as a house name to demonstrate the large number of children that reside within the house.*

The Crib
English/American Informal
Referring to a house or apartment; a place to sleep; a bed.

The Crypt
Latin/Greek/Old English
An underground chamber that is used as a burial place. *This is more informally used by Americans to describe an apartment, house or place to sleep.*

The Deep South
English/American
Remote part of the south. *This is usually in reference to the American 'Deep South' and its five major states, Alabama, Georgia, Louisiana, Mississippi and Tennessee which all share a rich culture, history and heritage.*

The Desert House
Home in the arid area.

The Dinkum Den
Australian/Old English
The genuine lair; a genuine, comfortable room.

The Dungeon
Latin/French/Middle English
Underground prison; an unpleasant place to live.

The Everglades
Old English
Open space in the forest. *The Everglades, in Florida, USA, is a swampy, partly forested area, lying mostly to the south of Lake Okeechobee. Harlan Howard's country and western song, 'Everglades', was a hit for the Kingston Trio in 1960. It tells the story of a fugitive who stays 'running like a dog through the Everglades' for many years, unaware that the jury has found him not guilty on grounds of self-defence.*

The Expanse
English
Wide and vast land.

The Experiment
English
A test. *A cheeky name for a house where the occupants are testing out living there or their relationship.*

The Fossil
English
A cheeky name for a very old house.

The Funny Farm
English/Old English
Odd ranch. *A humorous name for a house full of crazy people.*

The Gates
Old English
The entrance. *A name for a house with large front gates.*

The Gateway
Old English
The entrance through the gates.

The Gazebo
Latin
The summer house.

The Getaway
Old English
Place of relaxation. *The 'Getaway' has traditionally been a peaceful retreat that invigorates the mind, body and spirit.*

The Goldfields
English
Meadows of gold; gold rush meadows. *The goldfields is a collective name for the various sites of the Australian gold rush in the 1800s.*

The Golden Fleece
English/Australian Colloquial
Informally referring to the best. *This may be a name for the best house on the street. According to Greek legend, Jason and the Argonauts went on a quest to recover from King Aeëtes of Cholchis the golden fleece from the ram on which Phrixus had been carried to Cholchis and bring it back to Iolchos.*

The Guide Post
Old English
A guidance fence used to show where the road is situated.

The Habitat
Latin
A place where a plant or animal resides.

The Halfway House
Old English
Midway house; house for drifters.

The Hideaway
Old English
The retreat. *The hideaway has traditionally been a peaceful retreat that invigorates the mind, body and spirit.*

The Hilton
Old English
The hill town. *This would make an amusing name for a small or rustic house, the opposite of the famed Hilton hotels.*

The Hive
Old English
Beehive. *This would be a perfect name for a very busy household.*

The Home Front
Old English/English
This refers to the home and its inner circle.

The Home Stretch
English/American
The final stage of an event or project. *The name might also suit a home that has been added on to or 'stretched'.*

The Homeland
Old English
One's native land. *A home on the land.*

The Hut
Old English
A simply constructed shelter.

The Joint
English/American Informal
The house. *Since the 1960s, this name has acquired a further meaning and may invite the unwanted curiosity of the constabulary!*

The Jubilee
Hebrew/Greek/Latin//French/Middle English
Anniversary. *A name for a house celebrating its 25th, 50th or 60th anniversary of being built. The name derives ultimately from the Hebrew 'Yōbēl' meaning ram. The ancient Hebrews blew a ram's horn trumpet to herald the beginning of special years of celebration, during which fields were to be left untilled and slaves set free.*

The Lagoon
Latin/ Italian
The body of water separated by a sand bank from a larger body of water.

The Last Resort
English
The last option.

The Looker
English/Australian Colloquial
Good looking. *This may be used as a name for a beautiful home.*

The Metropolis
Middle English/Greek/Latin
The main city. *This may be used as a name for a very large house. It may also be used in an amusing way for a small house.* Metropolis *was a sci-fi movie made in 1927 written and directed by Fritz Lang. 'Metropolis' was also the city Superman resided in.*

The Moores
Old English
The marshlands.

The Nest
Old English
Where house a is made a home; a cosy retreat.

The Never Never
English/Australian
The outback; a home that is in a remote area. We of the Never Never *was a movie made in 1982, about a woman overcoming sexist and racial prejudice in outback Australia.* (See Never Never)

The Oasis
Latin
Fertile area in a desert or dry area.
This would be a perfect name for a home in an arid area with a section of lush green gardens or a pool.

The Odd Couple
English
Two people living together who are the opposite of each other, one may be tidy, the other may be messy; strange couple. The Odd Couple *was a movie starring Jack Lemmon and Walter Matthau (1968) based on the stage play by Neil Simon and later made into a television series starring Jack Klugman and Tony Randell.*

The Outlook
Old English
The view. A name for a house or property with a view.

The Pad
English/American Informal
An apartment or house.

The Pavilion
Latin/French/Middle English
A building on a sports ground containing changing rooms; an ornamental structure in a park; an exhibition tent.

The Pearly Gates
Old English
The entrance to heaven. *This may be used as a name for a property with gates that lead onto a beautiful acreage.*

The Play House
English/Old English
The theatrical place; a house of fun.

The Play Shed
Old English/Australian English
Small place where children play; a playroom for adults, a billiards room for example.

The Plaza
English/Spanish
Public square. *An amusing name for a large house that may resemble a shopping mall or hotel.*

The Pyramid
Latin/Greek/Middle English
A building that has a square base yet is made up of four triangles that meet at a point. *Used as a burial chamber for the Pharaohs in ancient Egypt. May also be used as a name for a home that is inspired by Egyptian design.*

The Raintree
Old English
Rain forest tree.

The Resort
English
A place of recreation. *May be used as a house name for a home that has resort-like facilities.*

The Round House/The Roundhouse
Old English
The circular house. *A name for an unusually circular shaped home. 'Roundhouse' is also a nautical term, denoting variously the captain's accommodation on the quarterdeck of Indiaman ships, the apprentices' accommodation on the afterdecks of some later sailing ships, and the toilets on the top deck of Royal Navy ships. Therefore the name might also be chosen for a houseboat.*

The Shack
English/American English
A simple constructed shelter. *May also be used as a tongue-in-cheek house name for a large and expensive house.*

The Shed
English/Australian
Small barn or covered a work area.

The Southern Cross
Latin/Old English
Crossing in the south. *The 'Southern Cross' is a star constellation most famous in southern skies and also features on the Australian and New Zealand flags.*

The Southern Cross Cottage
The small house by the crossing in the south. (See The Southern Cross)

The Spot
English
A good place to be.

The Taj Mahal
Persian Abbreviation
The light of the palace. *The 'Taj Mahal' is a building in India, built by the Emperor Shah Jahan in memory of his favourite wife, Mumtaz Mahal. The name is believed to have come from an abbreviated form of her name. It may be used as a name for either a large house, one influenced by Indian design, or as a bold name for a small house.*

The Treasure
Greek/French/Middle English
Hoarded wealth; cherished. *'The Treasure' may be an affectionate name for a very loved and cherished home.*

The Treasure Chest
Greek/French/Middle English
A place where valuables are contained within.

The Treasure Trove
Old French/English
A wealthy discovery.

The Tree House
Old English
Home among the trees; tall house. *A name for a house built on stilts or from wood in a forested area.*

Thorngarth
Old English/Scandinavian
Prickly enclosure.

Thunder Cloud
Middle English/Old English
Thunder in the clouds.

Thunder Cove
Middle English/Old English
Thunder in the bay.

Thunder Hill
Middle English/Old English
Thunder by the hill.

Thunderdome
Middle English/French/Latin
Stately home of thunder or loud noise. Mad Max: Beyond Thunderdome *(1985) starred Mel Gibson and Tina Turner*

Thunderhead
Middle English/Old English
Thick thunderclouds overhead.

Top Of The World
Old English
The highest summit.

Thunderhead Mountain
Middle English/Old English
Thick thunder clouds over the mountain. *Thunderhead Mountain is situated in South Dakota, USA.*

Tickled Pink
English
The owners of this house are very happy.

'Tilthen
English
Until then.

'Tilwemeetagain
English
Until we meet again.

Timbuktu
African Mali
Often meaning a far away place. *Also spelt Tombouctou, a city in the West African nation of Mali located on the southern edge of the Sahara.*

Tomatin
Gaelic
Hill with a juniper bush growing on it.

Touchwood
Old English
To pat or feel wood. *This house may be named after an old superstition. To touch wood is to ward off bad luck. It may also mean a crumby or decayed wood used for kindling. 'Knock on Wood' is the American version of this saying.*

Treasure Cottage
Small house of hoarded wealth; small, cherished house. *'Treasure Cottage' may be an affectionate name for a very loved and cherished home.*

Treasure Wood
Valuable forest; forest of hoarded wealth; cherished forest.

Tropica
English/Latin
Tropical home.

Tropical House
English/Latin/Old English
House in a tropical climate.

True Blue
English/Australian
Loyal. *If a house is named after this, the owners will appear to be faithful and genuine.*

True Grit
Old English/English
To have true determination. True Grit *(1969) starred John Wayne (1907–79) and Glen Campbell (b. 1936).*

Twilight Zone
Latin/English
A place of decline; an odd place. *Generally used as a reference to the television show* The Twilight Zone, *(1959–64 and 1985–7) created by Rod Serling. Because of this show, the name may suggest an unusual place to be.*

W

Wandah-in
English
To wander in.

Wander In/ Wander Inn/Wanderin/ Wanderinn
Old English
To wander in.

Warts 'n' All
Old English/English
May be used as a name for a house that is likeable, even though it has defects.

Weeds 'n' All
English
Weeds and all. *A house that is loved even if it has a large expanse of weeds.*

Welldon/Welldone/Welldonne/Welldun/ Welldunn/Welldunne
Old English
Well done.

Weowna
English/Australian
We own her, referring to the house. *This is a very popular name for Australian homes as it looks exotic but the meaning is very Australian.*

Whyworry
English
Why worry? *A name given to a home where the owners are easy going and free from worry.*

Witsend
Old English
At wits' end; about to go crazy.

Woodstock
Old English
Forest stockyard. *This name may be inspired by the huge 1969 rock concert held at Woodstock Bethel, in upstate New York. Woodstock was also a character in the Charlie Brown comic strip* Peanuts, *created by Charles M. Schultz on 2 October 1950.*

Woodwood
Old English
Many forests. *A name for a house nestled amongst many trees in a forested area. It*

may also reflect the owner's name, 'Wood', and the fact that they also live in a forest or a 'wood'.

Woop Woop
Australian
A remote place. *The perfect name for a house in a far away place.*

Y

Yesteryear
Old English
Years of the recent past. *A name for a house which was built in the recent past.*

Yworry
English
Why worry? (See Whyworry)

CHAPTER 13

WHO WE ARE TODAY

During the nineteenth century many placenames and house names in Australia and New Zealand reflected the nostalgia felt by people from Britain, Scotland and Ireland for the homes they had left behind. Indeed, many houses were named after the village or town where the settler had lived in the 'old country'.

Today our planet is often described as a global village. The Internet, chat rooms and email can unite people from opposite parts of the world, submerging them in different cultures and languages. Similarly, in recent times baby names and even house names have taken on a more exotic composition. These names are now proclaimed in confident celebration of a multicultural identity. The house names in this chapter come from many different languages including Gaelic, Spanish, Italian, Greek, French, Hebrew, and a variety of Indigenous languages. They reflect our changing sense of who we are today.

Gaelic

A

Abernnethy
Scottish
Mouth of the river.

Adair
Scottish
Oak tree by the shallow, river crossing.

Airleas
Irish
Promise.

Alina
Celtic
Harmonious.

Aneira
Welsh
Honourable; gold.

Argyle
Irish
From Ireland.

Argyll Manor
Gaelic/Old English
Estate house from Ireland. *The owners of this home maybe are originally from Ireland.*

Arianwen
Welsh
White; silver; white friend.

Athol Cottage
Old English
One who resides in the hollowed area; (Gaelic) from Ireland; the small Irish house. *The people who reside in this house may be Irish or have an Irish ancestry.*

Athol Lodge
Old English/North American
Irish cabin. (See Athol Cottage)

Avoca
Irish
Sweet. *Avoca is a popular holiday and surfing area on the central coast of New South Wales, Australia.*

Avoca Cottage
Irish/Old English
Small, sweet house.

Avocavale
Irish/Old English
Sweet valley.

Awena
Welsh
Poetry.

B

Baera
Irish
Brown/red-colour.

Balfour
Scottish
Village meadow.

Barren
Irish
Hilltop.

Boan
Irish
White cow.

Bonny
Scottish
Pretty; charming.

Bonny Cottage
Scottish/Old English
Pretty and small house.

Bonny Blue Cottage
Scottish/Old English
Pretty, small and blue-coloured house.

Bonnyville
Scottish/Old English
Pretty village.

Brae Cottage
Scottish/Old English
Small house on the hill.

Brae End
Scottish/Old English
Hill at the end of the property.

Braemar
Scottish/Old English
Hillside marshland.

Braeside
Scottish/Old English
Hill side.

Braeside Manor
Scottish/Old English
Hillside estate house.

Brangane
Irish
White raven.

Breen
Irish
Fairy palace.

Briar
Irish
Heather; wild rose.

Bryanna
Irish
Hill. *Also a girl's name.*

Brynmore
Welsh
Large hill.

C

Cailin
Welsh
Pure spring.

Camden
Irish
Windy valley.

Carey
Welsh
Castle on the rocky island. *Mariah Carey was the best-selling female singer in the 1990s and made history having more number ones than even the Beatles.*

Ceinlys
Welsh
Gem.

Ceinwen
Welsh
Beautiful; precious stone.

Celyren
Welsh
Holly.

Cheryl
Welsh
Love. *Also a girl's name.*

Cheyne
Scottish
Oak hearted.

Clunies
Scottish
Meadow resting place.

Cordelia
Celtic
Jewel from the sea.

Crisiant/Crysiant
Welsh
Crystal.

D

Dallas
Irish
Wisdom. Dallas *(1978–91) was a famous television soap set around J.R. Ewing (Larry Hagman) and the oil industry.*

Darby
Irish
Freedom.

Devony
Scottish
Loved.

E

Edana
Celtic
Desired.

Eibhlín
Irish
Shining light.

Eiralys
Welsh
Snow drop.

Erin
Irish
Western island; peace. *'Erin' is an archaic name for Ireland.*

Erskine
Scottish
High cliff.

Eveleen
Celtic
Pleasant life. *Also a girl's name.*

F

Fagan
Irish
Little fire.

Fergal
Irish
Strength.

Forbes
Irish
Wealthy fields. *Forbes is a town in the western slopes of New South Wales, Australia.*

G

Garvey
Irish
Peace.

Giorsal
Scottish
Graceful.

Glen/Glenn
Scottish
Valley.

Glendon
Scottish
Valley fortress.

Glenivan
Scottish
God's gracious valley.

Glenna
Irish
Valley.

Glenrowan
Scottish
Rowan tree valley. *Glenrowan is a small town at the foot of The Warby Ranges in Victoria Australia. It is infamously known as the place Ned Kelly had his 'last stand'.*

Glyn/Glynn
Welsh
Valley.

Glynnis
Irish
Valley.

Gold Rush Cottage
English
Small house built during the gold rush. *The gold rushes had a large effect on the growing Australian economy and brought a large consignment of new arrivals including Italians, the French, Americans, Germans as well as German and Polish exiles. The largest contingent came from the 40,000 Chinese who searched the fields in hope of making their fortune and a new life for themselves and their families.*

Graceland/Gracelands
Graceful meadows. *In 1957, Elvis Presley bought a stately colonial mansion on 14 acres on (then the) outskirts of Memphis. He named it 'Graceland'. Graceland is now a very popular tourist attraction in Memphis where Elvis fans pay homage to 'The King'.*

Hagan
Irish
Ruler of the house.

Highlander
Scottish/English
Person from the high mountain land.
A 'Highlander' is someone who resides in the mountainous region of central and northern Scotland, famous for its beauty and Scottish/Gaelic culture.

Idelle
Irish
Bountiful.

Ilene
Celtic
Light

Ireland
Irish
From Ireland; peace; western island. *Also known as 'Erin'.*

Irvin
Gaelic
Green river.

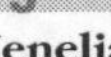

Jenelia
Welsh
White river.

Jennalee
Welsh
White meadow.

Kade
Scottish
Wetlands.

Kallen
Irish
Might warrior.

Kinnard
Irish
The king's high hill.

Lachlan
Scottish
Lake.

Lachlan
Scottish
Land of the lakes.

Laird
Scottish
Land owner.

Lennox
Scottish
Elm tree grove.

Lian
Irish
Protector.

Lightning Ridge
Old English
Lightning on the ridge. *Lightning Ridge, Australia yields some of the rarest and most beautiful fossils and opals in the world including the black opal.*

Loch
Scottish
Lake. *The most famous 'loch' would have to be Loch Ness, famed for its Loch Ness Monster, or 'Nessie' as it is more affectionately named. The first documented sighting was by Saint Columba in 565 AD.*

Lach Ness/Lachness/ Loch Ness/Lochness
Scottish
Lake. *Loch Ness is the second largest Scottish loch with a surface area of 56.4 square kilometres or 21.8 square miles.*

Lochacre
Scottish/English
Land with lakes.

Lachside/Lochside
Lakeside; hillside lake.

Lockley
Scottish
Meadow lake.

Locksley
Scottish
Meadow lakes.

Logan
Irish
Hollow. Logan's Run (1976) *starred Michael York and is set in an ideal world in*

2274, ideal except that once one hits thirty, one is exterminated. A new version of this movie is believed to be in production.

Loman
Celtic
Enlightened.

Lundy
Scottish
Island grove.

M

Marjorie
Scottish
Pearl. *Also a woman's name.*

Meave
Irish
Happy.

Morna
Gaelic
Beloved.

Morven
Scottish
Sea mariner.

Muir
Scottish
Marshland. The Ghost and Mrs Muir *(1947) starred Rex Harrison and Gene Tierney. It is about a young widow and her family who move to a seaside cottage only to find it haunted and a relationship between her and the ghost of Captain Daniel Gregg ensues.*

N

Neala
Irish
Champion.

Ogilvie
Welsh
High.

Oisin
Irish
Home where the small deer reside.

Paddy
Irish
Noble. *A popular male name, short for 'Patrick'.*

Peadar
Irish
Stone.

Pembroke
Welsh
Headland; hill stream.

Quinlan
Irish
Strong.

Rhidian
Welsh
River crossing.

Rhiannon
Welsh/Gaelic
Sorceress. *Rhiannon is part of Welsh legend. She was married to Pwyll and gave birth to a son who disappeared. The servants claimed Rhiannon killed him and her punishment was to carry strangers one her back as though she were a packhorse. The son Pryderi was found by a couple in the woods and raised as their own until his identity was discovered and he was returned. 'Rhiannon' is also the title of a song by Fleetwood Mac.*

Romney
Welsh
Curved river.

Sayers
Welsh
Carpenter.

Seafra
Irish
God's peace.

Shalyn
Welsh
Shade pool.

Shanahan
Irish
Large, stately house of wisdom.

Shannon
Irish
Slow moving stream.

Sheridan
Irish
Wild.

Siany
Irish
Health.

Skene
Irish
The bush.

Slavin
Irish
Man from the mountain.

Sloane
Irish
The warrior.

Sorcha
Irish
Bright.

Stratton
Scottish
The river valley town.

Sulwyn
Welsh
Sunny.

T

Tadleigh/Tadlea/Tadlee/Tadley
Irish
Poet from the meadow.

Tain
Scottish
Stream.

Taliesin
Welsh
Radiant top of the hill.

Tangwyn
Welsh
Peace that is blessed.

Tara
Irish/Gaelic
Rocky hill. *'Tara' is the name of the plantation in* Gone with the Wind, *a novel by Margaret Mitchell that in 1939 was made into a movie starring Vivien Leigh and Clark Gable.*

Tarrant
Welsh
Thunder.

Teagan-Evvron
Celtic
Beautiful doe.

Tearlach
Gaelic
Strong and courageous.

The Clunies
Scottish
Meadow resting place.

The Glen/The Glenn
Scottish
Valley.

The Lach/The Loch
Scottish
The lake.

Trevina
Welsh
Homestead.

Tudor
Welsh
God's gift.

Tullia
Irish
Peaceful.

Tyddyn
Welsh
Small farm.

U

Ula
Celtic
Jewell of the sea.

V

Vanora
Celtic
White wave.

Vaughan
Celtic
Small.

W

Weymouth
Celtic
Mouth of the river.

French

A

Amour
Love.

Au Sables
On the sand.

Auberte
Noble.

Avenall
Lives near the oat field.

B

Beauregard
Handsome.

Beaufort
From the fine or commodious fort.

Beaumont
Beautiful mountain.

Beauté
Beauty.

Beauvoir
Beautiful to look at.

Belda
Fair maiden.

Belle Vue
Beautiful view.

Belle Maison
Beautiful house.

Benoit
Blessed.

Blanche
White.

Bonbon
Sweet.

Bon Chance
Good luck.

Bon Vista
French/Italian
Good view.

Botanique
Botanical.

C

Caprice
Change of mind. Caprice *(1967) starred Doris Day and was about an industrial designer who sells a top-secret formula to a cosmetic company rival.*

Cavalier
Gentleman. *The Cavalier King Charles Spaniel is a breed of small dog.*

Cavalry
Mounted troop. *The Cavalry is a branch of an army made up of mounted troops. Many western fans would be familiar with various cowboy movies where the cavalry comes to the rescue.*

Cerise
Cherry.

Chantilly
Lace. *A town in northern France.*

Chez Nous
Our house.

Corinne
Girl, daughter. *Also a girl's name.*

Creola
Home raised.

D

Déjà vu
Having experienced the same thing before.

Desiree
The one desired.

Destiny
Fate.

E

Entrez
Enter.

F

Fontainebleau
Blue spring.

G

Gasparde
Guardian of the treasure.

Germaine
From Germany.

H

Haute Vue
High view.

Henriette
Ruler of the house.

I

Iolanda
Hyacinth; purple.

J

Joi
Joy.

La Maison
The house.

Laroux
Red.

Lasalle
Hall.

L'Amour
The love.

Le Cirque
The circus.

Le Grand
The great.

La Grande
The great.

La Loge
The hut.

La Medewe
Old French/Old English
The field.

Le Sandes
The sands.

Les Vins
The wines.

Lis
Lily.

Loup
Wolf.

Love Chalet
Small house of adoration.

M

Maison Pluviale
Rain house.

Maitland
Meadow pasture.

Mignonette
Little darling.

N

Neige
Snow.

Ninette
Little.

Notre Dame
Our lady. *Notre Dame is a gothic-style cathedral in Paris, France. Victor Hugo (1802–85) wrote the novel,* The Hunchback of Notre Dame *(first published in 1831), about Quasimodo and his love for Esmeralda.*

P

Paradis Maison
Paradise house.

Parc Floral
Floral garden.

Perry
Pear tree.

Platt
Flat land.

Porche du Nord
North porch.

Que Sera Sera
Whatever will be will be.

Roesia
Rose.

Saville
Village with willow trees.

The Esplanade
A paved or grassed area used for walking.

Vue Claire
Clear view.

Italian

Alcorso
By the main street or the stream that runs through the small town.

Amore
Love.

Angelucci
Angel of light.

Aria
Melody sung in an opera. *'ARIA' is an acronym for the Australian Record Industry Association.*

Arietta
Little melody.

B

Bella Vista
Beautiful view.

Belvedere
Beautiful to look at.

Bene Arrivate
Welcome.

Benito
Blessed.

Bianca
White.

Carino
Friendly.

Casa Azzurra
Blue house.

Casa Bella
House of beauty.

Casa Bianca
White house.

Casa Bramasole
House desiring the sun; yearning for the sun. *'Casa Bramasole' was the house in the movie* Under the Tuscan Sun *(2003), starring Diane Lane about a divorced writer who travels to Italy and on a whim buys a villa that changes her life for the better. The movie was based on the novel of the same title by Frances Mayes.*

Casa Gialla
Yellow house.

Casale
Farmhouse.

Casella
Pigeon-hole; gatekeeper's house; toll-house.

Castello
Castle.

Chiara
Clear; bright.

Cozzi
One who resides on the peak of the mountain.

Da Castello
At the castle.

Da Rango
One of rank; one of standing.

Da Buono
home of the good.

Dante
Enduring.

Della Bosca
Of the forest.

E

Enrico
Leader of the house.

F

Fiorillo
Little flower.

Fioritura
Flowering.

Fonte
Fountain.

G

Gelata
Icy weather.

I

Ilario
Cheer.

M

Montefiore
Mountain flowers.

Montagna
Mountain.

N

Nico
Victory of the people.

O

Othello
Prosperous.

P

Poeta
Poetry.

Primo
First.

Primavista
One view.

R

Riva
River; river bank.

Rocco
Stone.

Roma
Rome.

Romavilla
Rome village.

Romany
Gypsy.

Rome
Named after the famous city in Italy.

S

Salvestro
Found in the forest.

Sansone
Of the sun.

Selvaggio
Wild.

Saviero
New house.

T

The Villa
The country house.

Tuscan
A resident of Tuscany.

Tuscany
A region in Italy.

U

Ullivieri
Olive tree.

V

Valentino/Valentine
Powerful; healthy.
Valentine Rossi is a 500cc Grand Prix triple world champion. Rudolph Valentino (1895–1926) was an actor who starred in many movies including The Son of the Sheik *(1926) and* The Eagle *(1925). St Valentine's Day is celebrated by lovers on February 14.*

Venezia
Venice.

Villa Bianca
White country house.

Villa Fiorenda
Flowering country house.

Villa Vista
View of the country.

Vita
Life.

Z

Zanebono
The good one.

Middle Eastern

A

Amandeep
Punjabi
Light of peace.

Aparna
Persian
Religious waters.

Aslani
Turkish
Lion.

B

Babylon
Akhadian /Greek
Gate of the god Il. *Babylon was an ancient city of Mesopotamia that was famed for its sensual living. The Assyrians destroyed it in 689 BC. It was subsequently rebuilt and regarded as a great city when Alexander the Great visited in 339 BC.*

Bahar
Persian/Arabic
Glorious and valuable property.

Bibli
Arabic
Lady.

C

Cala
Castle.

Cantara
Small crossing.

D

Darice
Persian
Queen.

F

Farida
Unique.

G

Ghanei
Persian
Prosperous.

H

Hasna
Beautiful.

Haya
Arabic
Modest.

I

Iman
Believer.

J

Jalaad
Glory.

Jalal
Majestic.

Jamal
Beautiful.

Jinan
Arabic
Garden.

K

Kadar
Powerful.

Keshisha
Arabic
Elder.

L

Lateef
Subtle.

Layla
Persian/Arabic
Dark. *'Layla' was a hit song for Eric Clapton in 1992.*

M

Maimon
Lucky.

Makin
Strength.

Maysun
Arabic
Beautiful.

N

Nadira
Precious.

Noya
Beautiful.

Q

Qadir
Powerful.

Qusay
Arabic
Distant.

R

Raja
Hope.

S

Sahar
Dawn.

Saida
Lucky.

Sakhir
Arabic
Rock.

T

Tamir
Tall.

Thara
Wealth.

U

Umar
Longevity.

W

Wahida
Unique.

X

Xavier
Of the new house; bright; brilliant.

Y

Yasar
Wealthy.

Z

Zulema
Peace.

Hebrew

A

Abira
Strong.

Abra
Earthmother.

Ada
Ornament.

Adar
High.

Ahuda
Peaceful.

Anaïs
Graceful. *Anaïs Nin (1903–77) was a French writer of the erotic.*

B

Barukh
Blessed.

Bethel
House of God.

C

Carmel
Vineyard; garden.

Chaika
Life.

Chaya
Life.

D

Dorita
Generation.

E

Eban
Rock.

Endora
Fountain. *Agnes Moorehead (1900–74) starred as Endora, the meddling mother-in-law in the television series* Bewitched *(1964–72).*

G

Gana
Garden.

Geva
Hill.

Gilana
Joy.

H

Hadara
Adorned with beauty.

Hallelujah House
Hebrew/Old English
Praise the house of the Lord; praise the Lord.

Hasia
Protected by the lord.

Haya
Life.

I

Ilana
Tree.

Ilisha
Life.

J

Jada
Wise. *Also a green stone.*

Jonina
Dove.

K

Kalanit
Flower.

Kerenza
Light.

Korenet
Shining.

L

Leshem
Precious stone.

Lewanna
Moon; white.

M

Mazal
Lucky star.

Myer
Light.

N

Nir
Ploughed field.

Noy
Beautiful; bountiful.

O

Oren
Pine tree.

P

Poria
Fruitful.

R

Raphah
High.

Rivkah
Shore.

Rosenbaum
Rose flower.

S

Saloma
Peace.

Sela
Rock.

Shapiro
Beautiful.

Shara/Sharo/Sharon
Plains.

Sima
Treasure.

T

Tal
Rain; dew.

Talmai
Small hills.

Tamar/Tamara
Palm tree; date fruit.

Tilon
Hill.

Tove
Good.

U

Uri
God's light.

V

Varil
Water.

X

Xevulun
Home.

Xion
Guarded land.

Y

Yachne
Gracious.

Yaffa
Beautiful.

Z

Zebulo
Home.

Zephyrus
Western wind.

Zerikas
Rain storm.

Zevulun
House.

Greek

A

Agare
Noble.

Alpha
The first letter of the Greek alphabet. *This may have relevance for the first house the owner has ever bought.*

Alpha–Omega
The first and the last letters of the Greek alphabet. *This may have relevance for the owner; it may be the first and the last house they will buy.*

Aminta
Protector.

Anastasia
Resurrection; springtime. *Anastasia Romanov, born 1901 was the youngest daughter of Nicholas II. The mystery surrounding Anastasia's fate after the Russian Revolution in 1918 is one of the biggest mysteries of the twentieth century.*

Anemore
Wind; flower.

Annis
Complete.

Anstis
Resurrection.

Apolda
Sunlight.

Appollonia
Sunlight.

Areta
The best.

Argyro
Silver.

Ariandna
Holy.

Armide
Sorceress.

Aspasia
Welcomed.

Aspholdel
Flower.

Aster
Star.

Athea
Flowery.

Ava
Eagle. *Ava Gardner (1922–90) was an American actor who starred in movies such as* On the Beach *(1959) and* The Sentinel *(1977).*

B

Bassilla
Royal.

Berenice
Strength.

Bouno
Mountain.

C

Calandra
Carefree.

Calantha
Flower.

Calla
Beautiful.

Calypso
Greek
The hidden. *This was the name of the ship used by Jacques Cousteau, the famous Oceanographer. According to Greek mythology, the sea nymph Kalipsou detained Odysseus for seven years on the island of Ogygia. 'Calypso' is also the name of a terrestrial orchid found in the Northern Hemisphere.*

Celena/Celene/Celina/Celine
Moon; heavenly. *Celine Dion is a Canadian born singer and winner of many music awards including Grammies, People's Choice Award and American Music Awards. She is well known for songs such as 'My Heart Will Go On' and 'Beauty and the Beast' (1991), a duet with Peabo Bryson.*

Chrysanthe
Golden flower.

Chrysanthemum
Golden flower. *Chrysanthemums are flowers traditionally given to mothers on Mother's Day.*

Clematis
Brushwood; vine.

Cyma
Flowering.

D

Delpha
Dolphin.

Dianth
Divine flower.

Doris
Sea. *Doris Day (b. 1924, Doris Mary Ann Von Kappelhoff) is a movie actor/singer who starred in such movies as* Midnight Lace *(1960),* Pillow Talk *(1959) and* Move Over, Darling *(1963). She is also an avid animal lover and supporter of animal rights.*

Dorrit
Dwelling.

E

Eirene
Peaceful.

Eirpne
Peaceful.

Elidi/Elodi
Sun gift.

Eunice
Happy.

Eureka
Greek
Found. *It is believed that 'Eureka' was first uttered by Archimedes, (a mathematician and an inventor), when he found a method that determined the purity of gold.* (See also 'Eureka Stockade').

Eureka Stockade
Greek/Old English
The found enclosure. *The 'Eureka Stockade' is the name given to the armed rebellion of goldminers in Victoria in 1854. Many miners objected to paying taxes on gold and clashed with Victorian police and a garrison of soldiers. It was a key event in the development of Australian democracy. A movie of the same name starred Bryan Brown and Tom Burlinson (1984). The distinctive Eureka flag, which bears a white cross with a star at the end of each arm on a blue background and is now associated with the Australian Republican Movement, was first raised at the Eureka Stockade* (See also Eureka).

Eustacia
Productive.

Evanthe
Flower.

F

Fotini
Light.

G

Gaia
Earth.

H

Halo House
Circle of holy light around the home.

Hester
Evening star.

I

Idylla
Perfect.

Ione
Coloured stone.

Iris
Rainbow; flower.

Ismena/Ismene
Wisdom.

J

Jocasta
Shining moon.

K

Kaia
Earth.

Kalika
Rosebud.

Kaliope
Beautiful.

Kallirroe
Beautiful river.

Kallista/Calista
Beautiful. *Calista Flockhart (b. 1964) is an American actor most known for the television series* Ally McBeal *(1997–2002).*

Katoikia
Home.

L

Lais
Happy.

Larissa
Happy.

Libadi
Meadows.

Lotus
Flower.

Louloudi
Flower.

M

Melina
Gentle.

Metis
Wise.

N

Nea
New.

Nemo
Valley.

Nereus
By the water.

O

Oraios
Beautiful.

Orea
Mountain.

P

Panos
Rock.

Parthena
Purity.

Pedar
Stone.

Peri
Prosperous.

R

Rasia
Rose.

Rea
Poppy flower.

Reena
Peace.

Rhodes
One who resides where the roses grow.

S

Seba
Majestic.

Solon
Wise.

Spiti
House.

Syna
Together.

T

Tassus
Harvester.

Thalia
Flowering.

Thanos
Noble.

Timeus
Perfect.

U

Urana/Urania
Heavenly.

X

Xenia
Welcoming.

Xylia
Forest dweller.

Xylon/Xylona
Forest.

Z

Zeferino
Spring wind.

Zenia
Welcoming.

Zylon
Forest.

Nordic

A

Alpine Cottage
Nordic/Old English
Small house in the snow region; small house by the old pine trees.

Alpine House
Nordic/Old English
Home in the snow region; home by the old pine trees.

Alpine Mountain Ranch
Nordic/Old English
Mountain farm in the snow; mountain farm with old pine trees.

Arvid
Old Norse
Eagle forest.

Asplund
Swedish
Poplar tree grove.

Asta
Old Norse
Star.

B

Bo
Old Norse
House holder.

Booth
Old Norse
Shelter.

Brandy
Dutch
Burnt. *Also a distilled wine.*

Busby
Old Norse
Thicket farm.

C

Cadby
Old Norse
The Warrior's town.

Carr
Old Norse
Marshland.

Colby
Old Norse
Dark country; coal town.

Crosby
Old Norse
Village with a cross. *Bing Crosby (Harry Lillis Crosby 1903–1977) was an American actor/singer who starred in many movies including* White Christmas *(1954).*

D

Dag
Old Norse
Day.

Dagmar
Old Norse
Glorious day.

F

Finn
Old Norse
From Finland.

G

Garton
Old Norse
Fenced farm.

Gerda
Old Norse
Protected. *Also a girl's name.*

Gulla
Norse
Devine sea.

H

Halsten
Old Norse
Rock.

Howe
Old Norse
Hill.

I

Inge
Old Norse
Meadow.

Ingram
Old Norse
Raven.

K

Karr
Old Norse
Marsh.

Kell
Old Norse
One who resides near the spring.

Kelsey
Old Norse
One who resides at the island of ships.

Kerr
Old Norse
Marshland.

Kirby
Old Norse
Church in the village.

L

Leif
Old Norse
Beloved. *Leif Garret (b. 1961) is an American actor who starred in such movies as* The Outsiders *(1985). He also released a cover of 'Surfin' USA' and 'Runaround Sue' and 'I was made for Dancin'.*

Lindstrom
Swedish
Lime tree stream.

Lunt
Swedish
Grove.

M

Midgard
Old Norse
Middle garden.

O

Odell
Old Norse
Wealthy.

R

Rigby
Old Norse
Farm on the ridge. *'Eleanor Rigby' is a song written by John Lennon and Paul McCartney and performed by the Beatles in 1966.*

Rigg
Old Norse
Ridge.

Roosevelt
Old Dutch
Rose field. *Franklin Delano Roosevelt (1882–1945) was elected President of the United States of America in 1932. He was also the fifth cousin of the earlier President Theodore Roosevelt (1858–1919).*

Roscoe
Old Norse
Deer forest.

S

Schofield/Scholey
Old Norse
Hut in the meadow.

Scholes
Old Norse
Hut.

Solveig
Old Norse
Strong house.

T

Tarn
Old Norse
Mountain pool or pond.

Tibor
Hungarian
Holy place.

U

Unni
Norse
Modest.

V

Vaal
Dutch
Valley.

Vaina
Finnish
One who resides at the mouth of the river.

Van
Dutch
From.

Varad
Hungarian
Fortress.

W

Walby
Ancient wall.

Welby
Old Norse
Farm by the stream.

Wyck
Old Norse
Village.

Spanish

A

Adonica
Sweet.

Aimon
Homebody

Alcazar
Place built by the Moors; castle.

Alvarado
White land or white hills.

Casa Amarilla
Yellow-coloured house.

Atalaya
Watchtower; lookout; sentinel.

Azella
Virgin.

B

Belicia
Dedicated to God.

Bello Casero
Beautiful home.

Bienvenida
Welcome.

Blanco
White.

Bonito
Pretty; nice; bonito, tunny fish.

Bunita
Pretty and little.

C

Calidad
Quality.

Carvalho
Oak tree.

Casa Azula
Blue-coloured house.

Casa Blanca
White house.

Casa Bonita
Pretty house; nice house.

Casa Flora
Flower house.

Chavella
Holy, sacred to God.

Conchita
Beginning.

D

Damita
Noble.

Da Sousa
Salty marshland.

Delmar
From the sea.

E

Engracia
Graceful.

Espinosa
One who resides at the thorny place.

F

Felicitas
Fortunate.

Feunsanta
Holy fountain.

Flor Bonita
Pretty flower.

Florus
Flower.

G

Galeno
Little and bright.

H

Hermosa
Beautiful.

Hogar
Home; hearth.

I

Isleta
Isle.

J

Javier
New house.

L

La Casa
The House

La Casa Blanca
The white house; the White House. *This is also the Spanish name for the residence of the president of the USA.*

La Casa d'España
The house of Spain.

La Casa Española
The Spanish house.

Latoya
Victory.

Licha
Noble.

Lina
Light.

Lindie
Beautiful.

Lona
Solitary.

M

Malaya
Free.

Mireya
Miracle.

Montana
Mountain.

Montez
One who resides on the mountain.

Mt Diablo
The devil's mountain. *'Mount Diablo' is a mountain state park of California, USA that first opened in 1931. It is known for its beauty, wildlife and unique rock formations. It got its name after Spanish soldiers chased some Native Americans into the thicket of the mountain. The soldiers camped overnight believing that they could capture them in the morning. The Native Americans had escaped during the night, a feat that was thought only possible by help from the devil, thus it became known as Monte del Diablo.*

N

Neper
New town.

Nevada
Snowfall. *Carson City is the capital of Nevada USA.*

Nevado
Covered in snow.

Noe
Peace.

O

Oro
Golden.

P

Pacifico
Peaceful.

Pasto
Meadow.

Pasto de Flores
Meadow of flowers.

Paz
Peace.

Q

Quinta
Country house; fifth; draft.

Quinto
Fifth; conscript.

R

Raeka
Unique and beautiful.

Ria
River.

Rio
River. *Rio de Janeiro was the capital city of Brazil until 1960 when it was moved inland to Brasilia to avoid naval attack. 'I Go to Rio' was a hit song for Australian singer and performer Peter Allen (1944–92).*

Rodas
Where the roses grow.

S

Santana
Saint. *Carlos Santana (b. 1947) is a renowned guitarist and has had musical success with songs such as 'Black Magic Woman' and more recently 'Smooth' (2000) featuring Rob Thomas (Matchbox 20) and 'The Game of Love' (2002) featuring Michelle Branch.*

Santo
Saint.

Sabana
Grassy meadows; savannah.

Solana
Sun.

T

Tago/Tajo
Day.

Tanno
Camp of glory.

Ticco/Tico
Noble.

Tierra
Land.

U

Umberto
Bright heart or mind.

V

Valencia
Valencia. *Valencia is a seaport in eastern Spain and capital of the province of the same name.*

Ventura
Lucky.

Australian Aboriginal

A

Akala
Parrot.

Amarina
Rain.

Arika
Water lily.

Aroona
Running water.

B

Bapp
Blue gum tree.

Bara
Dawn.

Beltana
Running water.

Berontha
Crow.

Billabong
Watering hole. *In Australian poet/author Banjo Paterson's story* Waltzing Matilda *(1895), the swagman jumped into the billabong to avoid arrest and drowned.*

Billabong Cottage
Small house by the watering hole. (See Billabong)

Billabong Gardens
Garden by the watering hole. (See Billabong)

Binda
Deep water.

Bombala
Where the waters meet.

Bonal
Place with lots of grass.

Bondi
Sound of tumbling water.

C

Calca
Star.

Caleena
Fresh water.

Curra
Water spring.

D

Daku
Sand.

Derain
From the mountains.

E

Ekala
Lake.

Elanoya
From the seaside.

Eleeban
Beautiful.

G

Ganan
West.

Girra
Creek.

Gurley
Willow tree.

Guyra
Fishing place.

H

Hanya
Stone.

Horah
Sky.

I

Iluka
By the sea.

Iona
Tree.

J

Jarralea
Jarrah wood meadow.

Jedda
Bird. Jedda *(1955) is a movie about an Australian Aboriginal girl who was brought up with white Australians and was torn between that life and her longings to be with her family and her people.*

Jerara
Waterfall.

Jiba
Moon.

Jungay
West wind.

K

Kalinda
View.

Kalyan
Stay near.

Kara
Possum.

Kareela
Wind from the south.

Karri
Eucalyptus tree.

Katyin
Water.

Kawana
Wild flower.

Keina
Moon.

Kirra
Magpie.

Kogarah
Place where rushes grow.

Koleyn
Winter.

Konol
Sky.

L

Lakkari
Honeysuckle tree.

Legana
Sea.

Lemana
She-oak tree.

Liamena
Lake.

Lilipili
Myrtle tree.

Lira
River.

Lutana
Moon.

M

Macalla
Full moon.

Manilla
Winding river.

Mara
Black duck.

Marbilling
Wind.

Merinda
Beautiful.

Midgee
Acacia tree.

Moorak
Mountain.

Mulga
Acacia tree.

Mulwala
Rain.

Myall
Drooping acacia tree.

N

Nalong
Source of the river.

Namur
Tea tree.

Nanda
Lake.

Nardoo
Nardoo. *Nardoo or Nardu is an Australian species of mud-loving and aquatic ferns, the sporocarps of which are ground into flour.*

Narooma
Magic stone.

Nerang
Little.

Nioka
Green grass.

Noora
Campsite.

Nyah
River bend.

Nyora
Cherry tree.

Nyrang
Little.

O

Oldina
Snow.

Olono
Hill.

Oonta
Star.

P

Padulla
Stone.

Parri
Stream

Pataya
Flower.

Pindari
High ground.

Pinterry
Star.

Pirrin
Cave.

Q

Quamby
Shelter.

R

Ranwul
Ancient.

Rewuri
Spring.

T

Tabulum
My home.

Tallara
Rain.

Tamago
Sweet water.

Tanundra
Place with plentiful waterfowl.

Tarcoola
River bend.

Taree
Fig tree.

Tarro
Stone.

Teangi
Earthy.

Thoar
Sunrise.

Thomar
Small river.

Tirranna
Running water.

Toolan
Wattle.

Turramurra
Big hill.

U

Uwan
Meeting area.

V

Vanda
Sandhill.

W

Wallah
Rain.

Wapin
Dawn.

Wirrin
Tea tree.

Wyuna
Clear water.

Y

Yaralla
Camping place.

Yileen
Dream.

Yooralla
Love.

Yuka
Plant.

Maori

A

Amiri
Eastern wind.

Aniwaniaw
Rainbow.

Aroha
Love.

Ataahua
Beautiful.

Ataahua Wahi
Beautiful place.

Atamai
Knowing.

Atarau
Moonlight.

Awa
River.

E

Emere
Hard working.

H

Haere Mai
Welcome.

Hikurangi
High mountain.

K

Kainga
Home.

Kirralee
Bark meadow.

Koa Whare
Happy house.

Kohanga
Nest.

Kura
Treasure.

L

Lulani
Highest point to heaven.

M

Maiki
High.

Manawa
Heart.

Manga
Stream.

Marama
Moon.

Matangi
Breeze.

Mawake
Breeze from the southern sea.

Moana
Sea.

Motu
Island.

N

Nui
Great.

Nyree
Sea.

O

Omaka
Flowing streams.

P

Pania
Sea woman.

Powhiri
Welcome.

R

Rahiri
Welcome.

Rangi
Sky; heaven.

Reka
Sweet.

Rere
Waterfall.

Rongo
Peace.

Roto
Lake.

T

Toku Kainga Noho
My home.

Totara
Rocky hill.

W

Wai
Water.

Whare
House.

Whanga
Harbour; bay.

Wharenui/Whare Nui
Meeting house.

Whare Whakairo
Carved meeting house.

Tongan

A

Api
Home.

F

Fale
House.

Funga Fale
House-top.

K

Komaki
Bay.

Konga
Field.

L

Langi
Heaven.

M

Maka
Rock.

Makamaka
Rocky.

Melino
Peace.

O

Oketa
Orchid.

P

Paini
Pine tree.

S

Sinou
Snow.

T

Toa
Casuarina tree.

Toafa
Field.

V

Vaha
Open sea.

Vaitafe
River.

Hawaiian

A

Ahulani
Heavenly shrine.

Akela
Noble.

Alamea
Precious.

Alani
Orange tree.

Alaula
Dawn.

Aloha
Greeting; farewell.

Ani
Beautiful.

Aolani
Heavenly.

B

Bleniki
White.

E

Elenola
Bright.

Eme
Loved.

Enakai
Sea of fire.

F

Felora
Flower.

H

Hale
Home.

Haleigha
House of the rising sun.

I

Ilima
Flower.

Iona
Dove.

K

Kahale
Home.

Kahua
Sea.

Kai
Sea; willow tree.

Kala
Sun.

Kalani
Sky.

Kalilinoe
Rain.

Kamakani
Wind.

Kamekona
Strength.

Kamoku
Island.

Kanale
Stony meadow.

Kauri
Forest tree.

Keala
Pathway.

Kilia
Heaven.

Koka
Scotland.

Konane
Bright moonlight.

Kuleana
Small property.

Kunani
Beautiful.

L

Lani
Sky; heaven.

Larni
Sky; heaven.

Lokalia
Rose garland.

Lulani
Highest point in heaven.

M

Malu
Serenity.

Mirena
Loved.

Moana
Ocean.

Mohala
Flowering.

N

Nahele
Forest.

Naia
Dolphin.

Nalani
Calm heavens.

Nani
Beautiful.

O

Okilani
Heaven.

Oliana
Flowering evergreen.

P

Pililni
Near heaven.

Pokaku
Stone; rock.

Puakai
Sea flower.

Punawai
Water.

R

Ruta
Friendly.

S

Sukey
Lily.

T

Tava
Fruit tree.

Toafo
Woods.

U

Ualani
Heavenly rain.

W

Wilikinia
Purity.

Native American

A

Alameda
Cottonwood.

Amayeta
Berry.

Amitola
Rainbow.

Angeni
Spirit.

Aponi
Butterfly.

Aquene
Peace.

B

Bly
High.

C

Chenoa
White dove.

Chilali
Snow bird.

Cholena
Bird.

Chooli
Navajo
Mountain.

D

Dakota
Friend.

Dohasan
Kiowa
Cliff.

E

Elu
Grace.

Eyota
Greatest.

G

Galilani
Cherokee
Friend.

Gomba
Kiowa
Wind.

H

Hachi
Seminole
River.

Halona
Lucky.

Hialea
Cherokee
Beautiful field.

Hiawasee
Meadow.

Hogan
Navajo
Home.

Hopi
Peace. *Also the name of a Native American Nation.*

Howi
Dove.

Hute
Star.

I

Immookalee
Cherokee
Waterfall.

Iskemu
River house.

Istas
Snow.

Ituha
Oak tree.

Izusa
White stone

J

Jacy
Moon.

Jolon
Valley of the dead oaks.

K

Kai
Willow tree.

Kiona/Kiowa
Brown hills.

Knoton
Windy.

Kokanee
Salmon.

L

Lakota
Friend. *Also the name of a Native American people belonging to the Sioux nation.*

Langundo
Peaceful.

Lokni
Moquelumnan
Rain coming in through the roof.

Lootah
Lakota
Red.

M

Mahpee
Lakota Sioux
Sky.

Mapiya
Heaven.

Minnehaha
Waterfall. *Minnehaha Falls is part of the Mississippi National River and Recreational Area of the USA. Henry Wadsworth Longfellow wrote* The Song of Hiawatha, *an epic poem about the lovers Hiawatha and Minnehaha who are believed to have lived around 1550. Hiawatha was instrumental in establishing The Five Nations of the Iroquois confederacy. There is a statue of Hiawatha and Minnehaha at the Minnehaha Falls Minneapolis USA.*

Miso
Rippling water.

N

Nawkaw
Winnebago
Woods.

Nebraska
Land with flat water.
Nebraska *is the title of one of Bruce Springsteen's early album releases (1982). It is also a state in the USA.*

Niagara
Thunder water. *The original Iroquois name for Niagara Falls was believed to have been 'Onguiaahra' meaning the strait; however, it became simplified to 'Niagara' as we know it today. Niagara Falls is located on the Canadian–USA border and made up of the Horseshoe Falls, the American Falls and the Bridal Veil Falls.*

Nodin
Wind.

O

Ogin
Wild rose.

Oheo
Beautiful.

Ohio
Beautiful river. *Olivia Newton John sang about the 'Banks of the Ohio' in 1972.*

Olanthe
Beautiful.

P

Paco
Bold eagle.

Pala
Water.

Pekabo
Shining water.

Petunia
Sweetly scented flower.

Pezi
Sioux
Grass.

Pocahontas
Playful. *Pocahontas is believed to have lived around 1595–1617. She saved Jamestown Virginia from starvation and is said to have saved John Smith (a colonist) from execution, though this account may be*

debatable. She married a colonist, John Rolfe taking the Christian name of Rebecca Rolfe and later, after a tour of England, died of smallpox. Disney came under scrutiny from Native Americans with its romantic distortion of Smith and Pocahontas's relationship.

Powhata
Algonquin
Meeting place.

Sakuna
Bird.

Sihu
Flower.

T

Tadan
Plentiful.

Tadewi
Wind.

Tainn/Tain
New moon.

Talise
Beautiful water.

Tallulah
Running water.

Talma
Crash of thunder.

Tarhe
Tree.

Tashunka
Sioux
Horse.

Tatanka
Sioux
Bull; buffalo. *Buffalo was a source of life and spiritual beliefs for the Native Americans. All of the buffalo was used by the people for food, clothes, warmth, shelter and tools.*

Tawa
Hopi
Sun.

Tepee
Dakota
Tent made of animals skins.

Tiba
Navajo
Grey.

Tsoai
Kiowa
Rock tree.

W

Waban
East wind.

Wahjan
Lakota
Sacred.

Wapi
Lucky.

Washta
Sioux
Good.

Wicahpi
Sioux
Star.

Wyoming
Algonquian
Broad plains. *Also a state in the USA.*

Yakez
Heaven.

Yamka
Hopi
Flower.

Yoluta
Summer flower.

Yottoko
Mud.

Zaltana
High mountain.

African

Aaliya/Aaliyah
Rising. *Aaliyah (1979–2001) was an African American singer who tragically died in a plane crash on the way home from a video shoot in the Bahamas.*

Abieyuwa
Nigerian
Born of a wealthy family.

Abimbola
Nigerian
Born into a rich family.

Abiona
Nigerian
Born into a famous family.

Agiya
Nigerian
One who defeated suffering.

Akili
Tanzanian
Wisdom.

Amlak
Ethiopian
Angel.

Azuka
Nigerian
The great supporter of the family.

Arziki
Prosperity.

Belebela
Bubbling spring.

Bron
Source of the river.

C

Cakusola
Loving.

Chipo
Gift.

D

Darari/Dakarai
Happiness.

Ebun
Nigerian
Gift.

Eca
Nigerian
Bird.

Edosomwan
Nigerian
The family that resides by the river.

Ega
Nigerian
Bird.

F

Faizah
Victory.

Fayola
Nigerian
Lucky.

Fola
Yoruba
Honour.

Foluke
Nigerian
In god's care.

H

Hadiya
Swahili
Gift.

Hasina
Swahili
Good.

I

Isoka
God's gift.

K

Kenya
Jewel.

Kesia
Favourite.

Krun
Mountain.

Kunle
Yoruba
Honourable home.

L

Lakenya
Jewel.

Latara
Rocky hill.

M

Mundan
Zimbabwean
Garden.

O

Odomn
Ghanian
Oak tree.

S

Saidah
Fortunate.

Sarai
Zimbabwean
Settler.

Segun
Yoruba
Conquering.

Senwe
Dry.

Setimba
Luganda
One who resides by the river.

Sipho
Zulu
Present.

Soja
Yoruba
Warrior.

Sultan
Swahili
Ruler.

T

Tale
Tswana
Green.

Tano
Favourite.

U

Umhlanga
Reeds.

Uzoma
Nigerian
Good path.

Z

Zaid
Growth.

Thai

A

Aran
Forest.

Aroon
Dawn.

Atid
Sun.

K

Kasem
Happy.

L

Lawan
Pretty.

M

Mali
Flower.

Mayoree
Beautiful.

N

Niran
Eternal.

R

Ratana
Crystal.

S

Sumalee
Beautiful flower.

Sunee
Good.

T

Tasanee
Beautiful view.

Chinese

A

An
Peace.

B

Beibei
Bud of a flower.

Bo
Precious.

C

Chen
Precious.

Cho
Butterfly.

Chu
Pearl.

Chung
Wisdom.

H

Ho
Good.

K

Kong
Hole.

L

Li
Strength.

Lian
Graceful willow tree.

Lim
Family.

Ling
Delicate.

M

Manchu
Purity.

Mee
Beautiful.

Meiying
Beautiful flower.

Q

Qua
Hill.

S

Shaiming
Sunshine.

Shing
Victorious.

Sya
Summer.

Sying
Star.

T

Tao
Longevity.

Tien
Heaven.

Y

Ye
Leafy place.

Z

Zan
Praised.

Zhen
Purity.

Japanese

A

Ai
Love.

Akako
Red.

Akeno
Shining field.

Akira
Intelligent.

Akiyana
Autumn; fall.

Anzu
Apricot.

B

Bokusouchi
Meadow.

C

Chika
Beloved.

Chiyo
Eternal.

Cho
Butterfly.

E

Enkai
Banquet.

F

Fujita
Meadow.

H

Hachimenreirou
Beautiful from all sides.

Hiroshi
Generosity.

Hisa
Longevity.

Hitogama
Mountain.

Hoshi
Star.

I

Ikka
House

Ikken'ya
Isolated house.

Ishi
Stone.

J

Jin
Silver.

Joben
Clean.

K

Kado
Gateway.

Kai
Forgive.

Kajitsu
Beautiful day.

Kazuo
Peace.

Kichi
Lucky.

Kiyoshi
Peace.

Kouzan
High mountain.

Kurao
Mountain.

Kurosawa
Black river.

M

Makiba
Meadow.

Mamoru
Earth.

Manshon
Apartment house.

Matsu
Pine tree.

Mika
New moon.

Miki
Tree.

N

Nara
Oak tree; strength.

Netsuai
Love.

Nishi
West.

Nozomi
Hope.

O

Ohara
Small field.

Okaerinasai
Welcome home.

S

Sachi
Bringer of peace.

Seki
Wonderful.

Sen
Magical forest fairy.

Shan
Beautiful.

Shima
Island.

Shina
Victorious.

Shoken
View.

Sugi
Cedar tree.

T

Takara
Treasure.

Takeko
Bamboo.

Takeo
Strength.

Taki
Waterfall.

Taku
House.

Tani
Valley.

Taya
Home in the valley.

Tomi
Wealthy.

U

Uyeda
Field of rice.

Y

Yasu
Tranquillity.

Yei
Flourishing.

Yori
Reliable.

Yoshi
Quiet; good; respected.

Yoshiko
Good.

Youkoso
Welcome

Yumi
Beautiful.

Hindi and Sanskrit

A

Ahimsa
Hindi
Peaceful.

Anil/Anila
Sanskrit
Wind.

Arun/Aruna
Sanskrit
Dawn.

Asha
Sanskrit
Hope.

B

Bel
Hindi
Apple tree in the sacred wood.

Bhima
Sanskrit
Mighty.

C

Chandra
Sanskrit
Moon.

D

Deepak
Sanskrit
Light. *Deepak Chopra (b. 1947) is the author of many self-help books. He was born in New Delhi and studied medicine there. In 1970 he moved to the USA.*

Divya
Hindi
Heavenly.

F

Fulande
Hindi
Flower.

J

Jalini
Hindi
One who resides by the ocean.

Jaya
Sanskrit
Victorious.

Jyoti/Jyotis
Sanskrit
Light.

K

Kaanan
Hindi
Forest.

Kabr
Hindi
Grass.

Kalyani
Sanskrit
Beautiful.

Kamala
Sanskrit
Lotus flower.

Karma
Sanskrit
Destiny.

N

Nadisu
Hindi
River of beauty.

Nanda
Sanskrit
Happiness.

P

Prasad
Sanskrit
Bright.

Prem
Sanskrit
Love.

Prya
Hindi
Beloved.

Purnima
Sanskrit
Full moon.

S

Sagar
Hindi
Sea.

Sala
Hindi
Sacred tree.

Sambhu
Sanskrit
House of happiness.

Satanvara
Hindi
Hope.

Sitara
Sanskrit
Morning star.

Sujata
Hindi
Noble.

Surya
Sanskrit
Sun.

T

The Bungalow
Hindi
Small house.

Tula
Hindi
Peace.

U

Uma
Sanskrit
Light.

V

Vanalika
Hindi
Sunflower.

Vandani
Hindi
Honourable.

Varana
Hindi
River.

Vasanti
Sanskrit
Spring time.

Vimal/Vimala
Sanskrit
Purity.

Y

Yamuna
Hindi
Sacred river.

CHAPTER 14

OH TO BREAK LOOSE . . .

Have you ever wanted to break loose? A weekend away? A holiday? Time to get away from it all?

Perhaps you have a favourite beach to which you like to escape for renewal and refreshment. You may even be fortunate to have your own beach house there.

If you'd rather be on the water than by the water, a houseboat might be for you. Or maybe your yacht, motorboat, or rowboat needs a name. Perhaps it's time to hit the road with a caravan. Whatever your home away from home, the following suggestions for naming beach houses, houseboats and caravans may provide inspiration.

Beach houses

Beautiful ocean vistas, sea creatures, marine animals and birds can be a great source of inspiration when choosing a name for a beach house or a house near the water.

A

Above The Bay
Old English
A home that overlooks an inlet.

Ahoy
Old English
This is a nautical term for 'hello' and may be used as a house name for a home by the sea or with a sea theme.

Anchorage
Old English
To be firmly in place; secure. *This is for the house owner who intends to stay where he or she is for long time.*

Angelfish Cottage
Old English
Small house where the angelfish are kept or bred.

Angelsea
Old English
An angel at sea.

Angler's Reach
Old English
The place where the fisherman casts his line and hook.

Aqua Shack
Latin/English
Water hut.

Atlantic Calm
Greek/Old English
The calm waters of the Atlantic Ocean.

Atlantic Heights
Greek/Old English
High views of the Atlantic Ocean. *A name for a home on a cliff top or with a sweeping view of the Atlantic Ocean.*

Atlantic Palms
Greek/Latin/Old English
Palm trees by the Atlantic Ocean.

Atlantic Views
Greek/Old English
Vista of the Atlantic Ocean.

Atlantica
Greek
The Atlantic Ocean.

B

Barracuda
Spanish
The barracuda fish. *A keen fisherman may wish to name their house after this fish.*

Bass Lake Cottage
Middle English/Old English
Small house on the lake, containing freshwater bass fish. *A house name for those fond of fishing.*

Bay Breeze
Old English
Soft wind on the inlet.

Bay Cottage
Old English
Small house by the inlet.

Bay Shore Manor
Old English
Estate house by the inlet shore.

Bay Vista
Old English/Italian
View of the inlet.

Baybrook/Baybrooke
Old English
Small stream by the inlet.

Bayside
Old English
Beside the bay.

Beach Break
English
Beachside getaway; where the waves break on the shore.

Beach Croft
English/Old English
Small pasture by the beach.

Beach Farm
English/Old English
Ranch by the beach.

Beach Grove
English/Old English
Small woods by the beach.

Beachlea Grove/Beachlee Grove/ Beachley Grove/Beachly Grove
English/Old English
Small wood meadow by the beach.

Beach Point
English/Old English
The beach headland.

Beach View
English/Old English
Vista of the beach.

Beach Vista
English/Italian
View of the beach.

Beach Walk Cottage
English/Old English
Small house with a path that leads to the beach.

Beachcomber
English
One who searches the beach for washed up articles. *This is a popular name for homes situated by the beach.*

Beachcroft
English/Old English
Small pasture by the beach.

Beachside
English/Old English
By the beach. *A good name for a home that is situated on or very near the beach.*

Beachside Villa
English/Old English/Italian
Small, country house beside the beach.

Beachton
English/Old English
Beach town.

Beachvilla
English/Italian
Small villa on or near the beach.

Beachville
English/Old English
Village by the beach.

Beachworth
English/Old English
Farm near the beach; valued beach.

Belle Island View
Italian/Old English
Vista of the beautiful island.

Blacksands
Old English
Dark-coloured sand.

Blue Pacific
Middle English/French
The blue, peaceful sea. *The Pacific (peaceful) Ocean was named by the Portuguese explorer Ferdinand Magellan, as he encountered no storms there.*

Blue Waters
Middle English/Old French/Old English
Blue-coloured water. A good name for a house or property that overlooks a lake, sea or river.

Bondi
Australian Aboriginal
The sound of tumbling water. *Bondi is a suburb of Sydney, Australia, famed for its beach.*

Bridgeport
Old English
A bridge close to where ships discharge their cargo.

Broadbeach Cottage
Old English
Small house on the wide beach.

Brown Sea Cottage
Old English
Small house by the brown-coloured sea.

By The Sea
Old English
Beside the sea. *A perfect name for a house situated close to the sea.*

C

Calm Waters
Old English
Calm and relaxed lake, sea or river.

Calypso
Greek
The hidden. *This was the name of the ship used by Jacques Cousteau, the famous oceanographer. According to Greek mythology, the sea nymph Kalipsou detained Odysseus for seven years on the island of Ogygia. 'Calypso' is also the name of a terrestrial orchid found in the Northern Hemisphere.*

Cape Valentine
Old English/Latin
Headland sweetheart. *A romantic name for a home on a cape. It may also have a reference to Saint Valentine's Day, February 14.*

Capeside
Old English
Headland by the hillside.

Capeside Cottage
Old English
Small house situated very close to the headland.

Cave Beach House
English/Old English
Home situated near the beach cave.

Coastal Bay
Old English
Inlet in the coast.

Coastal Cottage
Old English
Small house on the coast.

Coastal Cove
Old English
Bay on the coast.

Coastal Waters
English/Old English
Water on the coast.

Cockle Cottage
Middle English/French/Old English
Small house close to where molluscs are found.

Cockleshell Bay
Middle English/French/Old English
Molluscs inlet.

Cockleshell Cottage
Middle English/French/Old English
Small house by the mollusc shells.

Coconut House
English/Old English
Home by the coconut trees.

Cod Cove
Old English
The sheltered inlet where the codfish may be found.

Copper Beach
English/Old English
Golden/red-coloured sands.

Crab Cottage
Old English
Small house close to where the crabs are caught or cooked.

Crabwall Cottage
Old English
Crabs by the wall of the small old house.

Crayfish Cottage
English/Old English
Small house where crayfish may be cooked or found nearby.

Cruising Cottage
English/Old English
Small houseboat.

Deep Water Cottage
Old English
Small house by the deep water.

Dolphin Cottage
Latin/Greek/Old English
Dolphins may be seen in the waters by the small house.

Dolphin Cove
Latin/Greek/Old English
Dolphin bay.

Dolphin Point
Latin/Greek/Old English
Dolphin headland.

Dolphin Sands
Latin/Greek/Old English
Dolphin beach.

Dolphin Terrace
Latin/Greek/Old English
Dolphins may be seen from the courtyard.

Dolphin Waters
Latin/Greek/Old English
Dolphins may be found swimming in the water.

Drop Anchor
Old English
To be firmly in place; secure. *This house name is for the house owner who intends to stay where s/he is for a long time.*

Dune View
French/Dutch/Old English
Vista of the sand hills.

East Bay
Old English
Eastern inlet.

East Rocks
Old English
Rocks on the eastern side.

Eastport
Old English
The eastern place where ships discharge their cargo.

Edge of the Bay
Old English
Beside the inlet. *A name for a house that is situated very close to a bay.*

Edge Water
English/Old English
By the edge of the water. *For a house that is situated close to a river, lake or sea or for a houseboat.*

Endless Summer
English/Old English
Forever summer time. *A wonderful name for a house in a place with a year round warm to hot climate.*

Evening Tide
Old English
A tide that comes in at evening time. *This may also be used for retired house owners, as 'Evening' may also mean in the latter part of one's life.*

Fairwater
Old English
Light-coloured water; good water.

Fairweather
Old English
Good weather.

Fisherman's Cabin
Old English
Small house where the fish catcher resides.

Fisherton
Old English
The fishing town.

Fisherton Cottage
Old English
Small house in the fishing town.

Fishmore
Old English
Fish in the marshland lake. *This name could also be used in a humorous way, for those who feel the need to do more fishing.*

Forever Summer
English/Old English
Always summer time. *A wonderful name for a house in a place with a year round warm to hot climate.*

Freshwater
Old English
Fresh water lake or river.

Fun In The Sun
English
Joy may be found by being in the sunshine.

Golden Sands
Old English
Yellow-coloured sands. *A wonderful name for a house situated on or with views of yellow sand.*

Gone Fishin'/Gone Fishing
English
The owner of this house has gone fishing; absent. *This is a fun name for the home of a keen fisherman and need not be taking literally.*

Grand Atlantic
Old English/Greek
The great Atlantic Ocean. *A wonderful name for a house with a view of the Atlantic Ocean.*

Grand Pacific
Middle English/Latin
Great peaceful. *The Pacific (peaceful) Ocean was named by the Portuguese explorer Ferdinand Magellan, as he encountered no storms there.*

Hammerhead Point
English/Old English
Hammerhead shark by the headland.

Harbour House
Old English
House by the sheltered inlet. *Sydney Harbour is famed for being the most beautiful harbour in the world.*

Harbourside
Old English
Beside the sheltered inlet. (See Harbour House)

Harbourside Manor
Old English
Estate house beside the sheltered inlet. (See Harbour House)

Homeport
Old English
The house that is close to where the ships discharge their cargo.

Horseshoe Bay
English/Old English
Inlet that is shaped like a horseshoe.

I

Indian Ocean Views
English/Old English
Vista of the Indian Ocean.

Indian Summer
Old English/North American
A period of summer weather occuring after summer. *This may also refer to a happy time in the later period in life, therefore it would be the perfect name for a retiree's home.*

Indian Summer House
Old English/North American
(See Indian Summer)

Jetty Cottage
French/Middle English/Old English
Small house by the small pier.

Jolly Boat
Old English
Medium sized boat used for general work.

Kayak Cottage
Inuit/Old English
Small house with a canoe.

Kelp Cottage
Middle English/Old English
Small house by the seaweed.

Key Cottage
Old English
Small house on the low island.

Kyle Cottage
Scottish/Old English
Small house by the strait.

Lake Cottage
Old English
Small house by the lake.

Lake House
Old English
Home by the lake.

Lakeland
Old English
Acreage by the lake.

Lakeshore Estate
Old English
Large, stately house that stands by the bank of the lake.

Landbridge
Old English
Land that connects two pieces of land.

Landscape Island
Old English
Island of natural scenery.

Longbeach
Old English
Lengthy beach.

Mackerel Bay
Middle English/Old French
Mackerels in the cove.

Marina Lodge
Italian/Spanish/English
Cabin situated close to where the boats moor.

Marine Cottage
Italian/Spanish/Old English
Small cabin by the sea.

Mariner's Cottage
Latin/Old English
Small house where the sailor resides.

Mermaid Cottage
Old English
Small house where the mermaid resides. *This would be a good name for a house where the owner has a passion for the mythical tales of the mermaids.*

Moontide
Old English
Moon over the tide.

Moontide Lodge
Old English
Cabin where the moon shines over the tide.

N

Naval Cottage
Latin/Old English
Small house used by people in the navy.

Newport House
Old English
Home situated near the newly established place where the ships discharge their cargo.

North Bay
Old English
Northern inlet.

North Rocks
Old English
Rocks on the northern side.

Northport
Old English
The northern place where ships discharge their cargo.

O

Oasis
Latin
Fertile area in a desert or dry area. *This would be a perfect name for a home in an arid area with a section of lush green gardens or a pool.*

Ocean Calm
Latin/Greek/Old English
Calm ocean.

Ocean Dreaming
Latin/Greek/English
Dreaming of the ocean.

Ocean Glory
Latin/Greek
Splendour of the ocean.

Ocean Palms
Latin/Greek/Old English
Palm trees by the ocean.

Ocean Vista
Latin/Greek/Italian
Ocean view. *A house with a wonderful view of the ocean would suit this house name.*

Ocean Watch
Latin/Greek/English
Place from where the ocean can be seen.

Oceana
Latin/Greek/Middle English
The ocean.

Oceanfront
Latin/Greek/English
The shore or beach of the ocean. *A name that gives status to a home, as oceanfront property is usually very expensive and highly desirable.*

Oceangoing
Latin/Greek/Middle English/English
Going to the ocean. *This term is usually used for a ship that is designed for the ocean.*

Oceania
Latin/Greek/Middle English
The ocean.

Oceanview
Latin/Greek/Middle English/Old English
Vista of the ocean.

Oceanville
Latin/Greek/Middle English/Old English
Village by the ocean.

On Golden Sands
Yellow-coloured sands. *A wonderful name for a house situated on or overlooking gold-coloured sand.*

On the Beach
English
To reside on or very close to the beach. On the Beach *is a famous novel by Neville Shute (1889–1961), written in 1957 and set in Australia, about the effects of nuclear war. A movie soon followed the successful book and starred Gregory Peck and Ava Gardner.*

P

Pacific Grove
Middle English/French/Old English
Small, secluded wood by the peaceful ocean; small, secluded wood by the Pacific Ocean. *The Pacific (peaceful) Ocean was named by the Portuguese explorer Ferdinand Magellan, as he encountered no storms there.*

Pacific Heights
Middle English/French/Old English
High views of the peaceful ocean; high views of the Pacific Ocean. (See Pacific Grove)

Pacific Palms
Middle English/French/Latin/Old English
Palm trees by the peaceful ocean; palms trees by the Pacific Ocean. (See Pacific Grove)

Pacific Sands
Middle English/French/Old English
Sand by the peaceful ocean; sands by the Pacific Ocean. (See Pacific Grove)

Pacific View
Middle English/French/Old English
Vista of the peaceful ocean; view of the Pacific Ocean. (See Pacific Grove)

Pacifica
Middle English/French/Old English
By the Pacific ocean; by the peaceful ocean. (See Pacific Grove)

Palm Beach
Latin/Old English/English
Palm trees growing on the beach.

Paradise Palms
Middle English/French/Greek/Old English
The idyllic place with palm trees.

Park Beach
Old English/English
Recreational area by the beach.

Pebble Beach
Old English/English
The beach where many small stones may be found.

Point Pleasant
Old English
The lovely head of land. *This is a town in West Virginia that featured in the movie* The Mothman Prophecies *(2002), starring Richard Gere and about psychic visions and the appearance of bizarre entities by the town's people.*

Portland House
Old English
The house by the land where the ships discharge their cargo.

Quay Cottage
English/Celtic/Old English
Small house by the pier.

Quayside
English/Celtic/Old English
Land bordering a port.

Reef Cottage
Dutch/Old English
Small house by the ridge of rocks or coral under the surface of the water.

Regatta View
Italian/Old English
Vista of the boat race. *A great name for a home overlooking an area of ocean or a lake where boats compete against each other.*

Rock Oyster House
Old English/Middle English/Greek
A house that is situated by an oyster farm.

Rocky Beach
Old English
Beach with many rocks.

Salmon Stream Cottage
Old English
Small house by the salmon stream.

Saltwater
Old English
Salty water. *This name would be perfect for a house situated near the ocean.*

Sandcastles
Old English
Castles that are made of sand.

Sandcliff
Old English
The sand covered ledge.

Sandgate
Old English
The entrance to the sandy beach.

Sandhole
Old English
The sandy cavity.

Sandhurst
Old English
Sand bank.

Sandpiper
Old English
The wading bird.

Sandringham
Old English
Round, sandy and small village.

Sandrock Manor
Old English
Estate house by the sandy rock.

Sandy Banks
Old English
Sand dunes.

Sandyway
Old English
Path in the sand.

Sapphire Waters
Middle English/Greek/Latin/Old English
Blue-coloured sea, lake or river.
A wonderful name for a home with views of beautiful, blue water.

Sea Beach House
Old English/English
Home by the sea.

Sea Blue House
Old English
Home overlooking the blue sea.

Seaboard
Old English/North American
Land beside or close to the sea.

Sea Breeze
Old English
Soft sea wind.

Sea Change
Old English
To make a complete change; move to the sea. *The expression comes from Shakespeare's* The Tempest *and means a change brought about by the sea. In more modern times, this term is used for people who have had enough of living in the city and choose to move to a coastal area for a better lifestyle.*

Sea Court
Old English
Courtyard by the sea.

Sea Cow
Old English
Another name for a dugong or a manatee; cow by the sea.

Sea Dog
Old English
A veteran sailor.

Sea Dog Cottage
Old English
Small house owned by the veteran sailor.

Sea Eagle
Old English
Fish-eating eagle; eagle by the sea. *This could be used as a name for a home with a high view of the sea.*

Sea Gem
Old English
Sea jewel.

Sea Haze
Old English
Sea mist.

Sea Holme
Old English
Home by the sea; hamlet or village by the sea; inshore island; floodplain.
'Holm/holme' is also a form of 'hamlet'. Today the name is sometimes used as an alternative spelling of 'home'.

Sea Jewel
Old English
Sea gem.

Sea Lavender Cottage
Old English
Small, lavender-coloured house overlooking the sea; lavender plant growing by the sea.

Sea Lodge
Old English
Cabin by the sea.

Sea of Dreams
Old English
The best sea; dreaming of the sea.

Sea Shanty
Canadian French/Old English
Shack built by the sea; also a sailor's song.

Sea Shells
Old English
Place where seashells may be found.

Sea Shimmer
Old English/English
Shining sea.

Sea Treasure
Greek/French/Middle English/Old English
Sea wealth; cherished sea. *'The Sea Treasure' may be an affectionate name for a very loved and cherished home by the sea.*

Seabird Cottage
Old English
Small cottage by the sea birds.

Seabourn/Seabourne/Seaburn/ Seaburne
Old English/Scottish
Born to the sea; stream by the sea.

Seabreeze
Old English/English
Gentle sea wind.

Seacliff
Old English
Ledge by the sea.

Seacrest/Sea Crest
Old English
Sea summit.

Seacrest Cottage
English/Old English
Small house by the sea summit.

Seacroft
Old English
Small pasture by the sea.

Seacroft Manor
Old English
Estate house with a pasture by the sea.

Seafield
Old English
Meadow by the sea.

Seagate
Old English
Entrance to the sea.

Seakindly
Old English
Family residing near the sea meadow.

Seal Rocks
Old English
The place where seals rest on the rocks.

Seamist
Old English
Light sea fog.

Seanook
Old English
Small, secluded area by the sea.

Seascape
Old English/English
Sea painting or a view of the sea.

Seashell House
Old English
Home by the place where sea shells may be found.

Seashore Estate
Old English
Large, stately house by the shore of the sea.

Seaside Chalet
Old English/French
Small house by the sea.

Seatown
Old English
Town by the sea.

Seaview
Old English
Vista of the sea.

Seaward
Old English
Towards the sea; guardian of the sea.

Seaways
Old English
Crossroads by the sea; path to the sea.

Seaweed Cottage
Old English
Small house by the seaweed.

Seawinds/Sea Winds
Old English
Wind from the sea.

Shark Cove
English/Old English
Shark in the sheltered inlet.

Shark Point
English/Old English
Headland from which sharks can be seen.

Shelbourne Estate
Old English/Scottish
Small, shelly stream by the large, stately house.

Shell Beach
Old English
Shells on the beach.

Shell Harbour
Old English
Shells by the harbour.

Ship In/Ship Inn/Shipin/Shipinn
Old English
To move in; the place where the sailors stay when their ship is in port.

Ships Point
Old English
Point from which ships can be seen.

Shipshape
Old English
In good condition; organised.

Shipton
Old English
Ship town.

Shipwrecked Lodge
Old English
The cabin by the shipwreck.

Shoal Bay
Old English
Sandbank by the inlet; refuge in the inlet.

Shoalhaven
Old English
Sandbank near the refuge; refuge by the shallow water.

Shoalstone Manor
Old English
Sandbank near the stone estate house; estate house by the shallow water.

Shore Break
Middle English/Old English
The place where the waves break on the beach.

Snapper Cottage
Old English
Small house next to where the snapper can be caught.

South Bay
Old English
Southern inlet.

South Rocks
Old English
Rocks on the southern side.

Southport
Old English
The southern place where ships discharge their cargo. *Southport is a seaside resort in both England and on the southern coast of Queensland, Australia.*

Splashwater
English/Old English
The spatter of water.

Sunseeker
Old English
Searching for the sun.

Surf Beach
English
The beach where people surf.

Surfside
English/Old English
Beside the waves.

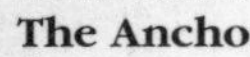

T

The Anchor
Old English
To be firmly in place; secure. *This is for the house owner who intends to stay where she or he is for long time.*

The Atlantic Manor
Latin/ Old English
Estate house by the Atlantic Ocean.

The Beach
English
Sandy place beside the sea.

The Beach Cottage
English/Old English
Small house by the beach.

The Beach House
English/Old English
Home by the beach.

The Beach Hut
English/French
Small and simply constructed shelter by the beach.

The Beach Shack
English
Small, simply constructed shelter by the beach.

The Beaches
English
A place where many beaches may be found.

The Blue Marlin
Old English/English
Where the blue marlin fish may be found or fished for.

The Boardwalk
English/Old English
Footpath made from boards by the beachside.

The Boat House
Old English
The place which houses a boat.

The Boat Shop/The Boatshop
English/Old English
The place where boats are serviced, made or kept.

The Buccaneer
French
The pirate.

The Clam Bake
English/American
Small house where clams are cooked. Clambake *was a 1967 movie starring Elvis Presley.*

The Coast
English
The coastal region.

The Coastal Cottage
Old English
Small house by the coast.

The Cove
Old English
Sheltered bay.

The Cove House
Old English
House by the sheltered bay.

The Deep Blue
English/Old English
A reference to the ocean; the blueness of the ocean.

The Dunes
French/Old English
Hills made of sand.

The Fish House
Middle English/Old English
The home where the fisherman resides; the place where fish are kept or bred.

The Fishing Net
Middle English/Old English
The net used for catching fish.

The Four Seasons
Old English
An area that experiences spring, summer, winter and autumn/fall.

The Hut
English/French
A simple constructed shelter.

The Jetty
English
The pier.

The Marina
English/Latin
Place where boats anchor or moor.

The Marina Cottage
Latin/Old English
Small house near to where the boats anchor or moor.

The Marine Lodge
Latin/English
Cabin by the sea or ocean.

The Oasis
Latin
The fertile area in a desert or dry area. *This would be a perfect name for a home in an arid area with a section of lush green gardens or a pool.*

The Old Port
Old English
The place where ships once discharged their cargo.

The Peninsula
Latin
Narrow land almost completely surrounded by water.

The Pier
Middle English/Latin
The jetty.

The Port
Old English
The place where ships discharge their cargo.

The Quays
English/Celtic
Piers.

The Round House/The Roundhouse
Old English
The circular house. *A name for an unusually circular shaped home. 'Roundhouse' is also a nautical term, denoting variously the captain's accommodation on the quarterdeck of Indiaman ships, the apprentices' accommodation on the afterdecks of some later sailing ships, and the toilets on the top deck of Royal Navy ships. Therefore the name might also be chosen for a beach house or a houseboat*

The Sails
Old English
Vista of the boat sails; a place where sails are made; a structure that resembles the sails of a boat or yacht.

The Sea Mariner
Old English/Latin
The sailor.

The Sea Shore
Old English
Where the sea meets the land.

The Seafront
Old English/English
Where the sea meets the land.

The Shack
English
A simply constructed shelter.

The Shell House
Old English
Home by the shell covered beach; house made out of shells.

The Shore
Old English
Beach bank; where the sea meets the land.

The Shore House
Old English
Home by the beach bank; the house near where the sea meets the land.

The Shoreline
Old English
Beach bank; where the sea meets the land.

The Shores
Old English
Beach bank; where the sea meets the land.

The Surfer's Cottage
English/Old English
Small house where the surfer resides.

The Waterfront
English/Old English
Where the sea meets the land.

The Waterside
Old English
Where the sea meets the land.

The Wharf
English
The pier or jetty.

Three Salmon Lodge
Old English
Three salmon were caught in the stream near the cabin.

Tidal Song
Old English
The sound of the tide rushing in.

Tidesong
Old English
The sound of the tide rushing in.

Trinity House
Latin/French/Old English
Three fold; house of the Father, the Son and the Holy Spirit. *'Trinity House' is a British maritime organisation responsible for licensing pilots, maintaining lighthouses and buoys. Accordingly the name might be chosen for a houseboat.*

Trout Cottage
Old English
Small house by the river where the trout swim.

U

Undertow House
Old English
Home by the hidden current. *An 'undertow' flows in a different direction to the surface current.*

Unity Island
Latin/Old French/Middle English/Old English
One island.

V

Viewside Cottage
Old English
Small house with a side vista.

W

Watersmeet
Old English
The place where the waters meet.

Waterview
Old English
Vista of the sea, lake or river.

Waverley
Middle English
Waves in the quivering meadow.

West Bay
Old English
Western inlet.

West Rocks
Old English
Western rocks.

Westport
Old English
The place in the west where the ships discharge their cargo.

Whale Cove
Latin/Old English
Whales in the sheltered inlet.

Whale Point
Latin/Old English
Whales by the headland.

Wharf View
English/Old English
Vista of the pier.

White Sands
Old English
White sand. *The perfect name for a home situated on or overlooking a white, sandy beach.*

Whitefish Lodge
Old English
The cabin where whitefish may be caught near by.

Whitewater
Old English
Rushing water; white-coloured water.

Wide Bay House
Old English
Home by the broad, sheltered inlet.

Y

Yacht View
Dutch/German/Old English
Vista of the sailing vessels.

Yellowfin House
Old English
Home where the yellowfin (tuna) is sold or cooked.

Sail Away

Living on a boat may be an unusual option but you need not be exempt from finding a name for your floating palace. People living in these circumstances are often avant-garde and are attracted to creative and individual names. For those a little more conventional, there are more traditional names in various other sections of this book that may suit you better.

A

A Habit
A Little Bit Crazy
Abracadabra
Abyss
Accelerate
Addicted To Love
Addicted To Surf
Addicted To The Ocean
Addicted To The Sea
Addicted To Waves
Addiction
Adelaide
Adios
Adrenaline
Adventure Bound
Adventure Seeker
Adventurer
Adventurous
Affirmation
Africa
After Five
After Glow
After Hours
After Shock
Afterglow
Afternoon Delight
Aggravation
Aggro
Ahoy
Ain't Misbehaving
Airborne
Aladdin
Alaska
Albatross
Algebra
Alibaba
Alibi
All Aboard
All That Jazz
Alligator
All-star
Almost There
Aloha
Alpha
Alpha Female
Alpha Male
Alter Ego
Alyssa
Amadeus
Amazing Grace
Ambassador
Amber
Ambition
Ambitious
America
American Beauty
American Pie
Amethyst
Amigo
Amore
Analyse That
Analyse This
Anastasia
Anchor
Anchorman
Anchors Away
Angel Eyes
Angel Fire
Angel Fish
Angelica
Angelo
Anglers
Annabelle
Annie's Song
Anniversary
Ann-Marie
Another Adventure
Another Chance
Antic...ipation
Aphrodite
Apple Pie
Aqua
Aqua Cat
Aqua Dog
Aqua Girl
Aqua Man
Aqua Therapy
Aqua-holic
Aquarium
Aquarius
Aqua-trails
Arcadia
Aries
Aristocrat
Arms Of The Angel
Arrival
Ashley
Asia
At Ease
Athena
Atlanta
Aurora
Aussie
Ava
Ave Maria
Avon
Away
Awestruck
Aye Aye
Aztec

B

Baby Blue
Baby Cakes

Baby Face
Bad Ass
Bad Boy
Bad Buoy
Bad Girl
Bad Habit
Bad To The Bone
Baffled
Bail Out
Bait
Bait Hunter
Ballet Dancer
Balmain Bug
Banana Boat
Bandit
Bank Note
Banshee
Bar Chaser
Barbarian
Barman
Barnacle
Barracuda
Bartender
Bath Toy
Bay Dreamer
Bay Runner
Bay Spirit
Beam Me Up
Beaming
Bear
Beautiful Dreamer
Beauty
Bedazzled
Been There, Done That
Beer-run
Bella
Bella Vista
Belle
Bellydancer
Bewdy
Bewitch
Bewitched
Big Ben
Big Daddy
Big Foot
Big Mama
Big Red
Big Toy
Bikini
Bikini Haven
Bikini Heaven
Birthday Present
Bit O' Heaven
Black Dog
Black Hole
Black Magic
Black Orchid
Black Star
Blackbeard
Blackhawk
Blackjack
Blade
Blazing Comet
Blessed
Bliss
Blitz
Blizzard
Blossom
Blowing In The Wind
Blown Away
Blue Angel
Blue Bottle
Blue Chip
Blue Cloud
Blue Devil
Blue Horizon
Blue Moon
Blue Skies
Bluegrass
Boat Of Us
Boat Whisperer
Boat-alicious
Bon Voyage
Bones
Boo
Boo Boo
Boomer
Boomerang
Born Free
Born To Run
Born To Try
Bossy
Bossy Boots
Both Of Us
Bottom's Up
Bound
Bounty
Bourbon
B-positive
Brass Bell
Brat
Brat Pack
Braveheart
Breaking Waves
Breathless
Brief Encounter
Broke
Bronco
Brumby
Buccaneer
Budget Surplus
Buffy
Buggaboo
Bugger
Bullwinkle
Bumble Bee
Bumpkin
Bunny
Bunyip
Buoy Crazy
Buoy Toy
Butterfly
Butterscotch
Byte Me

C

Cache 22
Cactus
Calender Girl
Calypso

Camelot
Camelot Cruiser
Canada
Cancer
Candy
Candy Monster
Caprice
Capricorn
Capricornia
Captain Nemo
Captive
Caress
Caribbean King
Caribbean Queen
Carmen
Carnival
Carolina
Caroline
Casanova
Cascade
Casper
Cast Away
Cat Tales
Catalyst
Catatonic
Catherine
Catherine The Great
Cavalier
Caveman
Cavewoman
C-bird
C-boat
C-boy
C-breeze
C-buoy
C-calf
C-captain
C-cow
C-cruiser
C-culture
C-curity
C-da-boat
C-dancer
C-doo
C-dragon
C-drive
C-eagle
Celebration
Celebrity
Celtic
Celtic Cross
Celtic Jewel
Celtic Sun
C-farer
C-fever
C-girl
C-guardian
C-gypsy
Cha-cha
C-hag
Champagne
Champion
Chance
Chances
Chaos
Chardonnay
Charisma
Charity
Charleen
Charlie's Angel
C-harmony
Chaser
Chelsea
Cherokee
Cherry Pie
Cheyenne
Chic
Chicken
Chilli
Chocoholic
Chocolate
C-horse
C-hunter
Ciao
City Slicker
C-king
C-kitten
Clamshell
Clarity
Clear View
Cleopatra
C-life
C-lion
Cloud Chaser
Cloud Nine
Cloud Nine Cruiser
Clueless
C-menace
C-mist
C-Nomad
Cobra
Cocktail
Coco
Codger
Comanche
Comfy
Commodore
Compass
Contagious
Content
Contessa
Cool Summer
Coral Reef
Coral Reef Diver
Coral Sea
Corkage
Cosmo
Cougar
Court Jester
Cowboy
Cowgirl
Coyote
C-passion
C-prince
C-princess
C-puppy
Crab Catcher
C-raider
Cranky

Crayfish
Crazy
Crazy Ass
Creepy Crawler
Cricket Player
C-rider
Crime Scene
Crocodile
Crooner
Crow
Cruise Control
Cruisin'
Cruising
Crystal
Crystal Ball
C-safari
C-sanctuary
C-scaped
C-seeker
C-sick
C-side
C-snail
C-snake
C-spray
C-style
C-time
C-toy
C-turtle
Cubism
CU-L8R
C-urchin
Curious
Current Affair
C-view
C-weed
C-witch
C-world
Cyclone

D

Daddy Long Legs
Daffodil
Dagger
Daiquiri
Daisy
Daisy Eater
Damsel
Dances With Dolphins
Dances With Fish
Dances With Waves
Dances With Wind
Dancing Bear
Dancing Pirate
Dancing Queen
Dandelion
Dandy
Daphne
Daredevil
Daring
Dashing
Dawn
Day Dream
Day Dreamer
Dead Calm
Deal Me In
Debit
Debt
Deckhand
Deep Blue
Deep Pacific
Déjà vu
Delilah
Deliverance
Delta
Demon
Dependable
Desired
Destiny
Devil In A Blue Dress
Dewdrop
Diamond
Diamond In The Rough
Diana
Digger
Dirty Harry
Disco Diva
Distraction
Diva
Dixie
Dixie Chick
Dollars And Cents
Dolly
Dolphin
Dolphin Chaser
Dolphina
Don Juan
Don Quixote
Double Trouble
Doufishtoo
Dove
Dragon
Dragonfly
Drake
Drama Queen
Dream A Little Dream
Dream Big
Dream Catcher
Dream Machine
Dream Maker
Dream Weaver
Dreamscape
Dreamy
Drift Wood
Driftaway
Drifter
Dropdead Gorgeous
Duchess
Ducky
Dumb Blond
Dundee
Dynamite

E

Eagle
Eagle Eye
Eagle Eyes
Eagle Spirit
Eagles Nest
Easterly
Eastern Waters
Easy Living

Easy Rider
Easy Sailing
Ebony
Eccentric
Eclipse
Edelweiss
Eden
Eden Found
Ego
El Relaxo
Elfin
Elixir
Elizabeth
Elvis
Emerald
Emmanuelle
Empty Pockets
Enchantress
Endeavour
Energetic
Engaged
Enigma
Enterprise
Eros
Escapade
Escape
Escape Da Blues
Esmeralda
Esperance
Espresso
Eternal Flames
Eva
Eve
Evening Star
Ever So Clever
Everlast
Evita
Evolution
Excalibur
Excellence
Exotic Dancer
Extraordinary
Extreme
Eye Of The Storm

F

Fair Maiden
Fair Play
Fair Weather
Fairy Slipper
Faith
Faithful
Falcon
Fallen Angel
Famous
Fancy
Fancy Face
Fancy Free
Fandango
Fantasia
Fantastic
Fantasy
Faster Than You
Fate
Favourite
Fear Knot
Featherstone
Felix
Fiesta
Filly
Finally Mine
Finally Ours
Fine Tune
Fire And Ice
Firecracker
Firefly
First Class
First Love
Fish Finder
Fish 'n' Chips
Fish Stalker
Fish Technician
Fishalot
Fisherman
Fisho
Fishtails
Fishtales
Fishy Business
Fishytales
Flamboyant
Flaming Heart
Flamingo
Flash Dance
Fleet Goddess
Fleet Street
Fleetwood
Fleur
Flipper
Floating Palace
Flutterby
Fly Me To The Moon
Flying beauty
Flying Eagle
Flying Fish
Follow Me
Fool's Gold
Footloose
Footsie
Forever
Forever Bliss
Forever Summer
Fortunate
Fortune Cookie
Fortune-8
Four Leaf Clover
Foxtrot
Foxy
Frangipani
Free Spirit
Freedom
Freshman
Freshwater
Freud
Freya
Frolic
Frozen Assets
Fudge
Fun At Sea
Funky
Furious
Fury

G

Gabriel
Gabrielle
Gaia
Galaxy
Galaxy Quest
Galileo
Gator
G'day
Gem
Gemini
Genevieve
Gentleman
Georgia
Geronimo
Get Wet
Getaway
Ghost Hunter
Ghost Orchid
Girl Crazy
Give Peace A Chance
Gizmo
Glamour Girl
Glass Slippers
Globe Trotter
Glorious
Glory
Glory Days
Gnome
Go Faster
Go Fish
Go For Gold
Go For It
Go Snap
Goblin
Goddess
God's Grace
Godspeed
Go-go
Goin' My Way
Golden Boy
Golden Buoy
Golden Girl
Goldfish
Goliath
Gone Fishin'
Gone Fishing
Gone With The Wind
Good Girl
Good Karma
Good Times
Goodbye
Goodbye Angel
Gotta Break
Gottago
Grace
Graceland
Grand Illusion
Greased Lightning
Green Emerald
Groover
Groovy
Growing Pains
Grumpy
Guardian Of The Sea
Gulliver's Travels
Gusto
Gypsy
Gypsy Of The C
Gypsy Of The Sea
Gypsy Queen
Gypsy Rose

H

H2O
Had To Get It
Hamlet
Hammerhead
Hammerhead Shark
Handy Man
Hangover
Hanky Panky
Happenstance
Happy Boy
Happy Buoy
Happy Camper
Happy Girl
Happy Hour
Happy Times
Happy Trails
Happy Vacation
Hardware
Hat Trick
Haunted
Have A Nice Day
Haven
He Devil
He Loves Me
Head Over Heels
Heart Breaker
Heart 'n' Soul
Heartbeat
Heat Wave
Heather
Heaven
Heaven Sent
Heavenly Prize
Heidi
Heiress
Hellraiser
Hemlock
Her Highness
Hercules
Hers
Hidden Treasure
Hide Out
Hideaway
High Flyer
High Heels
High Hopes
High Life
High 'n' Dry
High Roller
High Tech
High Tide
Highlander
Highlight
Hippie Heaven
His
His Highness

His 'n' Hers
Hocus Pocus
Hokey Pokey
Holly
Hollywood
Hollywood Star
Holme
Home And Away
Home Sweet Home
Homeless
Honey Bunny
Hoodoo
Hook
Hooked
Hot Diamond
Hot Dog
Hot Rod
Hot Shot
Huggy Bear
Hummer
Hung Jury
Hunter
Huntress
Hurricane

I

Ice Princess
Ice Queen
Iceberg
Iced Bear
Illusion
I'm A Celebrity
I'm A Star
Image
Imagination
Imogene
Impulsive
In Heaven
In Vogue
India
Indian Song
Indian Summer
Indigo
Infatuation
Inheritance
Innocent
Insanity
Inspector
Into The Wind
Intrigue
Intuition
Irish Eyes
Irish Lass
Irish Mist
Irish Rose
Ironman
Ironwoman
Isabella
Isabelle
Isadora
Isis
Island Hopper
Itsy Bitsy
Ivory

J

Jackaroo
Jackpot
Jade
Jaguar
Jalapeno
Jasmine
Java
Jaws
Jazz
Jazz Singer
Jazzman
Jazzstar
Jazzy Lady
Jellybean
Jennifer
Jessica
Jet Stream
Jewel
Jezabel/Jezabelle
Jigsaw
Jillaroo
Jiminy Cricket
Jolly Roger
Jonah
Jonah's Whale
Joyride
Jubilee
Juliet
Jumbo
Jumping For Joy
Jumpstart
Jupiter
Just Between You And Me
Just Chillin'
Just Chilling
Just Cruisin'
Just Cruising
Just Dandy
Just In Time
Just My Style
Just The Two Of Us
Justice
Just Us

K

Kaleidoscope
Karma
Karma Receiver
Kasimira
Katarina
Katie
Katinka
Katrina
Keep Sake
Kermit
Kimberly
King Neptune
King Of Kings
King Of The C
King Of The Sea
Kingfisher
Kiowa
Kismet
Kiss 'n' Tell
Kiss This

Kitty-Kat
Kiwi
Knight
Knight In Shining Amour
Knight Rider
Kookaburra

L

La-di-da
Lady
Lady Angler
Lady Bird
Lady Bug
Lady In Red
Lady Jane
Lady Like
Lady Luck
Lady Sings the Blues
Lady Slipper
Ladylove
Lakota
Lambada
Lancelot
Land 'n' Sea
Land's End
Laurel
Layla
Leader
Leakin'
Leaking
Leaky Boat
Leap Of Faith
Leather 'n' Lace
Legacy
Leo
Leopard
Levi
Liberty
Libra
Lifestyle
Lilibeth
Lily
Lilypad
Limited Edition
Liquid Amber
Liquid Assets
Liquid Courage
Liquorice
Little Lady
Little Man
Little Miss Magic
Little Retreat
Lobster Dreamer
Lobster Eater
Lobster Hunter
Loch Ness
Locomotion
Logistics
Lolly Monster
Lonely Heart
Lonesome
Look At Me
Lorelei
Lost
Lost In Space
Lothario
Lottery
Lotto
Lotus
Love In Motion
Love It
Love Monster
Love Potion
Love Shack
Love The C
Love The Sea
Lovelady
Love's Wish
Lovey
Lucifer
Lucky Chances
Lucky Charm
Lucky Dog
Lucky Dolphin
Lucky Lady
Lucky Star
Lucky Stars
Lucy
Lullaby
Lullaby Maker
Lunatic

M

Macbeth
Mad Dog
Madame
Madame Butterfly
Made Of Gold
Made Of Silver
Majestic
Maggie Mae
Magic Carpet
Magic Kingdom
Magic Trick
Magical
Magpie
Maiden
Major
Makin' Doo
Makin' Dough
Makin' Love
Makin' Waves
Making Love
Making Memories
Making Waves
Malibu
Mambo
Mambo King
Mambo Queen
Mandy
Mango
Marcus
Marigold
Marilyn
Marlin Eater
Marlin Hunter
Marry Me
Martini
Marylou
Masquerade

Master And Commander
Matilda
Matrix
Matthias
Maverick
Maximum Exposure
Maximum Power
Mayday
Medicine Man
Megabucks
Megabytes
Melissa
Melodrama
Melody
Melt Away
Memories
Mercury
Merlin's Magic
Mermaid Express
Mermaid Mist
Midnight Blue
Midnight Blues
Midnight Lady
Millennium Rose
Milo
Mine
Minnow
Miracles
Misadventure
Misbehavin'
Mischief
Mischief Maker
Miss Behaving
Miss Magic
Miss Piggy
Mistletoe
Misty
Mocha
Mohawk
Moisture
Molly
Monroe
Monster
Montana
Moody
Moon Dancer
Moonbeam
Moonlight Sonata
Moonshine
Moose
Morning Glory
Morning Mist
Morning Star
Mosquito
Mozart
Mr Big Shot
Mr Clean
Mr Cool
Mr Muscle
Ms Bigshot
Ms Cool
Much-ado
Muncho Man
Muscles
Mustang
Mustang Sally
Mutiny
Mutt
My Alibi
My Dream
My Favourite
My Gizmo
My Heart
My Jewel
My Liberty
My Mistress
My Obsession
My Play Thing
Mysterious Lady
Mystical
Mystico
Mystique
Mystro

N

Napoleon
Narcissus
Naughty
Naughty Boy
Naughty Buoy
Naughty By Nature
Naughty Girl
Naughty One
Nautica
Nautical
Nautical Express
Navajo
Navigator
Nemesis
Nemo
Neptune
Neptune's Boat
Neptune's Daughter
Neptune's Son
Nero
Never Never
Neverland
New Beginnings
New Start
Nicholas
Nicola
Nicole
Night Chronicles
Night Crawler
Night Owl
Night Rider
Night Shift
Night Watch
Nirvana
Nitro
No Drama
Nomad
Northerly
Northern Skies
Northern Waters
Nostradamus
November Rain
Nugget
Nutcracker
Nuts

O

O Sole Mio
Obsession
Ocean Crest
Ocean Dancer
Ocean Potion
Ocean Quest
Ocean Reef
Ocean Runner
Ocean Thrill
Octopus
Octopussy
Off Duty
Off Shore
Oh A Whim
O-joy
Old Codger
Old Lady Of The C
Old Lady Of The Sea
Old Man Of The C
Old Man Of The Sea
Olympia
Omega
OMG (Oh my God)
On Target
One Love
Onyx
OO7
Optimist
Orca
Orion
Oscar
OU812
Our Favourite
Our Jewel
Ours
Outcast
Outlaw
Outrageous
Outta Here
Outta Sight
Over My Head
Over Our Heads
Overboard
Overtime
Ozone

P

Pacific Popsicle
Pacifica
Paid For
Paid My Dues
Paisley
Pandora
Pandora's Box
Panther
Paradise
Paradise Found
Paradise One
Partners In Crime
Party Boy
Party Buoy
Party Girl
Passion
Passionate
Pathfinder
Patience
Patriot
Pay Day
Peace
Peace Maker
Peaceful
Peaches 'n' Cream
Pearly
Pebbles
Peek-a-boo
Pegasus
Pelican
Penelope
Penny
Perfect
Perfection
Petal
Petty Cash
Phantasmagoria
Phantom
Philosopher
Phoebe
Phoenix
Pia
Picasso
Piggy Bank
Pinch Me
Pinnacle
Pioneer
Piper
Pirate
Pisces
Pitch Master
Platinum
Play Boy
Play Buoy
Play Girl
Play Pen
Play Station
Play Thing
Play Time
Play Toy
Player
Pleasure
Poetica
Poetry in Motion
Poison
Poker
Popcorn
Popeye
Popsicle
Popsicle Toes
Popsy
Power
Precious
Predator
Pretty Boy
Pretty Buoy
Pretty Flower
Pretty Penny
Prince Charming
Prince Of The C
Prince Of The Sea
Princess Of The C

Princess Of The Sea
Pro
Prosperity
Providence
Prozac
Pumpkin
Pure
Purity

Q

Quality
Que Sera Sera
Queen Of Sheba
Queen Of The C
Queen Of The Sea
Queeny
Quickstar
Quit Wishing

R

Ra
Race The Moon
Race The Sun
Racer
Raider
Rain Dancer
Rainbow
Rainbow's End
Rainmaker
Rainy Days
Ranger
Ransom
Rascal
Rasputin
Raven
Raven Lunatic
Ravenstone
Razzle Dazzle
Razzmatazz
Rebecca
Rebel
Red Cloud
Red Sea
Redbeard
Red-C
Reel Dream
Reel Easy
Reel Fishy
Reel Love
Reel Lucky
Reel Therapy
Reflections
Refuge
Regal Classic
Regulator
Relaxation
Release
Relentless
Rembrandt
Remembrance
Renaissance
Rendezvous
Rescue Me
Respect
Restless
Restless Heart
Retired
Retiring
Retriever
Reverie
Rhapsody
Rhyme And Reason
Ring Master
Rip
Risky Business
Risqué
Rock 'n' Roll
Rocket
Rocket Girl
Rocket Man
Rocket Power
Rocky
Romeo
Rose Petal
Rosie
Rover
Roxanne
Roxy
Royal Star
Ruby
Rum Runner
Rumba
Runaway
Runner
Running Away

S

Sacred Spirit
Safari
Saffron
Sagittarius
Sails
Sails Away
Salmon
Salmon Hunter
Salt Eater
Salty
Salty Dog
Salty Miss
Salty Sir
Salvation
Samba
Samson And Delilah
Sanctuary
Sandpiper
Sapphire
Sassy
Satin
Savannah
Scallywag
Scandal
Scandalous
Scarlett
Scorpio
Scubadoo
Sea Angel
Sea Bird
Sea Boy
Sea Buoy
Sea Calf
Sea Captain

Sea Cow
Sea Cruiser
Sea Culture
Sea Dancer
Sea Doo
Sea Dragon
Sea Drive
Sea Eagle
Sea Fever
Sea Flower
Sea Force
Sea Force One
Sea Girl
Sea Guardian
Sea Gull
Sea Gypsy
Sea Hag
Sea Harmony
Sea Hoon
Sea Horse
Sea Hunter
Sea Huntress
Sea In The Blood
Sea King
Sea Kitten
Sea Life
Sea Love
Sea Lover
Sea Menace
Sea Mist
Sea Nomad
Sea Passion
Sea Prince
Sea Princess
Sea Puppy
Sea Queen
Sea Raider
Sea Rider
Sea Safari
Sea Sanctuary
Sea Seeker
Sea Sick
Sea Snail
Sea Snake
Sea Spray
Sea Style
Sea Toy
Sea Turtle
Sea Urchin
Sea View
Sea Worthy
Seabound
Sea-curity
Sea-dation
Sea-duced
Seafarer
Seafood
Seafood Catcher
Seafood Eater
Seagasm
Seahag
Seal
Sealion
Seascape
Seaside
Seatime
Sea-u
Seaward
Seaweed
Seaworld
Second Home
Seeker
Sellout
Senora
Senorita
Serenade
Serendipity
Serenity
Seven Seas
Sextant
Sexy Lady
Sexy Man
Shabby Chic
Shaboom
Shadow
Shaman
Shamrock
Shangri-la
Shania
Shanty
Shark Hunter
Sharkbait
She Devil
Shell Collector
Shooting Star
Show Me The Money
Showdown
Showgirl
Sierra
Siesta
Silence
Silhouette
Silicone
Silver Bass
Silver Bells
Silver Fox
Silver Lining
Silver Tide
Simply Irresistible
Simply Sensational
Sin Bin
Sinbad
Sinful
Single
Single And Lovin' It
Sink Or Swim
Sioux
Size Does Matter
Size Matters
Skipper
Skirt Chaser
Sky Dancer
Sleeping Beauty
Slice Of Heaven
Slick
Slippery
Slippery When Wet
Slow Dancer
Snake

Snap Dragon
Snowflake
Socialite
Sociometry
Soda Stream
Solitaire
Solitary
Solitude
Solo
Something Fishy
Sonnet
Sorcery
Sorrel
Soul Asset
Soul Mate
Southerly
Southern Belle
Southern Cross
Southern Skies
Southern Waters
Sparky
Spartacus
Spawn
Specialty
Speed Demon
Speedy
Speedy Gonzales
Spell
Spicy
Spider
Spider Man
Spirit
Spirit Of The West
Spirited
Spit And Polish
Splash
Splurge
Spot
Spray
Sprayer
Sprinter
Sprite
Spritely
Squeak
Squeaky Clean
Squid Kid
Squid King
Stallion
Star
Star Blazer
Star Gazer
Star Studded
Star Woman
Starbuck
Stardust
Starlight
Starward
Sterling
Stinger
Stingray
Stop Worrying
Storm Chaser
Storm Raider
Storm's Destiny
Strange Days
Stranger
Strawberries 'n' Cream
Strawberry Fields
Streaker
Stress Buster
Stress Queen
Stressing Less
Stubby
Stubby Holder
Stud
Style
Sudden Debt
Sugar
Sugarpie
Summer
Summer Joy
Summer Madness
Summer Magic
Summer Oasis
Summer Place
Summer Reign
Summer School
Summer Time
Sun Chaser
Sun Dancer
Sun God
Sun Goddess
Sun 'n' Sea
Sun Seeker
Sunbeam
Sunburn
Sunburst
Sunflower
Sunny Side Up
Sunrise
Sunscreen
Sunshine
Sunspot
Sunstroke
Supercalafrangilisticex-pialadotious
Superdog
Super-duper
Supergirl
Superman
Supermodel
Supernatural
Supernova
Superstar
Superstitious
Surprise
Survivor
Swash
Sweet As Candy
Sweet Child O' Mine
Sweet Lullaby
Sweet Thing
Sweetie
Sweetpea
Swell Dancer
Swimmingly
Sympathy
Symphony
Synchronicity

T

Tabasco
Talisman
Tangles
Tango
Tara
Tarot
Tarzan
Taurus
Teacher's Pet
Teaser
Telepathy
Temper
Tempest
Temptation
Tequila
Testosterone
That's Amore
The Abyss
The American Dream
The Ancient Mariner
The Angler
The Aquarium
The Atlantic
The Australian Dream
The Bank's
The Bear
The Best Present Ever
The Better Half
The Blues
The Boss
The Boss Lady
The Boss Man
The Both Of Us
The Bounty
The Breaks
The Buoy
The Cat's Meow
The Cat's Pyjamas
The Clam
The Clam Bake
The Clam Catcher
The Cleaner
The Cod Father
The Cod Mother
The Cork
The Cosmos
The Count
The Crew
The Crow
The Crustacean
The Dance
The Deep Blue
The Dingy
The Distraction
The Diva
The Dolphin
The Dragon
The Edge
The First Dive
The Flying Duck
The Fox
The Gale Hunter
The Gator
The General
The General's Daughter
The Getaway
The Goblin
The God Father
The God Mother
The Haven
The Heir
The Heiress
The Honeymooners
The Hound
The Hulk
The Hull
The Investment
The Joker
The Jalopy
The Judge
The Jury
The Kiwi
The Last Rebel
The Magic Touch
The Majestic
The Mariner
The Marlon
The Marlon Eater
The Marlon Hunter
The Mayflower
The Milky Way
The Mister
The Mistress
The Monster
The Mrs
The Native
The Navigator
The Nomad
The Odd One Out
The Old Crow
The Other Woman
The Palace
The Passion
The Patriot
The Pay Off
The Phantom
The Place To Be
The Potion
The Prawn
The Prayer
The President
The Prettiest Thing
The Quest
The Raven
The Rose
The Round House
The Roundhouse
The Sails
The Seekers
The Shanty
The Shrimp
The Star
The Sultan
The Surfer
The Thing
The Tortoise
The Turtle
The Vacationer

The Walrus
The Warrior
The Weekender
The Wench
The Witch
The Witch Doctor
The Wizard
The Yen
The Zoo
Therapy
This Side Up
Thisledoo
Thor
Thoroughbred
Three's A Crowd
Thrill Ride
Thumper
Thunder Chaser
Thundercloud
Thunderhead
Thyme
Tidal Song
Tiffany
Tiffany's
Tiger
Tiger Lily
Tigger
Tiki
Time Of Our Lives
Time Off
Time Out
Time Warp
Tinkerbelle
Tiny Dancer
Titan
Titanesque
Titanic
Toad
Together Forever
Top Deck
Top Gun
Topless
Tornado
Torque
Total Recall
Touch Down
Tough Love
Toxic
Trade Wind
Tranquilizer
Treasure
Treasure Chest
Treasure Island
Trial And Tribulations
Tribulation
Tribute
Trickster
Trouble
True Blue
True North
Tuna Fish
Tuna Warrior
Tuna Watch
Tuna Witch
Tunnel Vision
Twilight Zone
Twinkle
Twinkle Toes
Twisted
Twister
Two To Tango

U

U Boat
Ultra Violet
Unchained Melody
Under My Spell
Under The Southern Cross
Unicorn
United
Unsinkable
Untamed
Untouchable
Uranus
Utopia
U-wish

V

Vagabond
Valentine
Vampire
Vanilla
Velvet
Veronica
Veronique
Viagra
Victor
Victoria
Victoria's Secret
Victorious
Victory
Viking
Villain
Vintage
Virgin
Virgo
Vision Quest
Vitality
Vitamin C
Vitamin Sea
Vixen
Vodka King
Vogue
Voodoo
Voyager

W

Walrus
Waltzing Matilda
Wanderer
Wanderlust
Wannabe
Warp Speed
Warrior
Water Addict
Water Hog
Water Lover
Water Spout
Waterbed
Waterbug
Waterholic

Wave Crusher
Wave Eater
Wave Maker
Wave Runner
Wave Surfer
Wave Walker
Weather Shield
Wedidit
Weekend Cruiser
Weekend Escape
Weekender
Welcome
Weowna
Weownit
Westerly
Western Skies
Western Waters
Wet
Wet Bunny
Wet Debt
Wet Dream
Whacky
Whale
Whale Of A Time
Which Way
Whisky
Whispers
White Cloud
White Pointer
Who Dares Wins
Wicked
Wild At Heart
Wild Blue Yonder
Wild Child
Wild Days
Wild Is The Wind
Wild One
Wild Orchid
Wild Times
Wild Weather
Wild Weather Rider
Wild Wind
Wildfire
Wildflower
Wildside
Wind Breaker
Wind Charm
Wind Magic
Wind Rush
Wind Song
Wind Spirit
Wind Talker
Wind Walker
Wind Wench
Windborn
Windchime
Windcrest
Windfall
Windseeker
Windsong
Windswept
Windward
Windy
Windy Days
Wine Merchant
Wine-o
Wing And A Prayer
Winsome
Winter
Wish List
Wished For
Witch
Witchcraft
Witches
Wizard
Wolfen
Wolfman
Wonder Dog
Wonder Woman
Woodstock
Worryless
Worth It
Wrangler

X

Xanadu
Xander
Xcellence
Xcellerate
XLER8
Xtreme

Y

Yankee
Yearned For
Yellowbeard
Yeti
Ying And Yang
Yowie
Yo-yo
Y-worry

Z

Zany
Z-breeze
Zebra
Zeus
Zia
Zig Zag
Zodiac
Zoo
Zoom
Zoomer
Zorro
Zulu

Home on the Move

Many people all over the world enjoy the easy escape of a caravan. It is a home away from home and the trend of naming your caravan is becoming more and more popular. To personalise a name adds to its individuality and allows it to stand apart from all those other caravans.

A

Adelaide
Adventure Bound

Adventure Seeker
Adventurer
Adventurous
Ain't Misbehaving
All Aboard
Almost There
Ambassador
Amigo
Anastasia
Angel Eyes
Anniversary
Another Adventure
AWOL

B

Bay Dreamer
Beautiful Dreamer
Bedazzled
Bella
Belle
Bit O' Heaven
Black Orchid
Blessed
Bliss
Blossom
Boomerang
Born Free
Both Of Us
Braveheart
Brumby
Buccaneer
Bugger
Bunyip
Bushman
Butterscotch

C

Calypso
Camelot Cruiser
Caprice
Carnival
Casanova
Celtic Jewel
Celtic Sun
Chances
Chaos
Chardonnay
Charisma
Ciao
City Slicker
Clarity
Cloud Nine
Codger
Compass
Contessa
Cosmo
Crooner
Cruise Control
Cruisin'
Cruising
Curious

D

Daddy Long Legs
Daffodil
Daisy
Dances With Wind
Dancing Bear
Dandelion
Daphne
Daiquiri
Day Dream
Day Dreamer
Déjà vu
Delilah
Delta
Dependable
Destiny
Diamond In The Rough
Digger
Don Juan
Don Quixote
Doufishtoo
Dream A Little Dream
Dream Big
Dream Catcher
Dream Machine
Dream Maker
Dream Weaver
Dreamscape
Dreamy
Driftaway
Dundee
Duchess

E

Eagle Eye
Easy Living
Easy Rider
Eccentric
Eclipse
Edelweiss
Eden
El Relaxo
Endeavour
Energetic
Enigma
Enterprise
Escapade
Evening Star
Evolution
Exceller-8
Explorer

F

Fair Weather
Family Cruiser
Fancy Face
Fancy Free
Favourite
Finally Mine
Finally Ours
First Class
First Love
Fishy Business
Fleur
Flutterby
Fly Me To The Moon
Follow Me
Footloose
Forever Bliss
Forever Summer

Fortune Cookie
Four Leaf Clover
Free Spirit
Freedom
Frolic

G

Galaxy Quest
G'day
Gem
Getaway
Gizmo
Glorious
Go Faster
Go For It
Goblin
God's Grace
Godspeed
Goin' My Way
Gone Fishin'
Gone Fishing
Gone With The Wind
Good Karma
Good Times
Grumpy
Gypsy
Gypsy Caravan
Gypsylore

H

Have A Nice Day
Head Over Heels
Heartbeat
Heaven Sent
Hidden Treasure
Hideaway
High 'n' Dry
High Roller
Highlander
Hippie Heaven
His Highness
His 'n' Hers
Holiday
Home And Away
Home Sweet Home
Homeless
Hoodoo
Hooked

I

In Heaven
Indian Summer
Inheritance
Insanity
Into The Wind
Irish Eyes
Irish Lass
Irish Mist
Irish Rose

J

Jellybean
Jewel
Jubilee
Just Cruisin'
Just Cruising
Just Dandy
Just My Style
Just Our Speed
Justice
Just Us

K

Kaleidoscope
Karma
Keep Sake
King of the Road
Kismet
Knight In Shining Armour
Kookaburra

L

Lady Jane
Leap Of Faith
Legacy
Liberty
Lifestyle
Little Retreat
Lonely Heart
Lost
Lottery
Lotto
Love In Motion
Love Shack
Lovey
Lucky Stars
Lullaby
Lullaby Maker

M

Majestic
Magic Carpet
Makin' Doo
Making Memories
Matilda
Maverick
Medicine Man
Memories
Miracles
Misbehavin'
Mischief Maker
Molly
Much-ado
My Dream

N

Navigator
Neverland
New Beginnings
Nomad

O

Old Codger
One Love
Optimist
Our Favourite
Outta Here

P

Paid My Dues
Partners In Crime
Pathfinder
Phantom

Pioneer
Play Time
Prosperity
Providence

Q

Queen of the Road
Quest
Quiet Time

R

Rascal
Ravenstone
Rebecca
Reflections
Refuge
Release
Remembrance
Renaissance
Rendezvous
Restless
Restless Heart
Retired
Retiring
Reverie
Rhyme And Reason
Rock 'n' Roll
Rocket Power
Romeo
Rose Petal
Rosie
Rover
Ruby
Rum Runner
Runaway
Runner
Running Away

S

Sacred Spirit
Safari
Salvation
Sanctuary
Scallywag
Scandalous
Second Home
Serenade
Serendipity
Serenity
Shabby Chic
Shaman
Shamrock
Shangri-la
Shooting Star
Silver Bells
Silver Fox
Silver Lining
Simply Sensational
Skipper
Sleeping Beauty
Slice Of Heaven
Slow Dancer
Socialite
Solitaire
Solitude
Sonnet
Soul Mate
Spartacus
Spirit Of The West
Spit And Polish
Star Blazer
Star Gazer
Stardust
Sterling
Storm Chaser
Strange Days
Stress Buster
Stressing Less
Summer Place
Sun Chaser
Sunflower
Sunny Side Up
Sunshine
Supernatural
Superstitious
Sweet Lullaby
Sweet Surrender
Sweet Thing

T

Talisman
Tarot
Temptation
Tequila
That's Amore
The American Dream
The Best Present Ever
The Boss
The Both Of Us
The Bounty
The Cat's Meow
The Cat's Pyjamas
The Distraction
The Fox
The Gator
The Getaway
The Happy Camper
The Haven
The Honeymooners
The Investment
The Last Rebel
The Milky Way
The Navigator
The Palace
The Pay Off
The Phantom
The Prayer
The Quest
The Raven
The Rose
The Sultan
The Tortoise
The Vacationer
The Weekender
Therapy
This Side Up
Thisledoo
Three's A Crowd
Thunder Chaser
Tiffany
Time Of Our Lives
Time Off

Time Out
Tinkerbelle
Tiny Dancer
Titan
Toad
Together Forever
Tornado
Tough Love
Toy
Tranquilizer
Travelling Gypsy
Treasure Chest
Trial And Tribulations
Trickster
Twilight Zone
Twinkle Toes
Two To Tango

U

Unchained Melody
Under The Southern Cross

V

Valentine
Vagabond
Veronica
Viking
Vision Quest
Vitality
Vogue
Voodoo
Voyager

W

Waltzing Matilda
Walkabout
Wanderer
Wanderlust
Warp Speed
Weather Shield
Wedidit
Weekend Cruiser
Weekend Escape
Weekender
Weowna
Weownit
Who Dares Wins
Wild At Heart
Wild Blue Yonder
Wild Is The Wind
Wild Orchid
Wild Weather
Wild Weather Rider
Wildfire
Wildflower
Wind Charm
Wind Charmer
Wind Magic
Wind Song
Windcrest
Windfall
Windseeker
Windsong
Windward
Wing And A Prayer
Winsome
Wish List
Wished For
Witchcraft
Wizard
Worryless
Wrangler

X

X-cellerate
X-cellent
X-treme

Y

Yearned For
Ying And Yang

Z

Zigzag

ACKNOWLEDGEMENTS

Thanks to Jason Howarth for his love and support. Thanks also to Joyce and Myra Cooper; Ken and Maureen Howarth; Jeanette and Henry Birett; John and Vicky Cooper; Kia, Lucy and Larni Marsterson; Nicole McLaughlin; Jean van Asperen; Georgina Papaioannou; Danielle Ryan; Garry, Colleen, Marian and Darren Howarth; Chloe and Chris Hearn; Cass, Josh and Brielle; and Pia Bjorkland. Special thanks to Valina Rainer and Amy Thomas for their enthusiasm, assistance and encouragement.

Thanks also to the following people of Wagga Wagga: Rodney Parsons, Lonny and Mavis Williams, Mary Breckenridge, Raymond Quarmby, Linda and Graham Hulford, Margot Brissenden, Annette and Dale Youngs, Bill and Heather Harris, Grant Jarich, Elizabeth Holders, Graham Hardwick, Ned Smith, Marjorie Hoare, Brooke Curry, Victoria Collins, Natasha Fitzsimmons, G. and S. Lidden, Marie Movon, Chris Buckland and Cathy Toole.

While researching this book, I was also searching for a name for my own house and discovered there was much more involved with the naming process than I first thought. I went through stages of considering *Lavender Cottage*, *Wisteria House* and even *Mandalay* after the mansion in *Rebecca*, a favourite movie of mine. After considering all avenues for house names including foreign languages, colours and flora, I finally came to the end of my many months of search. *Biggletree* is my choice of house name, simply for the *big old tree* in my front yard. It never fails to bring a smile to people's faces when they say it!

I hope reading this book gives you as much inspiration as it did for me to write it, and remember, house names are only limited by your own imagination.